W9-CLM-730

Making *Roots*

ALSO FROM UC PRESS BY MATTHEW F. DELMONT

*The Nicest Kids in Town: American Bandstand, Rock 'n' Roll, and the Struggle
for Civil Rights in 1950s Philadelphia*

*Why Busing Failed: Race, Media, and the National Resistance to School
Desegregation*

Making *Roots*

A Nation Captivated

Matthew F. Delmont

UNIVERSITY OF CALIFORNIA PRESS

University of California Press, one of the most distinguished university presses in the United States, enriches
lives around the world by advancing scholarship in the
humanities, social sciences, and natural sciences. Its
activities are supported by the UC Press Foundation
and by philanthropic contributions from individuals and
institutions. For more information, visit www.ucpress.edu.

University of California Press
Oakland, California

Library of Congress Cataloging-in-Publication Data

Names: Delmont, Matthew F., author.
Title: Making *Roots* : a nation captivated / Matthew F.
    Delmont.
Description: Oakland, California : University of
    California Press, [2016] | "2016 | Includes bibliographical
    references and index.
Identifiers: LCCN 2016002212 (print) | LCCN 2016004108
    (ebook) | ISBN 9780520291324 (cloth : alk. paper) |
    ISBN 9780520965133 (ebook)
Subjects: LCSH: Haley, Alex. Roots. | Roots (Television
    program : 1977)
Classification: LCC E185.97.H24 D45 2016 (print) |
    LCC E185.97.H24 (ebook) | DDC 973/.0496073—dc23
LC record available at http://lccn.loc.gov/2016002212

Manufactured in the United States of America

25 24 23 22 21 20 19 18 17 16
10 9 8 7 6 5 4 3 2 1

In keeping with a commitment to support environmen-
tally responsible and sustainable printing practices, UC
Press has printed this book on Natures Natural, a fiber
that contains 30% post-consumer waste and meets the
minimum requirements of ANSI/NISO Z39.48–1992 (R 1997)
(*Permanence of Paper*).

CONTENTS

AT MAKINGROOTS.NET

Video Clips
Images
Selected Research Materials

ILLUSTRATIONS

ACKNOWLEDGMENTS

I am fortunate to have received encouragement from family, friends, mentors, and colleagues for as long as I can remember. My mom, Diane Delmont, did an amazing job of raising me, and I am eternally thankful for her love and support. Thank you also to Frank Bowman, Bobbie and Lindy Stoltz, Katie Stoltz, Leari Jean and Jewel Anderson, and my late grandmother Kaye Henrikson, for their love and support.

I've found at Arizona State University a wonderful place to teach history and American studies. Thank you to Matt Garcia, Desiree Garcia, Bambi Haggins, Aaron Bae, Karen Leong, Calvin Schermerhorn, Chris Jones, Sujey Vega, Lee Bebout, Don Fixico, Victoria Thompson, Don Critchlow, Gayle Gullet, Pen Moon, Catherine O'Donnell, Paul Hirt, Rashad Shabazz, Marlon Bailey, Gaymon Bennett, Julian Lim, and my other colleagues in history and American studies at Arizona State University for discussing my research and helping me strengthen my arguments.

Thank you to Alexus Stewart, Elizabeth Blevins, Maggie Yancey, Don LaPlant, Amanda Daddona for working as research assistants on this project.

Thank you to Dean George Justice, Vice Provost Patrick Kenney, Provost Mark Searle, and President Michael Crow for welcoming me to Arizona State University and for supporting my research.

Thank you to Niels Hooper, my editor at University of California Press, for supporting this project from the earliest proposal. Thank you to Jessica Moll, Bradley Depew, and Ryan Furtkamp for guiding this book through production and to Elisabeth Magnus for her careful copyediting. Thank you to Cynthia Savage for preparing the book's index. Thank you to Lorraine Weston, Kate Pinnick, and Elizabeth Shreve for their work promoting this book.

Thank you to Cynthia Hunt, Sona Basmadjian, and the other archivists and librarians at Goodwin College, the Schomburg Center for Research in Black Culture, the University of Tennessee-Knoxville, and the University of Southern California for their invaluable assistance. Thank you to Erica Ball, Adam Bradley, Kimberly Juanita Brown, Marcia Chatelain, Kellie Carter Jackson, Bambi Haggins, Alondra Nelson, and other scholars for taking the time to talk with me about *Roots*.

Thanks to my friends from the Jackal club: Shawn Anderson, Tim Arnold, Victor Danh, Jessie Davis, Jake Ewart, Kara Hughes, Jake Lentz, Ken Miller, and Cabral Williams.

Finally, thank you to Jacque Wernimont, Xavier, and Simone for their love.

Introduction

"You know who we have on the show tonight?" Johnny Carson asked his audience during his monologue on February 2, 1977. "We have the author who wrote that amazing, wonderful novel, *Roots*. Alex Haley is with us tonight." Haley, the author of the best-selling book in the country, appeared on the *Tonight Show* just days after the *Roots* television miniseries completed its record-breaking run on ABC. "If there's anyone watching who does not know about *Roots,* you must have either been out of the country or on Mars someplace," Carson joked. As Haley waited in the green room while actor Tony Randall and singer Mel Tillis performed and bantered with Carson, he must have thought of how far he and his family story had come over the past fifteen years. If he was nervous, it did not show. Haley settled into the guest's chair and soon started telling Carson about how he had come to write his multigenerational story, tracing his family's history from West Africa through emancipation in the United States. "The thing that actually did it for me was that my grandmother in Henning, Tennessee ... told me, all while I was growing up, a story about the family, about where her parents had been slaves in Alamance County, North Carolina, and about the families preceding them," Haley told Carson. "I didn't really understand much of the story. It was like biblical parables." It was a story Haley had told hundreds of times to audiences all across the country. Haley described how he had found information about different members of his family in archival records before reaching the most remarkable part of his story: "Ultimately, that research over the nine years would take me back to my fourth great-grandfather, seven generations back, an African who was named Kunta Kinte. He was born and reared in a little village called Juffure, in the Gambia, West Africa. He was brought here on a ship called the *Lord Ligonier*. And it left Africa July 5, 1767."[1] With *Roots* Haley achieved two incredible feats. He tracked his family's history across the abyss of transatlantic slavery to a specific ancestor, and, almost as improbably, he made the slave trade and black history inescapable parts of national popular culture.

Roots, published by Doubleday in the fall of 1976 and broadcast by ABC in the winter of 1977, was read by millions and watched by millions more, but today *Roots* is neither acclaimed by critics nor much studied by academics. *Roots* fell out of favor in part because Haley's story started to unravel as soon as it was in print. Haley fabricated parts of his story, paid over half a million dollars to settle a plagiarism suit brought by Harold Courlander, and relied heavily on an editor, Murray Fisher, to finish *Roots*. Other people were upset with how ABC, Doubleday, Haley, and associated parties seemed to be wringing money from the history of slavery. This explicit commercialization allowed *Roots* to reach millions of people, but it has made it difficult to see the book or the television series as a serious contribution to our nation's understanding of the history of slavery.

Making "Roots" explores how Alex Haley's idea developed from a modest book proposal into an unprecedented cultural phenomenon. This book is guided by two themes. First, I emphasize how *Roots* demonstrates the importance, contradictions, and limitations of mass culture. Alex Haley always approached his family history as a story that had both emotional and economic value. There would have been no *Roots* without Haley, but there also would have been no *Roots* without white publishers and producers who pitched the work primarily to white audiences. It is likely that Haley never would have finished *Roots* without the financial incentive and pressure offered by his deal with television producer David Wolper and ABC. *Roots* never existed wholly apart from the mass market. This was and is uncomfortable for many critics, readers, and viewers to acknowledge. Rather than lamenting that *Roots* was somehow sullied by Haley's relationships with *Reader's Digest,* Doubleday, the W. Colston Leigh speakers' bureau, and ABC, it is more interesting and productive to consider how Haley, especially as a black writer in the 1960s and 1970s, created a story that could be successfully marketed to so many people.

Roots began as a book called *Before This Anger,* which Alex Haley pitched to his agent in 1963. Haley signed a contract the following year to write the book for Doubleday, while he was also finishing work on *The Autobiography of Malcolm X.* Haley originally planned for *Before This Anger* to focus on his hometown of Henning, Tennessee, in the 1920s and '30s, and to use this nostalgic vision of rural southern black life as a contrast to the urban unrest and racial tensions of the 1960s. Haley's vision for the book expanded after family elders told him about someone they called "the Mandingo," who had passed down stories of having been captured in Africa and sold into slavery. This initial family story sent Haley on a research quest motivated by both personal and financial concerns. On a personal level, Haley felt a natural human desire to understand his family's history. For Haley, like other descendants of enslaved people, this desire for genealogical knowledge was thwarted by the fact that his ancestors had been forcibly uprooted from Africa and treated as property for generations in America. The Middle Passage, where enslaved people were transported from Africa to the New World, both claimed lives and ruptured histories. When Haley eventually identified Kunta Kinte, from the Gambian village of Juffure, as his family's "original African," he felt as if he had reclaimed something that had been stolen from him.

Haley also understood that searching for and finding Kunta Kinte made for an amazing and lucrative story. Money problems followed Haley for the years he worked on *Roots*, and Haley supported himself during these years by lecturing across the country. Haley was a dynamic speaker, and on the lecture circuit he turned his search for his family's history into a detective story. He described traveling across continents and racing from archive to archive in search of clues. In Haley's detective story all of the pieces remarkably fell into place so that the stories he heard from his family elders matched up perfectly with legal deeds, shipping records, and Gambian oral histories. Much of what Haley told audiences was true; other parts were exaggerated, embellished, or fabricated. More importantly, Haley's story of his search for roots captivated audiences. As Haley crisscrossed the country in the late 1960s and early 1970s, he told the story of his search for roots to hundreds of thousands of people, earning $500 to $1,000 per appearance.

Haley was constantly selling *Roots*. His busy speaking schedule made it difficult for him to finish his epic book, but the lectures amounted to one of the longest advance promotion tours in the history of publishing or broadcasting. Haley used his storytelling skills, honed in front of lecture audiences, to successfully pitch *Roots* to *Reader's Digest,* which published a condensation of the book in 1974; to producers David Wolper and Stan Margulies; and to ABC television executive Brandon Stoddard. Whether Haley was speaking to college students, church groups, or television professionals, he understood that audiences responded to *Roots,* first and foremost, as a good story. Telling and retelling his story taught Haley to focus less on the boundaries between fact and fiction, or between history and literature, and more on making a connection with his audience.

The second theme of this book is how *Roots* pushed the boundaries of history. Historians have shied away from *Roots* because the story's relationship to history is messy, but it is this messiness that makes *Roots* so interesting. Alex Haley mixed archival research, oral traditions, and fiction into a narrative he described as "faction." The television version of *Roots* complicated matters further, insisting that the production was based on a true story while billing the series as an "ABC Novel for Television." Critics have noted several examples of how Haley played fast and loose with historical evidence, and one need not search too long online before seeing *Roots* described as a "hoax," "fraud," or "lie." At their worst, these criticisms of *Roots* reassure people who would like to deny or minimize the history of slavery. Even at their best, the critiques do not explain why so many people were eager to read, watch, and listen to the story Haley created. *Making "Roots"* carefully traces when, how, and why Haley made up parts of his story, but this book is not an exposé. Rather, I argue that we need to pay more attention to the emotional and economic investments that led Haley to believe the remarkable story of Kunta Kinte he heard in the Gambia and the similar investments that led publishers, television producers, and audiences to believe in *Roots*. Dividing *Roots* into discrete columns of fact and fiction does not explain why it was precisely the parts of Haley's story that most strained credibility that most moved audiences.

Americans choose to remember slavery at some moments and collectively forget it at others. *Roots* arrived in an era when academic and popular audiences were paying renewed attention to the history of slavery, including books such as John Blassingame's *The Slave Community: Plantation Life in the Antebellum South* (1972); Robert Fogel and Stanley Engerman's *Time on the Cross: The Economics of American Negro Slavery* (1974); Eugene Genovese's *Roll, Jordan, Roll: The World the Slaves Made* (1974); Herbert Gutman's *The Black Family in Slavery and Freedom* (1976); Lawrence Levine's *Black Culture and Black Consciousness: Afro-American Folk Thought from Slavery to Freedom* (1977); Edmund Morgan's *American Slavery, American Freedom* (1975); George Rawick's *From Sundown to Sunup: The Making of the Black Community* (1972); and *The Black Book* (1973), a scrapbook put together by collector Middleton Harris and Toni Morrison, who was then an editor at Random House. *Roots* benefited from and contributed to this interest in the history of slavery, but it reached millions more people and changed the way Americans viewed slavery in ways that a historical textbook or monograph never could. None of these historians, for example, were going to be interviewed by Johnny Carson on the *Tonight Show*, be featured in *Reader's Digest*, or make the cover of *Time* magazine. *Roots* was unapologetically commercial history and was pitched to everyday American readers and viewers rather than to scholars. Popular and academic reviewers who dismissed the book and television series as too middlebrow or criticized its historical accuracy largely missed the point. *Roots* asked viewers, across racial lines and national borders, to see slavery as a story about black people and black families and to identify with the sorrow, pain, and joy of enslaved people in ways that were unusual in commercial literature and unprecedented in broadcast television. There was power in the level of popularity *Roots* achieved. "The mass catharsis of 'Roots' has at last formulated a weapon equal in power to *Birth of a Nation*," *Los Angeles Times* critic Mary Beth Crain argued.[2] *Roots* encouraged more people to engage seriously with the history of slavery than anything before or since. There are many valuable histories of slavery, but there is only one *Roots*.

Representations of race have played an important role throughout the long campaign for African American freedom. In the nineteenth century, Frederick Douglass and Sojourner Truth made extensive use of photography and the circulation of their images to create public selves and make a case for the humanity of black people.[3] Similarly, W.E.B. DuBois compiled several hundred photographs of affluent African American women and men and displayed them in the "American Negro exhibit" at the 1900 Paris Exposition.[4] DuBois's remarkable collection of images testified to the diversity of African American identity and challenged the dominant racial ideologies of black inferiority. At the outset of the twentieth-century civil rights movement, the National Association for the Advancement of Colored People (NAACP) led protests against D.W. Griffith's *Birth of a Nation* when it opened in 1915 and again in later years when the film was rereleased.[5] In the early years of television, the NAACP protested the caricatures of black people on *Amos 'n' Andy* (1951–53 broadcast; 1954–66 syndication) and civil rights advocates and entertainers called for more and better representations of black people on the small screen.[6] Still, American culture continued to be enamored with retrograde depictions of race. Most people do not realize that before *Roots* the most watched television program in American history was *Gone with the Wind,* the 1939 historical epic film that NBC broadcast over two nights in 1976.[7] With *Roots,* Haley tried to marshal the power of history, at an epic and mythic scale, to advance black history in the mainstream of American culture. Over the course of the twentieth century many civil rights advocates and media critics lamented the power of racist fictions like *Gone with the Wind* and *Birth of a Nation* to "write history with lightning," to quote the phrase President Woodrow Wilson is said to have used to praise Griffith's epic. Few people have had the audacity, as Haley did with *Roots,* to create a larger lightning storm.

If *Roots* was too fictional for most historians to take seriously, its version of historical fiction was not literary enough to be dissected in English departments. *Roots,* for example, is notably absent from the *Norton Anthology of African American Literature,* which runs to nearly three thousand pages.[8] Despite his embrace of "faction," Haley was dedicated to fitting all of the pieces of his genealogical puzzle together neatly. Literary critic Arnold Rampersad described *Roots* as being "so innocent of fictive ingenuity that it seldom surpasses the standards of the most popular of historical romances."[9] Over nearly six hundred pages, Haley's narrative unfolds in a straight line from Kunta Kinte in the 1760s across seven generations to Haley in the 1970s, with little sense that there were questions Haley's research could not answer. Creative work and scholarship since *Roots* by Toni Morrison, Kara Walker, Saidiya Hartman, Tiya Miles, and many others have found new and profound meanings in the fissures and erasures in the historical record of slavery.[10] Haley's archived letters, notes, and drafts make it clear that he encountered hundreds of these gaps in his research but that he preferred to make his family story one of continuity. This commitment to continuity almost immediately put Haley out of step with how sophisticated writers and artists approached the subject of slavery. The long-term critical evaluation of *Roots* suffered in the exchange, and *Roots* has not found a place in the literary canon. But millions of readers and viewers enjoyed Haley's narrative style, and its massive popularity makes the work a baseline from which to appreciate more nuanced and challenging treatments of slavery.

This book draws on new and underutilized archival sources to tell the story of the making of *Roots*. I have examined tens of thousands of pages of Alex Haley's letters, notes, and manuscript drafts in the collections housed at the University of Tennessee, the Schomburg Center for Research in Black Culture, and Goodwin College. These documents show, sometimes on a day-by-day basis, how *Roots* took shape from the early 1960s through the late 1970s. At the University of Southern California, the archived papers of David Wolper and Stan Margulies offer similar insights into how these television producers adapted Haley's story for the screen, as do Archive of American Television oral histories. In this book I foreground the voices and perspectives of the people who played a role in creating *Roots*: Haley, literary agent Paul Reynolds, Doubleday editors Ken McCormick and Lisa Drew, Haley's editor Murray Fisher, Wolper, Margulies, screenwriter Bill Blinn, and actors like LeVar Burton, John Amos, and Leslie Uggams. Despite the tremendous success of Haley's book and ABC's television miniseries, *Making "Roots"* is the first book-length study of *Roots*.

As a scholar of popular culture and African American history I wanted to research and write this book because we know remarkably little about one of the most recognizable cultural productions of all time. One could fill a shelf with books on recent critically lauded television shows like *The Sopranos, The Wire, Breaking Bad,* and *Mad Men,* but there is a curious lack of scholarship on *Roots.* When *Roots* is discussed, it is routinely described as a "phenomenon," which suggests that it came out of nowhere or that it is inexplicable. By focusing on the fifteen-year period over which *Roots* developed, this book tries to ground this phenomenon in the specific decisions and actions of Haley and his collaborators.

Alex Haley never published another book after *Roots.* He loved talking to people but found himself overwhelmed by the praise, criticism, and legal troubles *Roots* generated. "He made history talk," Jesse Jackson said of Alex Haley at the author's funeral in 1992. "He lit up the long night of slavery. He gave our grandparents personhood. He gave *Roots* to the rootless."[11] In this light, pointing out the flaws in Haley's family history feels like telling your grandmother she is lying. Fortunately, Haley's fabrications are only a small part of a much larger, more interesting, and more complicated story of the making of *Roots.* This book tells that story.

CHAPTER ONE

Before This Anger

The story of the making of *Roots* begins at Le Marmiton, a French restaurant in midtown Manhattan. Over lunch on August 5, 1964, Alex Haley told Doubleday editor Ken McCormick and literary agents Paul Reynolds and Phoebe Larmore about an idea for a book about life in his hometown of Henning, Tennessee.[1] Haley arrived at lunch without a formal book proposal, but he was a great talker and he entertained his lunch companions with stories about growing up in the rural South. McCormick loved the book idea, and Haley signed a contract with Doubleday later that month to write *Before This Anger*. No one at the table could have anticipated how this project would grow over the next decade into *Roots*.

Alexander Murray Palmer Haley was born in 1921 and raised partly in Henning, a small town on the eastern edge of Tennessee. Haley's mother, Bertha (Palmer) Haley, was from a well-to-do black family that owned a lumber business. "When most kids were out pulling cotton she was virtually being pampered," Haley recalled.[2] Haley's father, Simon Haley, was a professor of agriculture who had served in World War I and worked as a Pullman porter. The family, which included Alex's younger brothers George and Julies, moved regularly to follow Simon's teaching appointments at different black institutions in the South, including Lane College in Jackson, Tennessee; Oklahoma Colored Agricultural and Normal University in Langston, Oklahoma; and Alabama A&M University in Huntsville, Alabama. Bertha died when Alex was ten, and Simon Haley was remarried a year later to Zeona Hatcher, an English teacher at Alabama A&M. Zeona ran a strict household and did not favor Alex. "By the time he was a teenager in Alabama," Haley's biographer, Robert Norrell writes, Alex Haley "was practicing the art of avoiding conflict."[3]

The family returned to Henning, Tennessee, every summer, where Alex enjoyed a more relaxed schedule in the company of his maternal grandmother, Cynthia Palmer, and her sister, Alex's "Aunt Liz." These elders regaled him with stories about the family's history, fostering an early appreciation for storytelling that eventually became his livelihood. Years later, in a Smithsonian Institution speech during the nation's bicentennial, Haley reflected on what he thought of as a simpler time. "Older adults of today can remember their childhood evenings when the kith and kin would gather in their homes, the entertainment mostly was that the elders would talk, and the young would listen," he told the audience. "Those elder ones' very presences evoked within all of the younger family members an ingrained sense of family continuity, and lineage and heritage."[4] Alex also made summer friendships with both black and white children, including George Sims, a tall light-skinned African American young man who was raised in Henning and who later became Alex Haley's research assistant and traveling companion. Memories of these comfortable summers in Henning animated Alex Haley's romantic vision of southern life and his initial approach to *Before This Anger.*

Alex graduated from high school in 1937 and finished his freshman year at Alcorn A&M in the Mississippi Delta before transferring to Elizabeth City State Teachers College in North Carolina.[5] Alex dropped out of Elizabeth City College after a year to join the US Coast Guard, which deeply disappointed his father. "When I went into the service ... it was the patriotic thing to do," Haley said, "but when the war was over and I didn't come out and go back to school and get my Ph.D., my dad became furious and he refused to have anything to do with me for a long time."[6]

Haley was twenty years old when he met his first wife, Nannie "Nan" Branch, in Beaufort, North Carolina, where he was stationed in the Coast Guard. The couple married in the wake of Pearl Harbor in what Haley later described as "a kind of marrying time for military people."[7] The couple had two children, Lydia and William, but Haley became increasingly invested in his writing career and was not an attentive father or husband. While he became obsessed with his family's history, Haley admitted he was not cut out for day-to-day family responsibilities. When "I am honest with myself," Haley later wrote, "I just ain't that domesticated. I too often yen to range and roam."[8]

Haley started writing in the Coast Guard. To stave off boredom at sea, he wrote letters to everyone he knew and penned love letters for shipmates to send to their girlfriends. "The fellows began to have phenomenal success," Haley said of these personalized love letters. "And to a bunch of sailors you are Merlin when you achieved that."[9] This success convinced Haley to submit stories for publication in pulp magazines like *Modern*

Romances and *True Confessions.* Haley wrote constantly and shared his writing with his Coast Guard commanding officer, who was a former sportswriter.[10] Haley had dozens of stories rejected before finally placing a story about the Coast Guard in *This Week* magazine, a newspaper supplement.

Haley began his Coast Guard career as a mess boy, cleaning the ship and serving dinner to the officers, but by 1949 he was promoted to chief petty officer with the previously nonexistent title Chief Journalist of the Coast Guard. The position was an office job that called for Haley to write press releases, speeches for officers, and stories for Coast Guard publications. Though Haley attended to his Coast Guard duties during the day, he woke up early and stayed up late working on freelance stories for national magazines. Haley lived with his wife and children in Harlem in these years, but his energies were focused on becoming a professional writer.[11]

Haley published his first national magazine article in *Reader's Digest* in July 1954. In "The Harlem Nobody Knows," Haley surveyed the economic potential of New York's historic black neighborhood and described how "racial pride and the desperate fight for survival" were being "channeled in more disciplined ways to shape Harlem's future." "Man for man, as a community, we are ready to be compared with other communities," Julius Adams, executive editor of the black newspaper *New York Age*, told Haley. "What we need is a crusade of public relations. Harlem's biggest trouble now is that in too many minds the Negro remains a stereotype."[12] Adams could not have known that Haley would do as much as any writer to challenge stereotypes of black people.

Haley's optimism and upbeat attitude made him well suited to public relations work but could not protect him from racism.

In the summer of 1954, Haley was transferred to the Coast Guard office in San Francisco. "It was a big adventure for me and my wife Nan and the two kids," Haley remembered. "We piled into the car and happily set out to drive from New York to San Francisco.... After a day's driving and now about sundown, you start looking for where you're going to stay. The first night we were in New Jersey. All these signs: motel, motel, vacant, vacant and you go up and suddenly the people are telling you, 'Oh, I'm so sorry, we just rented the last one.' ... We crossed [the] country, every single night it was the same thing." Haley started wearing his Coast Guard uniform with his service ribbons prominently displayed, but "They didn't mean a thing." Haley recalled it was particularly hard to explain to his children that "vacant" did not always mean "open." He described this experience as similar to one recounted by Martin Luther King in "Letter From a Birmingham Jail." King described the feeling of finding "your tongue twisted and your speech stammering as you seek to explain to your six-year old daughter why she can't go to the public amusement park that has just been advertised on television, and see tears welling up in her little eyes when she is told that Funtown is closed to colored children."[13] This everyday sort of racism was familiar to black people across the United States in this era, but that did not make it any easier for Haley to accept. By the time the family drove over the Bay Bridge into San Francisco, Haley said, "I was as angry as I'd ever been in my life."[14]

Despite this humiliating trip, San Francisco gave Haley his first glimpse of what it meant to be a professional writer. Haley met Barnaby Conrad, a writer who owned a popular nightclub in San Francisco called El Matador, frequented by writers like Truman Capote, William Saroyan, Budd Schulberg, and John

Steinbeck. Conrad and Haley became friends, and Haley spent hours talking with the writers he met through Conrad. "It was the first time I had been in a community of selling writers," Haley recalled.[15] By the time he retired from the Coast Guard in 1959 to become a full-time writer, Haley had published pieces in *Reader's Digest,* the *Atlantic Monthly,* and *Harper's.*[16]

Haley, Nan, and the children moved from San Francisco back to New York City in 1959. The couple soon separated, with Nan moving in with family in Harlem and Haley finding a small apartment in Greenwich Village (92 Grove Street), a building where his friend George Sims worked as the janitor.[17] Haley felt that Greenwich Village was "where a writer belongs," though he did not know any professional writers in New York at the time. Haley wrote to a half-dozen black artists in the city whom he hoped could give him advice. Only one writer replied, but that one was James Baldwin. Haley recalled, "It is a warm dear thing with me that that man at that time, who got this letter from an utterly unknown not only as a writer but utterly unknown to him, took the trouble to walk from where he lived to over to where I was and sat down and talked with me a couple of hours."[18] Haley found talking with Baldwin to be nourishing. "Baldwin talked of what he knew so well, and I so little—of the Civil Rights struggle, and of the black writers' responsibilities to articulate the man [*sic*] facets and complexities of it," Haley said. "He had psychologically put an arm about my shoulders and given me the encouragement I needed, and the confidence to work."[19] The two men developed a friendship, and Baldwin became Haley's most high-profile literary supporter.

Haley struggled to find his footing as a writer in New York. He briefly worked as a bank messenger, running cancelled checks from one branch to another. "People dealt with me as if they didn't even see me—I was just a cipher," Haley remembered. "People would just see your color and they didn't see any more."[20] Haley said he experienced his racial identity differently in New York than he had in the South. "I had always up to that time been somebody, wherever I had been.... Even if somebody was racially very intensely against you, hostile toward you, was calling you names or whatever, they were aware of you.... But it was more of something simply to be totally ignored.... It was a shock."[21] Haley's memory of his time in New York echoed Ralph Ellison's classic novel, *Invisible Man:* "I am invisible, understand, simply because people refuse to see me.... When they approach me they see only my surroundings, themselves or figments of their imagination, indeed, everything and anything except me."[22] The racism and invisibility Haley experienced fueled his desire to become a well-known author.

Haley's break as a writer came at a boxing gym in Harlem. Haley enrolled at Wiley's gym to meet the jazz trumpeter Miles Davis, who trained there.[23] Haley briefly sparred with Davis in the ring and persuaded the press-shy musician to be interviewed for a new celebrity interview feature in *Playboy* magazine. The Miles Davis interview, published in September 1962, was a wide-ranging discussion of race and racism in American culture. Haley took notes as Davis described the lack of black people in film and television. "Take the movies and TV," Davis said. "How many times do you see anybody in the films but white people? You don't dig? Look, the next movie or TV you see, you count how many Negros or any other race but white that you see.... If movies and TV are supposed to reflect this country, and this country's supposed to be democratic, then why don't they do it? Let's see all kinds of people dancing and acting."[24] For Haley, the Miles Davis interview was the start of his education in what it meant to be a black artist and celebrity. No one would ever mistake Haley for a cool jazz musician, but, like Davis, Haley came to understand the pressures of producing work in the public spotlight and creating art for black and white audiences. Haley's second *Playboy* interview, with Malcolm X, received even more attention and prompted Doubleday to approach the black leader about partnering with Haley on an "as told to" autobiography. Malcolm X and Haley signed a contract with Doubleday for *The Autobiography of Malcolm X* in June 1963.

By summer 1963, Haley had secured one of the top literary agents in New York, Paul Reynolds. Paul Revere Reynolds (a distant relative of Paul Revere) joined his father's literary agency in 1926 after graduating from Williams College. Reynolds, who wrote *The Writer and His Markets* (1959), *Writing and Selling Nonfiction* (1963), and *Writing and Selling Fiction* (1965), was a tough negotiator who introduced Haley to the business of publishing.

Haley first mentioned *Before This Anger* to Reynolds in early September 1963. Hard at work on the Malcolm X book, Haley sent Reynolds a few pages from the new project to highlight how his views differed from those of the black Muslim leader. *Before This Anger,* Haley wrote, would portray "the pastoral simplicity and the root Christian culture of the 1930s Southern Negro— who migrated to the ghettos where he was fermented into today's black racism that has given us Malcolm X."[25] "You mentioned that after this project, we would talk of others," Haley wrote. "I have it, Mr. Reynolds. I guarantee you a fine book, perfect for these times, its title to be 'Before the Anger.' Whenever we have lunch, I will want to tell you about it."[26] Haley's staid demeanor and political views (he was a moderate Republican) made it easy for him to distinguish himself from Malcolm X. While the two men grew closer during the months they worked together on the autobiography, Haley regularly used Malcolm X and the fury of black militants as foils to advance *Before This Anger*.

Reynolds met Haley in the midst of changes in the author's personal life. In fall 1963, Haley got engaged to Juliette Collins, an airline stewardess he had met while traveling for a magazine assignment. The couple was married in 1964 just months after Haley ended his marriage to his first wife, Nan. (Haley and Nan were still married when he and Juliette became engaged, and Nan later claimed that she never signed divorce papers.)[27] Reynolds hosted a surprise engagement party for the new couple at his home in Chappaqua, New York. "I so much enjoyed your surprise party, and so did Julie, who is so impressed with sudden entry into a world where she meets such important people," Haley wrote. In his library, Reynolds displayed books dedicated to him by the authors he had represented. Haley noted the names—Richard Wright, Irving Wallace, Conrad Richter, William Shirer—and resolved that he too would write significant books. I "so much enjoy being your client," Haley wrote, and "it shouldn't be any secret that it's my full intent to make your investment of time and interest in my development as an author prove to be variously worthwhile."[28]

Haley also kept Reynolds apprised of his money problems, which fluctuated between moderate and severe over the next decade. "I'm plain broke," Haley admitted in the fall of 1963. "I am hoping that this dramatic Malcolm X book will end this for me from here in."[29] In addition to the Malcolm X project, Haley and Reynolds communicated regularly about *Before This Anger* and other book and magazine ideas that could lead to book contracts and advances to pay Haley's bills.

After a walk on a cold January morning in 1964, for example, Haley wrote to Reynolds to pitch an idea for a book called *How to Co-exist with Negroes.* "Visualize this title on paperback stands, Paul. Instantly, to white people, it evokes their own subjective concerns, and that subject in the air ... all around them.... Inevitably, the 300+ years of segregation have caused average white people to know little of the 'inside' of Negroes. This book, in some ways, is a kind of manual." Haley also expected black readers to be drawn to the book, through in a sort of sideways manner. "Negroes will consider much of the book naïve," Haley wrote. "The title, to the average Negro, certainly at least to this one, sounding so gratuitously condescending, would spark irritation, with which motivation we'd also get the Negroes' 75 cents."[30] Haley saw *How to Co-exist with Negroes* as perfectly suited to the state of race relations in America in 1964. "Harmful emotions are attached to 'integration' and 'Civil Rights,'" Haley wrote. "To drain some of these emotions is among this book's chief ambitions. I have the temerity to feel that, for harmony, much more the *true* goal, the *true* perspective, should be white-Negro Co-Existence."[31] While *How to Co-exist with Negroes* never advanced beyond the idea stage, this pitch outlines how Haley saw an untapped market for books that were about race relations but that would not be particularly challenging to readers' sensibilities. Haley, in short, wanted to start conversations about race rather than arguments.

Haley initially approached *Before This Anger* with similar ambitions. "I *know* what this book will do, in these times," he wrote to Reynolds in the summer of 1964. "I know what I have to say, and that it needs to be said. I know, I feel, the strength of my position as a Negro, writing, who is not given to violent protest, but who can say powerful things of a nature that people will think about, say them to both white people, today the fad, and also to Negroes, who need, amid the fad today, need [*sic*] very badly to look squarely at themselves, and see *their* mistakes."[32] As Haley wrote these words in the summer of 1964, black freedom struggles gripped the nation. Thousands of young people traveled to Mississippi for Freedom Summer to join local grassroots activists in a campaign to register African American voters. In Washington, D.C., President Lyndon Johnson signed the Civil Rights Act of 1964 after a lengthy filibuster by southern congressmen. Racial uprisings drew attention to long-simmering racial tensions in several northern cities, such as Chicago, Harlem, Philadelphia, and Rochester. Against this backdrop, Haley pitched himself as a moderate black author who could tap into the national interest in race relations without turning off white readers. The *New York Times,* for example, asked Haley to write an article regarding the racial unrest in Harlem in the summer of 1964. "They wanted a piece wherein Harlem's 'responsible' citizens would condemn the riots," Haley recalled. "I asked and asked different such citizenry, who didn't condemn them as the Times desired. So the Times paid my expenses and I told them and they told me no hard feelings."[33]

At the end of the long hot summer of 1964, Haley had a contract from Doubleday for *Before This Anger.* He initially promised Doubleday that he would finish *Before This Anger* by the end of the year, describing it as "Doubleday's softly powerful Christmas 1964 release."[34] "The country needs this book, I think—with its healing nature."[35] In reality, Haley had not yet written more than a few pages of *Before This Anger* when Doubleday offered him an advance contract for the project. The book existed only in Haley's letters and spoken presentations to his agent and editors. Reynolds had previously cautioned Haley about the danger of signing contracts for books that were not close to being finished. "I think it's not very good business," Reynolds told Haley when the author considered an offer from Putnam Publishing for a different project. "I think you can get more money than Putnam offers and what will happen is you will have used up the money and will have an obligation on your shoulders to write the book and nearly all books take longer than the author thinks." Reynolds concluded, "I know it's tough but signing contracts long before you can do the books is just a form of borrowing and you're paying the equivalent of a terribly high interest because you're not getting the best kind of contracts."[36]

Reynolds offered sound advice, but Haley was not in a financial position to take it. Haley signed a contract with Doubleday for *Before This Anger* in August 1964, agreeing to a $5,000 advance to be paid in segments after he completed parts of the manuscript. Upon signing the deal he received a check for $900.[37] Haley signed the contract at an airport awaiting a flight back to New York after interviewing Reverend Martin Luther King Jr. for *Playboy*. "I think it's a fine contract, and I intend with this book to go for recognition as an author who has something to say," Haley wrote to Reynolds.[38] While Haley was initially happy to sign the contract and receive the much-needed money, he quickly came to feel Doubleday did not value the scope of the project he was undertaking. This bad contract left Haley scrambling for the money he needed to research and write his major book. Over the coming years Haley's excitement with the commercial potential of *Before This Anger* and his frustration with Doubleday grew simultaneously.

In Haley's early vision for the book that became *Roots,* Africa is barely mentioned. This is especially curious since Haley spent hours discussing, recording, and interpreting the life of Malcolm X. After breaking with the Nation of Islam, Malcolm X took two trips to Africa and the Middle East in 1964 that shaped many of his ideas about religion, race, history, and politics. Malcolm's travels to

Africa were among the most important events in his life, but to Haley they were an inconvenience that would potentially delay their work on *The Autobiography of Malcolm X*. "Malcolm X is apparently now, for the last several weeks, involved in skip-about visiting of some fifteen countries," Haley wrote to Reynolds. "I am a little irked at him that such protracted absence from this country with very spotty contact with us isn't the kind of cooperation that is needed with a very large book being dealt with.... I am a little put-out that he has rather crossed up the project by, one, staying away so long and, two, his new conversion, but certainly both are his business, I suppose."[39]

Despite the popular idea that Malcolm X turned Haley on to Africa, nothing in Haley's correspondence or interviews suggests that he was deeply influenced by Malcolm X's travels to the continent. Malcolm X did inspire Haley in other ways, however. Haley watched Malcolm X speak on several occasions, before both black and white groups, and must have come to appreciate his ability to captivate an audience. Haley came from a family of storytellers, but Malcolm X taught him to move a crowd through pacing and the careful sequencing of details, arguments, and anecdotes. Haley developed his own unique style on the lecture circuit and joined Malcolm X as one of the great public speakers of the era. Malcolm X's personality also captivated Haley. *Reader's Digest* had a feature called "My Most Unforgettable Character" that profiled celebrities and interesting people, and in many ways Haley adopted this model for his own writing. Haley considered Malcolm X to be a "maverick," a character type he held in the highest regard. "The mavericks keep our society aerated," Haley wrote. "They keep us from settling into deteriorating apathy, lethargy, complacency. The mavericks test us, spur us, irritate us; they prick, and nudge, goad, and prod at our tendency—which can be so fatal—to 'hide' behind semantical words, and phrases, to be lulled by 'Big Brother' politically and in our customs and institutions ... while our dangerous, growing problems are thus obscured."[40] It was not a coincidence that Haley also described his original African ancestor as a "maverick."

While Malcolm X traveled to Africa in 1964, Haley turned his attention elsewhere, traveling to Henning, Tennessee. "I'm going coach on the train, with a whole box full of fried chicken and sweet potato pie, to be authentic in nostalgic return," Haley wrote to Reynolds in October 1964. "For that's the way virtually all Negroes in the 1930s left their little Hennings all over the South and went North dreaming to 'do good' in Chicago."[41] Haley left New York for Tennessee just days after his wife Julie gave birth to a baby girl, Cynthia, the couple's first child and Haley's third.[42] In Henning, Haley interviewed dozens of senior citizens about southern life in the 1920s and 1930s. Haley was entranced by the small town of his youth and was excited to write back to New York on forty-year-old stationery he found from his grandfather's lumber company. "I'm talking with the old people—some, now, are up into their 90s, and I'm getting just great additive material," Haley wrote. "More than ever I'm confident that this will be a successful, significant, needed book."[43] Back home in New York, Haley remained excited about how the Henning stories he heard were shaping up into a book. "It was just terrific there!" he wrote. "I got material far surpassing what I had remembered, or expected. We've a great book coming up in this 'Before This Anger.' You just watch. It's one of the kind of jobs where you tap the keys of the typewriter gently, watching the words form before your eyes."[44]

In January 1965, Haley traveled to Kansas for a family reunion and to celebrate his younger brother George's election as a

Republican state senator. Talking with aunts, uncles, and cousins sparked Haley's imagination and expanded his ambitions for *Before This Anger*. Haley wrote a long letter to Paul Reynolds to describe the "exhilarating" conversations with his family's elders:

> Paul, incredible as it seems, I am going to be able to start that family story with the original African who was taken into slavery. Two lucky facts make this possible: He happened to be one of the later slaves taken—one of the Mandingo tribe. Secondly, the family, all the way back, has been blessed with story-tellers, who passed the stories down. The Mandingo (isn't that an odd way to have to refer to your great-great-great-great grandfather?) was, it is passed down, "a mean critter." He was one of a cargo of slaves taken from interior West Africa circa 1780. They were taken first to the British West Indes [*sic*] where they were "broken" for slavery, then he sailed to the U.S. For some reason, seemingly precise and correlated as the story is in some of its details, his name no one seems ever to have heard.[45]

This story of the "original African" dramatically shifted the center of gravity in Haley's book project. "The Mandingo," whom Haley later identified as Kunta Kinte, was not part of the book Haley had sold to Doubleday just five months prior. This meant that *Before This Anger* would start, not in Henning in the 1920s, but several generations earlier.

Haley continued to outline for Reynolds the genealogy he had heard at the family reunion. "The Mandingo sired a number of children on the several plantations to which he was successively sold," Haley wrote. "He was still 'mean,' he was beaten a good deal, but he was, the story goes, extremely strong and resilient. It was one of his last children, a daughter, who subsequently told the story of her father to *her* son, a slave lad who grew up, being sold only once, to the Master of a North Carolina tobacco plantation, where this slave lad reached adulthood, with the story intact. This slave lad became known on this plantation, in mid-to-late 'teens as 'Chicken George.'"[46] Haley described to Reynolds how, shortly before the Civil War, "'Chicken George' wandered off, leaving behind a wife and seven children." Haley explained this by noting, "Slave family-ties were not very binding in those days."[47]

Haley came away from this family reunion with the skeletal structure for his family genealogy, but there are several important differences between this early version and the story he later told on the lecture circuit and published in *Roots*. In *Roots*, a slave ship takes Kunta Kinte directly from the Gambia to Annapolis, without a stop in the West Indies. In *Roots*, rather than fathering "a number of children on several plantations," Kunta Kinte is celibate until his late thirties and has only one daughter, Kizzy. Most notably, Haley's early version of his family's story makes no mention of the words *Kin-tay*, *Ko*, or *Kamby Bolongo*. In the story Haley told about his search for his ancestors, these k-words were the key linguistic clues that had been passed down across generations. "In the oral history that Grandma, Aunt Liz, Aunt Plus, Cousin Georgia, and the others had always told on the boyhood Henning front porch, I had an unknown quotient in those strange words or sounds passed on by the African," Haley wrote in *Roots* in 1976. "'Kin-tay,' he had said, was his name. 'Ko' he had called a guitar. 'Kamby Bolongo' he had called a river in Virginia. They were mostly sharp, angular sounds, with *k* predominating."[48] Haley described in *Roots* how he brought these "phonetic snatches" to Dr. Jan Vansina, an anthropologist at the University of Wisconsin who was an expert on African linguistics and oral traditions. "The most involved sound I had heard and brought was Kamby Bolongo, my ancestor's sound to his daughter Kizzy as he had pointed to the Mattaponi River in

Spotsylvania County, Virginia. Dr. Vansina said that without question, *bolongo* meant, in the Mandinka tongue, a moving water; preceded by 'Kamby,' it could indicate the Gambia River. I'd never heard of it."[49] Vansina did host Haley at his home in Madison in the fall of 1967, but at that point Haley had already made two research trips to the Gambia and had traveled by boat up the Gambia River in search of stories about his ancestors.

It is difficult, even in Haley's earliest versions of the story, to separate fact from fiction. The elders' stories blend into Haley's story and both borrow liberally from popular narratives about slavery. "There are fascinating stories of the decline of the plantation during the war," Haley told Reynolds in recounting the family reunion. "The Master and Mistress had no children, only their slaves. There is a misty drama of how, the war over, the slaves were assembled in the yard and the Master and Mistress on the Big House portico read (the Master did) that the slaves were now free. The Master and Mistress, and the slaves, were crying. 'I—I guess it means … you all … don't have to call me … "Master" … no more'—I tell you, Paul, what a *scene!*"[50] Here Haley's family story resembles the romanticized stories of the antebellum South and kind slave owners that *Roots* would later challenge.

If the accuracy of these stories is difficult to judge, one thing that emerges clearly is that Haley always thought about his family history as a story he could sell. Haley believed that being able to trace his story back to the "original African" would make *Before This Anger* even more appealing to readers and more important to the country. "You know, Paul? In America, I think, there has not been such a book," Haley wrote to his agent. "'Rooting' a Negro family, all the way back, telling the chronicle, through us, of how the Negro is part and parcel of the American saga. Without rancor, which I do not feel, which has not been my experience in any influencing way. It is a book which I so deeply feel that America, the world, *needs* to read. For its drama, for its authentic image, for other reasons. I shall write it, when I get to the writing, with love."[51] Reynolds responded quickly and enthusiastically. He encouraged Haley to "do some research work on the Mandingo" and wrote, "This book is going to be a beauty.... Everything isn't money, but I think this book is going to make you a great deal of money and a great deal of prestige."[52]

In Haley's vision for the book that grew into *Roots,* emotions and economics were always intertwined. He was emotionally moved by the idea of being able to identify his family's "original African," and he was excited by the money that such a story might bring him. Haley's eagerness to profit from genealogy and the history of slavery is probably discomforting to many people, but it is important to recognize that *Before This Anger/Roots* was always a commercial venture. Everything that happened with the project from 1963 to 1977 was about bringing Haley's family story to larger and more remunerative audiences. What is surprising is not that financial motivations propelled Haley but that his story's ability to move people emotionally grew apace.

When Haley returned from his family reunion, Malcolm X was at John F. Kennedy Airport to pick him up. The two men had worked together on the autobiography for over two years and, despite their political and religious differences, considered each other friends. This airport meeting was the last time Haley saw Malcolm X alive. Days before the two were scheduled to meet at Haley's home in Rome, New York, to review the final manuscript, Malcolm X was assassinated at Harlem's Audubon Ballroom by members of the Nation of Islam's Newark mosque.[53] Haley wrote to Paul Reynolds the next day to discuss how the royalties from the book might help Betty Shabazz and the couple's five daughters

(Haley and Malcolm X had agreed on a 50/50 split of royalties). "I'm just glad that [the autobiography is] ready for press now at a peak of interest for what will be international large sales, and paperback, and all. I'm just glad that it isn't a 'little' book, but one that can well really provide for his family as he would have wanted."[54] While Haley was eager to forecast royalties for the autobiography, the manuscript was not close to being ready to submit to the press. Complicating matters further, a week later Doubleday cancelled its plans to publish the book, fearing that Malcolm X's story would be too controversial. Reynolds shopped the book to other publishers, eventually making a deal with Grove Press. Reynolds pushed Haley to finish the epilogue to the autobiography and dissuaded the writer from also trying to write a biography of Malcolm. "People who read the autobiography I don't think a few months later are going to rush to read a life of Malcolm X," Reynolds told Haley. "That would be too much Malcolm X for most readers."[55] To the end, Haley viewed Malcolm X more as a fascinating and profitable character than as an inspiration for thinking about black culture, politics, and history in new ways.

Through the summer of 1965, Haley continued working on *Before This Anger*, often writing late into the night. He was convinced that the book would have broad appeal. "I've got, taking shape here under my hands, day by day, nights, too, a book 'Before This Anger,' Paul, that's gonna rock 'em. Black. White. Overseas. Everybody. There has never been published, on this subject, this *sweep* of subject."[56] Haley also felt himself being drawn into the story of his forebears. "This night's session, up until this letter, I've been with that wagon train, wrenching and creaking over that Cumberland Trail, into Tennessee—where, with whoops of joy they found old crusty, promoter, entrepreneur 'Chicken George' waiting," Haley wrote. "And I tell you, I was there! There were *my* folks. They were *us!* The Murrays, slavery behind them, who have trekked Westward, and now are about to prosper. And in the wings ... await the Haleys—a separate saga. And then Phase Two. The Henning I grew up in. And then Phase Three. The adult me, looking back as a writer upon it all, from The Mandingo down over seven generations to me now."[57]

At this stage, Haley also began to compile and synthesize assorted research notes to provide historical context and anecdotes for his family saga. Haley's childhood friend George Sims spent hours at libraries and archives copying sections of books and articles in longhand to deliver to Haley. "All night until the birds began chirruping in the dawn just outside the window," Haley wrote, "I sat here just entranced with the material I was copying from my collection of notes for this forthcoming magnificent book. The sweep of it! The saga of it! That Mandingo maverick black human animal as he was described by his daughter.... Oh, I tell you it's a great one, Paul! You just wait!"[58] Sims worked closely with Haley over the next decade, traveling with him to the Gambia and elsewhere. Haley eventually paid Sims several thousand dollars a year in compensation for his research assistance.[59] "A Latin phrase, fidus achates—devoted companion—accurately describes our relationship," Haley noted.[60]

The publication of *The Autobiography of Malcolm X* in the fall of 1965 increased Haley's profile as a writer and commentator on black culture, and Haley used the book as a stepping-stone to promote himself and *Before This Anger*. He wrote to Ken McCormick, his editor at Doubleday, to report, "I've recently returned from something of a tour of air, TV and newspaper promotion of the Malcolm X book, and during it I haven't been able to resist putting in wherever I could some substantial advance plugs for the forthcoming 'Before This Anger."[61] Doubleday had passed on publishing the Malcolm X autobiography, but Haley assured the publisher that their commitment to his new book would pay dividends. "I'll tell you something, though: privately, I think the Malcolm X book is going to be outsold by 'Before This Anger' probably something at least like ten to one. I base this on how I, as the writer, *feel*, down deep in my self about the material."[62]

By August 1966 Haley had completed the preface to *Before This Anger*. "This book aspires not only to tell the story of my family, which has treasured its past, and passed it down, and had coalesced around it, and had been inspired by it," Haley wrote. "But through the actual, and concurrently symbolic experiences of our family, this book aspires to reflect the physical and cultural assimilation of the Negro race, in a microcosm way, from slavery to today. For when you tell the story of one Negro, in the essence you tell the story of all Negroes. We all have essentially the same background: we came in the forebears' seeds from Africa, and we have physically and culturally been assimilating here since." Haley's vision for his project embraced a monolithic view of black history and culture that overlooked the vast diversity of experiences of black people in the United States. Religion, gender, sexuality, ethnicity, and other aspects of identity were absent from Haley's formulation of what it meant to write black history. At the same time, this monolithic view of black history appealed to many people, and Haley found publishers and producers especially receptive to the idea that his story could tell the story of all black people. "We Negroes lack nothing today so much as we lack a sense of history," Haley continued, paraphrasing Malcolm X's lecture on Afro-American history. "As badly as we need more education, and more housing, and more jobs, we need yet worse some more sense of history under us. You cannot make a slave of someone who knows his past." Haley outlined the stakes of appreciating and elevating black history and not so subtly aligned his project with great works of Western art. "When you are securely anchored in history, through literature, you demand respect," Haley argued. "The English, today poor, still are proud and condescending: they have Shakespeare. The Germans, defeated twice in their lifetimes, are anchored in Beethoven, Goethe, Kant, Schiller, Heine. It is no accident that the Jewish people are planting their roots in Israel." Haley concluded his pitch for black history by suggesting that he could tell this story in a way that would make readers receptive. "The struggle of the Negro is implicit, or implied, in this book," he wrote. "I have made effort that it is told by a Negro without undue bitterness, or rancor. My reasons for this are hope that I will retain the documentary value, that readers will not 'tune out' but will bear with us."[63] While Haley was still a decade away from finishing his book, this preface outlined a clear vision for the book's mission. After reading Elia Kazan's *America, America* (1964), the filmmaker's story of his uncle's immigration from Greece, Haley scribbled a note that foreshadowed the eventual title of his own family story: "The Negro has been in the bark, trunk, roots, leaves—throughout the family tree of America."[64]

The path to *Roots,* however, was not smooth. Haley's financial trouble grew increasingly dire in the fall of 1966. An outstanding tax debt led the IRS to take all of Haley's royalties ($1,432.83) from the Malcolm X book for that period. Haley was philosophical about his debt issues but recognized that dealing with the IRS took time away from writing. "I feel that I am still lucky in a way, though," he wrote to Reynolds. "Early in the game, before I make any real money, which I will be doing, *lots* of it—I am learning, the painful way, about how debts can be not only a nuisance day by day, but worse, in the process they *eat up* time one *could* be spending writing. I would be willing to bet that since that tax lien went on, forcing me to scrabble hither, thither to earn living money, at least one-fourth of my time has gone to writing letters to creditors, or otherwise trying to assuage and piecemeal pay them—at least enough time to have written some kind of book."[65]

With these tax troubles looming, *Before This Anger* was Haley's light at the end of the tunnel. Haley promised Reynolds that the book would establish him as a major author. "Here's a prophecy for your memoirs: I'm nursing a great book, Paul. It's going to be a landmark work; a major award-winning, world best-seller. With this one, I'll curtsy to no author you ever handled. My simple reduction: I, too, can *write*. And none of them have worked with material any more powerful, if *as* powerful, as mine."[66] Reflecting on how well *The Autobiography of Malcolm X* had sold, Haley continued, "I *know* I will make my family name, Haley, famed far beyond Malcolm X."[67]

Haley's hubris seems laughable today given that Malcolm X is regarded as an iconic figure. While Haley never lacked for self-assurance, this particular emphasis on making his family name famous may have been fueled by his father's deteriorating health. Simon Haley was hospitalized in 1966 for cerebral arteriosclerosis (hardening of the walls of the brain arteries) and congestive heart failure.[68] Alex's brother George visited their father at the Veterans Administration hospital. "We have a problem," George wrote to his siblings. "It is an extremely painful experience for me to visit Dad. Most of the time when I've been there, his mind is perfectly clear and then he starts hallucinating."[69] Alex Haley and his father corresponded regularly in the mid-1960s, and Simon, when his health allowed, helped gather family pictures and stories for his son's book. Simon understood why Alex would focus on his maternal lineage ("The Murrays are remarkable," Simon wrote at one point) but hoped that Alex would also consider writing about the Haley side of the family.[70] "As your book Before This Anger is due in 1967," Simon wrote, "I think the Haley book should follow soon after as a story available for all the Haley clan. You remember we both are in Who's Who in Colored America."[71] Simon Haley was disappointed that his oldest son had not finished college, but the success of the Malcolm X autobiography made him appreciate Alex's career as a writer. His father described the book as "equivalent to getting your Ph.D."[72] Alex Haley was certain that Before This Anger would make his father even more proud.

Haley's confidence that Before This Anger would be a best seller and his tax troubles made him increasingly frustrated that Doubleday was reluctant to advance him any more money for the project. He told Reynolds that the scope of the book project was much larger than when he had signed the contract with Doubleday and that he needed to travel to Africa and Europe for research. "Time and again, I tried to convey to Doubleday that as I kept up research, based upon my seminal data, the book kept growing in its scope, and stature," Haley wrote. "It has become a 200-year chronicle, a sweeping saga; time and again I have tried to convey that to accomplish its research, I need more than $2200! I was trying to suggest, like, Look, fellows, you're publishing this! The contract's amendable. It's not the Constitution. Support me, help me—it's going to be a great book, a great seller!"[73]

By March 1967, Haley was unsure when he would ever be able to finish the book. "Before This Anger simply isn't going to get written, under my circumstances at present," he told Reynolds. "It won't get written until I can get enough money, at one time, to pay off sundry debt harassments, to be able to do the sustained *concentrating* on this book.... I hate all of this floundering around, necessitated by money-need.... The point is I need money, now, to write the book.... If I'd had operational money, this book now could have been in bookstores."[74]

Reynolds told Haley that one way to get more money would be to sell the paperback rights to *Before This Anger.* "I love your idea of proposing the book to several major paperback houses—for their making bids," Haley replied. "So its squarely up to me to present the most exciting possible package. You know that I can verbally present the book effectively, to these various paperback people you select to hear and bid."[75] Haley told Reynolds that if Doubleday would not approve the paperback sale, "well, then, tonight I am going to put my 'Before this Anger' materials carefully back into their cartons, and carry them upstairs. And I'm going to start tomorrow working on some magazine stuff. And I will resume work on the book when I get—enough—working money."[76] Frustrated with his Doubleday contract and facing pressure from the publisher for already missing three deadlines to complete *Before This Anger,* Haley was defiant. "I just happen to be that necessary evil, the writer," he told Reynolds. "Nobody is going to get this book *until* I write it. And the book that is here, the Olympian chronicle, *my* family, *my* forebears, I am not going to half-write. It is going to have from me what its magnitude demands, and that is the very uttermost that I can give to it. I hope Doubleday sees fit to help."[77]

Reynolds tried to talk Haley out of walking away from the project. "I don't want to argue with you, I want to help," Reynolds began. "The contract with Doubleday for 'Before This Anger' was signed the summer of 1964, long before your autobiography of Malcolm X was published and long before you could get the kind of money you can get today. People weren't paying in '64 what they're paying today and you were relatively unknown. Let's grant it was a mistake if you want to. It was also stipulated that the book would be delivered January 1, 1966, fourteen months ago.... When a publisher has a firm contract at one price it's awfully hard to make him pay more money. From his point of view why should he?"[78] Reynolds reminded Haley that finishing the book was the best solution to his money problems. "We've got to get Before this Anger done," Reynolds wrote. "It's a potential enormous money maker."[79] Reynolds urged Haley to start showing Doubleday some manuscript pages soon because they "are beginning to get scared you'll never write the book."[80]

Haley's experience in developing *Before This Anger* taught him that for commercial writers words equal money. He cared deeply about tracing his family's history and was energized by reading histories of West Africa, slavery, and early America. At the same time, Haley never stopped thinking of his family history as a story to be pitched, polished, and sold. These motivations eventually led him to take his first trip to Africa. In the Gambia Haley heard stories that gave his book even more emotional and economic potential than he had dreamed.

CHAPTER TWO

The Gambia

"The Union Jack fluttered down over Gambia at midnight this morning," the *New York Times* reported on February 18, 1965, "bringing an end to the last outpost of colonial rule in West Africa and giving Africa its smallest and poorest independent state."[1] From its coast on the Atlantic Ocean, the Gambia stretches three hundred miles east in a narrow strip of land surrounded by Senegal. (The country is referred to as "the Gambia" to differentiate it from the river after which the country was named.) The Gambia River made the country a small but important trading post, first for the Portuguese and later for the French and British. These European powers fought over control of the territory and transported hundreds of thousands of enslaved people from the country's ports from the mid-1600s to the early 1800s. In 1965, the British paid for half the cost of the fireworks display to celebrate Gambia's independence but left the country politically and economically unstable. "We are entering into independence with many grave problems," said David Jawara, the Gambia's first prime minister.[2] When Alex Haley's ancestral quest led him to the Gambia two years later, Gambian officials were eager to help and hoped that the author's search for roots would benefit the newly independent nation.

Haley first identified the Gambia as his ancestral home while touring the West Coast to promote *The Autobiography of Malcolm X* in December 1965. Haley told *San Francisco Chronicle* literary editor William Hogan that he believed his ancestor had arrived in South Carolina from the Gambia in 1766.[3] Haley had previously identified his original African ancestor as "the Mandinka" (or simply "the African"). While Haley later claimed that several fortuitous research finds in 1966 pointed him to the Gambia, it is likely that he identified the Gambia, among other West African nations, because the Mandinka ethnic group made up a large percentage of the Gambia's population. He may also have focused on the Gambia after reading the work of Scottish explorer Mungo Park, who focused on the Gambia River in parts of *Travels in the Interior of Africa* (1799) and later works (Haley's archives include several photocopies from Park's books, and Park is the source that appears most frequently in Haley's notes on the history of the Gambia).[4] Whatever the case, once Haley settled on the Gambia the country assumed a mythic importance in his research for *Before This Anger*.

In August 1966, Haley wrote Ken McCormick, his editor at Doubleday, to promise that the manuscript would be completed soon and mentioned his intention of traveling to the Gambia. "I plan to travel-write the last chapter—to Gambia, Africa," Haley wrote, "to walk by the river where the old slave-loading station is located; thence by ship across the old slave-trade route; thence by car, to walk on the ground of each of the former plantations where my forebears were slaves." Haley called this chapter "Sentimental Journey" and anticipated that writing it would be an "emotional experience."[5] To prepare for his trip, Haley went to the Gambian embassy in Washington, D.C., and sought out Gambian exchange students, both in the nation's capital and closer to his new home in upstate New York, to talk with them about his research. "All are fascinated," he said. "They assure me high-level entrée in their country, assure me every cooperation. I have just got to get there, symbolically to visit physically where that slave ship loaded my great x7-grandfather."[6]

Funding for the trip would come not from Doubleday but from an agreement Haley's agent Paul Reynolds negotiated with *Reader's Digest*. In exchange for the rights to publish advance excerpts of *Before This Anger*, *Reader's Digest* provided Haley with much-needed money for research travel and living expenses. "I couldn't tell you, really, how much this whole arrangement means to me, both the subsidy and the heightened incentive!" Haley told Reynolds. "Working with the meager resources I had, the more I researched, the more I came to realize what I *could* have as a book, if I could go all out. And now I can! Golly, even the travel: to Africa, and other places I need to go, for this, for that—to make this book a landmark. I make you a prediction, friend. I won't come right out and call the name of the Prize. I just say to you: you just watch what we are going to win! Because just ain't never *been* a book like this one!"[7]

In the story Haley told on the lecture circuit and repeated in the last chapter of *Roots*, he described how he had fortuitously met a student from the Gambia. Haley said that after anthropologist Jan Vansina had deciphered the Mandinka words from Haley's family stories and pointed him toward the Gambia, a professor who invited Haley to speak at Utica College mentioned that there was an outstanding student from the Gambia at nearby Hamilton College. According to the account in *Roots*, Haley drove the half hour to Hamilton College in Clinton, New York, to ask about this student. "Before I could finish asking, a Professor Charles Todd said, 'You're talking about Ebou Manga.' … Ebou Manga was small of build, with careful eyes, a reserved manner, and black as soot. He tentatively confirmed my sounds, clearly startled to have heard me uttering them.… In his dormitory room, I told him about my quest. We left for The Gambia at the end of the following week."[8] Ebou Manga did play a crucial role in facilitating Haley's research in the Gambia, but Haley's story compressed several months of planning into a fictionalized week of lucky coincidences.

In October 1966, Ebou Manga was a junior at Hamilton College and a member of the Utica chapter of the Congress of Racial Equality (CORE). An economics professor at Utica College, who knew Manga through CORE, gave Manga's name and phone number to Haley when the author spoke at the college regarding the Malcolm X book and *Before This Anger*. Haley called to invite Manga to dinner with him and Haley's friend and research assistant George Sims. The three talked late into the night about the Gambia and Haley's research.[9] "I just cannot tell you how delighted I am over our last night's meeting," Manga wrote the next day. "You have embarked on a very worthy venture, and I shall do my best to give you my fullest assistance." Haley described Manga as "a gentleman, quiet of manner, extremely capable, diligent, dependable, [and] loyal."[10] The young Gambian became Haley's mental model for creating the character of Kunta Kinte: "Kunta to me became Ebou. Ebou to me became Kunta."[11] More immediately, Manga opened doors for Haley in the Gambia. Manga, whose father, a pharmacist, worked for the Gambian government, told Haley how he hoped the project would benefit his home country. "Your book is going to be of tremendous importance to The Gambia," Manga wrote. "As I told you last night, it will be the main vehicle that will bring The Gambia to the front-line of world attention. The benefit that The Gambia will derive from it is unlimited. I assure you that you will have a very enthusiastic reception whenever you go to The Gambia. Furthermore, you will never be short of the necessary assistance from both official and private sources while you are there."[12] Manga helped Haley make connections in the Gambia over the next several months before Haley's first trip to Africa in the spring of 1967. As Manga predicted, Gambian officials saw Haley's research as a potential boon to the small and newly independent African nation.

Interestingly, Haley traveled to Ireland to search for his Irish ancestry before he traveled to the Gambia. James Jackson, a second-generation Irish immigrant, owned Haley's great-grandmother, Easter Jackson, and fathered a child with her, "Queen" Jackson Haley. "You know that my mission [to Ireland] was a facet of the research of the paternal side of my family's history," Haley wrote to *Reader's Digest* editor Maurice Ragsdale after returning from Ireland. "Most Negroes' U.S. lineage will include, somewhere during slavery, a white-sired child; it was thus that my father's mother was the child of a white plantation owner. In the U.S. Archives in Washington I had found that this family—Jacksons—originated in Carrickmacross, Ireland; and now I was going there to learn whatever more details I could about the Jacksons—in order to take that side of the forebears back as far as I can take the maternal-side African."[13] Haley initially included these Irish ancestors and anecdotes in his lectures, but they eventually became a footnote as the Gambian part of his story grew in importance.

Haley stopped in London on his return trip from Ireland, where he visited the office of the high commissioner of Gambia and made preliminary visits to archives and libraries in the city. These research leads made him increasingly excited for his planned visit to the Gambia. "I am told there are still present at

Gambia—or on James Island, hard by Gambia's capital city of Bathurst—the *ruins* of that centuries-old slave fort," Haley told Ragsdale in December 1966. "I am told that I very well may be able to obtain for a keepsake there, if I dig a bit, a link or two of the heavily rusted chain with which the slaves were chained."[14] In addition to the possibility of securing material artifacts to connect to his genealogy, Haley was optimistic that he would be able to find the specific slave ship that had carried his ancestor away from the Gambia some two hundred years earlier. "I am told that the township of Bathurst has ancient 'village records,' in Arabic, going back *before* 1766—supposedly recording chronological events of local interest," Haley wrote. "Suppose I can there find the name of *that* ship! (It really isn't impossible!) In fact, I *may* be able to find the name of it in London; the Admiralty Shipping records are so exhaustive and meticulous. I know the year. I know that not many ships went into Gambia, as into other ports. Either in London, or at Gambia, it's just *possible*."[15] Haley's optimism was partly aimed at convincing *Reader's Digest* that their travel funds were being well spent and that the magazine's condensation of *Before This Anger* would be successful. "I surely don't intend to miss with this book," Haley concluded. "It just seems to me to get more and more gripping the more I round out the research."[16]

As he prepared for his trip to Africa, Haley sent letters to a dozen Gambian officials whose names Manga had given him. "I think you will be pleased to know that my project promises to bring great international attention to The Gambia," Haley wrote. "*Reader's Digest* already has contracted to condense my book into its 24 million issues in 13 languages about the world." Haley also noted that filmmaker Elia Kazan had inquired about making *Before This Anger* into a film. "America's greatest cinema director has announced plans to film from this book a major motion picture," Haley promised. "A sizeable portion will be filmed in The Gambia, employing many Gambians as actors. I think it's safe to predict that by 1969, The Gambia will enjoy world recognition—and tourism."[17] M. D. N'Jie, an official in the Gambian Information Office who had known Ebou Manga since childhood, wrote back to Haley with promises of support. "I assure you that you will receive the fullest co-operation possible in your mission. We are indeed proud to learn that someone of your eminence can trace his descent from The Gambia."[18]

Haley made his first trip to the Gambia in late March 1967, the first time he had touched African soil. After a long flight from New York to Dakar, Senegal, Haley prepared to board a Nigerian Airlines connecting flight to Yundum Airport in Bathurst, Gambia. When the customs representative handed him a form, Haley recalls staring at the "name" section and thinking, "I really don't know my real name, as you who never left Africa know yours. Then I wrote 'Haley,' thinking how virtually all of us U.S. blacks bore the names, actually, of whom ever [*sic*] had happened to own our slave forebears."[19] After reaching the Gambia, Haley connected with Ebou Manga, who had arrived in the country several days earlier. Manga told his contacts about Haley's research and helped Haley secure time on Radio Gambia to describe his mission.[20] Haley stayed in the Gambia for a week, visiting local archives and talking with anyone who might offer insight into his family's history. His visit was front-page news in the *Gambia News Bulletin:* "Mr. Alex Haley, one of the top magazine writers in the United States, and perhaps the best known Negro journalist in America, is here on a short working visit—and with the news that The Gambia will be one of the most talked about African countries once his next book 'Before This Anger' appears next Spring." The goals of Haley's trip were widely circulated in the country.

The *Gambia News Bulletin* informed readers that Haley's book "will tell the story of how an American Negro family rooted itself in the United States over a 200 year period from the time an African slave was taken from The Gambia to work in the plantations of South Carolina in 1766."[21] Haley talked with dozens of people about the details of his genealogical search, which helped his hosts in the Gambia find someone who could tell a story of the capture of Haley's ancestor that would fit the dates Haley had already identified.

Back in the United States, Haley wrote to his agent Paul Reynolds with excitement about the developments in the Gambia. "I am about to produce the single *biggest* book success of 1968," Haley wrote. "You watch! Can you imagine that in Africa, they were able to determine for me even the very *village* from which my 1760's forbear was taken! And the history of that *village* can authentically be taken back to about 1600! Ain't *never* been a book like this! We're going to hang a Pulitzer Prize copy on that Reynolds' office hallway wall!"[22] Here again, the personal and professional meaning of Haley's search converged. Curiosity fueled his travels to the Gambia, and he was sincerely enthusiastic about finding his furthest-back person. At the same time, Haley knew that he was putting together a remarkable story and that, if he could pull it off, he would reap critical and commercial success. By this point Reynolds had heard Haley promise several times that *Before This Anger* would be a major book. Reynolds wanted to hear fewer promises and to see more writing. "Your experience in Africa is magnificent," Reynolds told Haley, before reminding him that he still had to write the book. "The time must come very soon when you'll be doing the weary labor of sorting out your notes and organizing them, and start writing. When can you promise me the first 10000 words?"[23]

Haley had been home for a month when he received a phone call from the Gambian High Commission in London. After Haley's first visit several Gambian officials organized a "Haley Committee" to aid the author's search for his ancestors. The official in London told Haley that they had found something "very worth your while" and encouraged him to return as soon as possible. "Knowing the Africans—that they never would make such a phone call, or statement, unless it really *was* something, without a second's hesitation I said yes," Haley wrote to Reynolds on a plane en route to the Gambia.[24] Haley said he had been "devouring facts about Africa" since his first trip. On the Pam Am flight from New York to Dakar, he read E. W. Bovill's *The Golden Trade of the Moors* (1958) and Sir John Milner Gray's *History of the Gambia* (1940).[25] Haley's first trip had generated significant interest in the small country, and dozens of people were now invested in making his family quest successful. "I thought about how it was good that I had made the first trip with Ebou Manga, meeting people," Haley wrote. "Then, when I had left, they had begun to spread my mission. The African grapevine had gone to work, abetted by traveling inspectors, and some telephone calls."[26]

In notes typed shortly after the second trip to the Gambia, Haley described himself as an "apprentice Mandinka" and wrote in vivid terms about what the trip meant in his family saga. "It seemed incredible that I, from Henning, Tennessee, actually was here, having employed an African safari of a dozen people to take me to see what Grandma used to sit me down in the kitchen and give me cookies and jelly biscuits and tell me about," Haley wrote. "Cousin Georgia had died the morning I was on the plane to Dakar; and her funeral services were being held the day I was there on the launch in the river, hunting what Grandma and she had told me about.... She had ... via me ... re-opened the long, dark corridors of those 200-odd years from our African forebears, in whom we had been semen."[27]

Haley's use of *semen* is a good indication that he thought of his genealogical search in paternal terms. Indeed, there are several notecards in his archived research materials across the top of which Haley wrote "semen."[28] While Haley described his female elders as the most influential storytellers in his family, he always expressed the most interest in and identification with the men in his family's history, especially "the Mandinka" (later Kunta Kinte) and "Chicken George." By thinking of his story in terms of forefathers "in whom we had been semen," Haley imagined his female ancestors (the characters Belle, Kizzy, and Tildy) as little more than receptacles who served as bridges from one generation of men to the next. Even when Haley used *semen* in more challenging ways, such as to describe how white slave owners had fathered "Chicken George" and "Queen" Haley, he evinced more interest in asserting paternity than in what this meant for the women involved, Kizzy and Easter Jackson. Haley underdeveloped the female characters in *Roots* because he approached his family history from the earliest stages as a search for semen.

It was on his second trip to the Gambia that Haley first heard the story of the most important man in his story, Kunta Kinte. After Haley's first visit Gambian officials had searched throughout the country for someone who knew the Kinte family history. Some of these officials carried pictures of Haley and his American family members. A man named Demba Kinte, who resembled a picture of George "Chicken George" Lea, Haley's great-great-grandfather, pointed officials to the village of Juffure, where his uncle, Kebba Fofana Kinte, could tell the family history going back several generations.[29] "I have to say that I am totally overwhelmed at the work that the Committee has done

Figure 1. Alex Haley with children in the Gambia, 1967. Image courtesy of Dr. David P. Gamble.

since I was here last, in the Gambia," Haley told the officials at the start of his second visit. "I understand that there has been one rather epochal development that you have made in your own local research since I left—and that was concerning a story which was told by an elderly man, which seems incredibly to tie in with the information that I have had, all my life, from my own parents, or grandparents." Incredible as it was, Haley was eager to believe that he could trace himself back to a specific Gambian ancestor. He promised to make sure that this amazing story would also benefit his hosts in the Gambia. "The only thing that I can say, in turn, is that ... I shall make every effort to write a book which will recompense the efforts that you have made in behalf of The Gambia, as overwhelmingly," Haley told the officials. "I believe that world attention focused upon this country will bring the community many benefits."[30]

Figure 2. Alex Haley takes notes on boat en route to Fort James in the Gambia, 1967. Gambian kora player Jali Nyama Suso is seated to Haley's right. Image courtesy of Dr. David P. Gamble.

After Gambian officials told Haley about Kebba Fofana Kinte and described what this elder had said about the Kinte family history, they took Haley to meet him. Haley, George Sims, and ten Gambian officials, interpreters, and musicians took a boat up the Gambia River to the village of Juffure. As they approached the village, Haley saw for the first time Fort James, from which slave ships had once departed. "I began to experience almost hallucinatory visions," Haley wrote. "It was as if I began to *see*, ahead, some of the things which had happened.... I could *see* the slave ships drawing out, heavily laden. I could imagine the confusion, the blood, on the decks. I could *see* the black forms wrestling loose and diving over the side. I could imagine the horror below the decks. I rapidly wrote in my notebooks." Haley started to cry. "I could feel the Africans staring at me," he wrote. "It was not the first time that tears were in my eyes in Africa."[31]

In *Roots,* Haley described the safari to Juffure as the "peak experience" of his life, "that which emotionally, nothing in your life ever transcends."[32] A crowd of villagers greeted Haley and his traveling party. Among the villagers was Kebba Fofana Kinte, whom Haley described as "a small man wearing an off-white robe, a pillbox hat over an aquiline-featured black face," who had "about him an aura of 'somebodiness.'"[33] With dozens of villagers gathered around, Kebba Fofana Kinte began to tell Haley about the Kinte clan's ancestral history. Haley considered Kebba Fofana Kinte a griot, a traditional storyteller and musician skilled at performing the oral history of the village. "The *griot* would speak, bending forward from the waist, his body rigid, his neck cords standing out, his words seeming almost physical objects," Haley wrote. Kebba Fofana Kinte spoke in Mandinka and would speak one or two sentences and then lean back, while an interpreter translated his words into English for Haley. "Spilling from the *griot's* head came an incredibly complex Kinte clan lineage that reached back across many generations," Haley wrote, "who married whom; who had what children; what children then married whom; then their offspring. It was all just unbelievable."[34]

After speaking for almost two hours, Kebba Fofana Kinte reached the part of the story that Haley had traveled four thousand miles to hear. He told Haley that Omoro and Binta Kinte had four sons, Kunta, Lamin, Suwadu, and Madi, and that one day Kunta went out to find firewood and disappeared. "The family believed he was caught," the interpreter told Haley. "Because then, you know the slave trade was going on."[35] "I sat as if I were carved of stone," Haley wrote in *Roots.* "My blood seemed to have congealed. This man whose lifetime had been in this back-country African village had no way in the world to

Figure 3. Alex Haley listens to Kebba Fofana Kinte, seated with white hat, tell the story of the Kinte family. George Sims, Haley's friend and research assistant, is seated to Haley's right. Image courtesy of Dr. David P. Gamble.

Figure 4. Kebba Fofana Kinte, the Gambian elder who told Haley the story of Kunta Kinte. Image courtesy of Dr. David P. Gamble.

know that he had just echoed what I had heard all through my boyhood years on my grandma's front porch in Henning, Tennessee ... of an African who always had insisted that his name was 'Kin-tay'; who had called a guitar a '*ko*,' and a river within the state of Virginia, 'Kamby Bolongo'; and who had been kidnapped into slavery while not far from his village, chopping wood, to make himself a drum."[36]

After *Roots* was published in 1976 and broadcast the following year to international acclaim, British journalist Mark Ottaway and others raised questions about the reliability of the Kinte family history Haley had heard in the Gambia and about whether Kebba Fofana Kinte was actually a griot.[37] Gambian scholar Bakari Sidibe cautioned Haley as early as 1973 about relying too heavily on Kebba Fofana Kinte. Sidibe, for example, wrote Haley with more information on Kebba Fofana Kinte and his relationship to the griot tradition. "Family *griots,* as part of their hereditary profession, must learn the stories of their patron family," Sidibe told Haley. "For this reason, the ambitious ones go for detail, chronology, praises, and drama. It is impossible to represent a griot's performance in writing, which loses much of his style, voice quality, and general showmanship, for they are entertainers."[38] Although Kebba Fofana Kinte adopted this style and was a respected elder in Juffure, Sidibe said that he was not of the specific class of family griots but was instead a drummer and substitute imam. "By birth and by his own views he is not a griot," Sidibe wrote. Sidibe had sought out an elder from a different branch of the Kinte family and had noted "some glaring contradictions" between the different family histories. To figure out the "contradictions in names, places, and generations," Sidibe encouraged Haley to interview "members of the five Kinte branches in Gambia ... including at least one *griot* from each house" and to put these oral sources together with the available written documents in Gambia.[39]

While Kebba Fofana Kinte may not have been a griot, he was clearly a skilled storyteller. The "griot embodies entertainment," Haley later noted. "He was the story-teller, carrier of news. He was the television of his time."[40] For Haley, listening to Kebba Fofana Kinte tell the story of the Kinte clan must have been like looking in a mirror. After pitching *Before This Anger* for several years, Haley understood that people enjoyed stories that were almost unbelievable, that suspending disbelief was part of the pleasure of the story he was selling. The appeal of Haley's story was that it was supposed to be impossible for an African American to trace his or her history back, through the abyss of slavery, to a specific African ancestor. Haley traded on this impossibility in developing *Roots*. In the Gambia, Kebba Fofana Kinte told a compelling and persuasive story that, incredible as it was, Haley was eager to believe. "I attached myself like a mollusk to the mystery," Haley said.[41] Over the next decade, Haley found that agents, publishers, lecture audiences, film producers, readers, and television viewers were also eager to be moved by this remarkable story.

CHAPTER THREE

Speaking *Roots*

Alex Haley returned from the Gambia in May 1967 with what he knew was a very valuable story. While *Roots* was still almost a decade from being published, Haley's incredible research saga paid immediate dividends on the lecture circuit. Haley started lecturing as a client of the W. Colston Leigh speakers' bureau in the fall of 1966. Over the next decade he crisscrossed the country, speaking at colleges, libraries, historical societies, and corporate meetings. Haley later recalled that rather than marching in "civil rights demonstrations, I marched from airport to airport dragging the ever-present enormous leather bag of *Roots* research data."[1] Some of his first lectures described the story behind *The Autobiography of Malcolm X* or featured anecdotes from his *Playboy* celebrity interviews. Soon, however, Haley started describing his research for *Before This Anger* in lectures titled "Myth of the Negro Past?," "Black Heritage," and "Saga of a People."[2] "When I was asked to speak on another topic designed by my hosts, within five or ten minutes I always managed to shift the ground to *Roots*," Haley remembered. "I was obsessive about it. And everywhere I spoke, I found audiences who were moved with me as the story unfolded."[3] A Leigh Bureau brochure assured prospective clients that "Alex Haley has made a remarkable and unique contribution to the American lecture platform through his unfailing gift of saying strong things in a quiet way, and by his ability for holding audiences spell-bound."[4] Haley earned $500 to $1,000 for these early lectures, money he desperately needed to pay for living expenses, research travel, and child support. While Paul Reynolds, Haley's literary agent, recognized the author's need for the money, he worried that these lectures would keep Haley from finishing his book. "I dread your spending the time away from the main tent," Reynolds wrote to Haley after Colston Leigh called Reynolds to ask Haley to accept more lecture bookings. "It is really so vital to you and your career, and your piece of mind with regard to money to get [*Before This Anger*] done this year."[5] Reynolds was right that lecturing would make it more difficult for Haley to write, but he did not anticipate how important the lectures would be in creating interest in Haley's story. At each lecture stop Haley also tapped into local media. "I would fly to the place where I was to speak and usually spent the morning taping a television show or doing a live local talk show on television or radio," Haley recalled. "I met local reporters for interviews in the early afternoon, dined with my hosts and their local committee, gave the lecture, and went on to a reception afterwards."[6] Hundreds of thousands of people heard Haley tell the story of his search for his family's roots before they read *Roots* or watched the television series. Neither Doubleday nor ABC could have asked for better promotion. Haley's extensive advanced marketing of *Roots* was unprecedented in the history of publishing or television. It is impossible to understand how *Roots* became a cultural

Figure 5. Alex Haley gave hundreds of lectures across the country as a client of the W. Colston Leigh speakers' bureau. Image courtesy of Leigh Bureau.

phenomenon in 1976 and 1977 without appreciating how Haley hustled across the country for a decade to build an audience for his story.

Haley was a dynamic speaker, and on the lecture circuit he fashioned his research into a dramatic detective story that captivated audiences. He embellished and resequenced events so that he could tell his audiences a story that found him moving quickly (by plane, boat, taxi, and foot) from amazing research discovery to amazing research discovery. "Through his lecturing, Haley has created an oral tradition of his own," Michael Kirkhorn wrote in the *New York Times*. "The story of his ancestry is so intimately Haley's own story that Kunta Kinte seems almost his contemporary; bits of narrative are threaded through his conversation."[7] Just as Haley wanted to believe the Kinte family story he heard in the Gambia, lecture audiences found Haley's story compelling and persuasive because it was wonderful how all of the pieces of this puzzle fit together just so. Haley told audiences a story that they wanted to believe. For his part, Haley thrived on the energy of sharing his remarkable story with more and more people. "I really do not feel as if I am lecturing, but rather that I am sharing an experience with friends," Haley wrote to one fan.[8]

The stories Haley gathered in the Gambia were a sort of currency that increased the value of his lectures. Haley's research finds in the Gambia also made him bolder in negotiating with people who wanted to buy the film rights to his family saga. Elia Kazan, the prominent stage and film director, was the first to approach Haley about the film rights to Haley's book. In 1966, Kazan optioned *The Autobiography of Malcolm X* and started working with James Baldwin and Haley on making the book into a film. Haley and Kazan became friends in the process. Haley called Kazan by his nickname "Gadge" (short for gadget), and Kazan offered Haley his house on Montauk, Long Island, to use as a writer's retreat. Hearing Haley describe *Before This Anger*, Kazan thought this family history had the potential to be a motion picture, and he made an offer for the film rights to Haley's yet-to-be-written book. "Elia Kazan told me that he cannot get the book out of his mind, the motion picture that it will make, which he wants to be the one to produce and direct," Haley told Reynolds in April 1967, shortly before Haley took his second trip to the Gambia.[9] Given his constant financial problems, Haley was particularly excited about the money to be made from a film. "I think that literally millions will be made by the motion picture, playing, as it will, all over the world.... So if we get a good percentage of this movie ... we just about can't avoid becoming durably rich!"[10]

When Haley received Kazan's offer, it was much lower than expected. On Reynolds's advice, Haley turned down the bid, which would have paid him $2,500 in advance and another $20,000 if the film was made. (Kazan had previously offered Haley $350,000 if the Malcolm X book was made into a film.)[11] "Gadge— Kazan—and I are good, warm friends," Haley told Reynolds. "I have heard him say, regarding other deals, that friendship and money deals should not be mixed. I know I ain't even about to, ain't even thinking about any such price for the motion picture rights of *this* book.... Hence, the thing, obviously, to do is to wait until the book is done; until its momentum is avalanching—when we will have the seller's market."[12] Haley had a keen sense that each research discovery added additional emotional and economic value to his story.

Haley's second trip to the Gambia and the story he heard there about Kunta Kinte made him certain that *Before This Anger* was worth much more than what Kazan had offered. "I know, better than anyone else, better than even you can (since it isn't readable yet), the book that's here," Haley wrote to Reynolds. "Even I don't fully know yet, because so much is going to happen on that paper. But I know we are going to see this book achieve at least a reception comparable to 'In Cold Blood,' and, in fact, probably considerably greater. My theme is vastly greater, and more powerful, and I know the portent of the things I now am feeling as more, more impact material gets added, such as with this last trip. Never before anything like it! Not in its area."[13]

In the thousands of letters he wrote, Haley rarely mentioned other books, so it is interesting that he cited Truman Capote's

In Cold Blood (1966), a story about the murder of a Kansas farm family and the search for their killers, as the book he wanted to match or surpass. It is easy to understand why Haley would see Capote as someone to emulate. Capote called *In Cold Blood* a "nonfiction novel," and the book mixed journalism with fictional techniques.[14] While Haley did not reference New Journalism explicitly, he found common ground with writers like Capote, Gay Talese, Hunter S. Thompson, and Tom Wolfe who popularized a blend of journalism and fiction in these years. Haley embraced this mixture of fact and fiction and ended up referring to *Roots* as a work of "faction" and a "novelized amalgam." Haley also appreciated and envied the commercial success *In Cold Blood* had achieved. Columbia Pictures bought the film rights to Capote's book and released a film version in 1967, the *New Yorker* published the entire story across four issues, and New American Library paid $500,000 for paperback rights. All together, the *New York Times* calculated that "Mr. Capote is being paid $14.80 a word for his 135,000-word book."[15] These numbers convinced Haley that he too was writing a potential blockbuster and that he needed to negotiate accordingly. Haley told Reynolds that he planned to take William Fitelson, Kazan's lawyer, up on Fitelson's invitation to have dinner with Ralph Ellison, the acclaimed author of *Invisible Man* (1953). "I am going to whet their appetites a bit," Haley said. "I am going to take up this invitation after I have some photographs now in development and a few other little handy exhibits, and I'll do some talking about what I've got, just among friends. And let him do some subsequent thinking."[16] It is telling that Haley viewed a dinner invitation with Ralph Ellison, one of the greatest American novelists, as an opportunity to improve his negotiating position with Kazan for the film rights to *Before This Anger.* Haley never considered himself to be a literary writer on par with Ellison and never aspired to this type of greatness. He chased commercial success of the sort Capote had achieved with *In Cold Blood,* and if this resulted in literary awards, all the better.

Reynolds was encouraged by Haley's confidence but wanted to see Haley get *Before This Anger* down on paper. "Research is essential for any good book," he told Haley. "It looks to me as if you had magnificent research. There is almost no limit as to the amount of research one can do. Now you must keep your nose to the grind stone and get the book done. When will I be able to see the first 100 pages?"[17] While Haley had made little progress on actually writing the book by the summer of 1967, he still promised Doubleday that the final manuscript would be ready by the end of the year. Haley told Lisa Drew, who had started as Ken McCormick's assistant at Doubleday before becoming an editor, that *Before This Anger* would be ready "for that August 1968 publication, which will make its appearance most timely—in the nerve-wracking time of these summers, which I truly believe my book is going to do as much as one book can do toward helping positively."[18] Haley was eternally optimistic about his ability to meet deadlines and finish his book. He was also consistently wrong. "I never really thought I was saying what was not accurate," Haley later said. "I really felt I'd be finished with it in six months."[19]

Haley prepared an eighteen-page "working report" on *Before This Anger* to show Doubleday, *Reader's Digest,* and prospective film rights bidders that he was making progress on the book. The report was essentially a book proposal for a book that was already under contract. Haley was desperate to get more money out of the story, whether from the film, paperback, or serialization rights to the book. The report included color pictures of Haley's trip to the Gambia, including one with Haley, Kebba

Fofana Kinte (the elder who had told Haley the Kinte family history), and other members of the Kinte clan. The pictures offered visual evidence to shore up Haley's compelling stories. "Though distant, by two centuries, we are cousins," Haley wrote. If *Roots* was about establishing continuities in black kinship across generations, these photos of Haley surrounded by distant Gambian relatives offered proof of the tremendous genealogical breakthrough Haley claimed to have achieved. In the report Haley also argued that his family's history was about more than his specific ancestors. "The story tells fundamentally, too, the history of all African slave-descent peoples," Haley wrote. "For only the slaver ships, and the African-thence-American (or Brazilian, or West Indian) names would differ. So the book I now am writing has a hope to help render a better perspective to the black present, through presenting a black past that is a true, inherently deeply-moving human drama.... And my book's chief goals include something which our total international society has long badly needed: a buoy for the self-esteem, and for the esteem all others hold for, the slave-descent peoples."[20]

By the summer of 1967 all of the pieces Haley needed to create this symbolic and uplifting story were falling into place. In addition to the Kinte family history he had heard in the Gambia, Haley pinpointed the specific slave ship, *Lord Ligonier*, that he believed had transported Kunta Kinte to America. A *Reader's Digest* researcher working on Haley's behalf identified the *Lord Ligonier* in a London archive.[21] With the help of archivists, scholars, and research assistants working in London, Washington, D.C., and Annapolis, Maryland, Haley found more information on the slave ship. These documents tracked the ship's voyage from London to the Gambia and from the Gambia to Annapolis,

Figure 6. Alex Haley seated with members of the Kinte clan in the Gambia, 1967. Image courtesy of Dr. David P. Gamble.

where the *Lord Ligonier* arrived with a cargo that included ninety-eight enslaved Africans (forty-two Africans had died as the ship traversed the Middle Passage).[22] Not coincidentally, the dates of the *Lord Ligonier*'s arrival and slave sale fit perfectly with a deed Haley had found showing John Waller transferring to William Waller an enslaved person named "Toby," whom Haley believed to be Kunta Kinte. Haley wrote to one of his Gambian collaborators in July 1967 to convey the exciting news about the ship: "The key thing for me is that she [the *Lord Ligonier*] sailed for Annapolis, Maryland—which is central in the Tidewater Virginia area where I know that Kunta Kinte was landed and bought and taken to a plantation nearby. She was the only vessel within about a two-year period which sailed to that particular place, having come directly from James Fort [in the Gambia]."[23]

Like much in Haley's research story, these pieces of evidence do not fit together as neatly as he suggested. Genealogists Gary and Elizabeth Mills examined pre-1767 records from Spotsylvania County, Virginia, and found that while "the document which Haley found does show one Toby in the possession of one John Waller ... this Waller slave Toby appeared in at least six documents prior to the arrival of the *Ligonier*." "Clearly, if Kinte was captured in 1767," the Millses concluded, "he was not the Waller slave Toby."[24] It is important to remember that Haley was not trained as a historian or genealogist. When he found archival materials or heard stories that fit together he did not wait to pursue different leads or look for conflicting evidence that might trouble the neatness of his story. From Haley's perspective, he was stitching together disparate documents with oral histories from Tennessee and the Gambia with much larger cultural and commercial goals. "I am thrilled anew each time I work this with material," Haley wrote to Gambian officials after he identified the *Lord Ligonier*. "By golly, it never had been done before! How wonderful to think how, via this book, the black people of America will be thrilled (for symbolically it is *all* of our heritage), and the white people of America will be so vastly educated (for until this very time in history, it popularly has been dismissed that we, the black people, *had* any heritage to speak of)."[25] Haley was less focused on rigorous scholarly accuracy than he was on creating a dramatic and plausible narrative that would be culturally and commercially enriching.

Talking about his search for his family's roots helped Haley improve his story. Author Frank Chin, who worked in 1969 as a screenwriter for a film version of Haley's story that was not produced, heard Haley tell his story before three different audiences. "You say that you enjoy telling the story over and over again before different people because the process of questions and answers that follows the telling often gives you new insight into your story ... somehow makes it grow in implications and meaning," Chin wrote to Haley. "[This] seems to me to be a way of saying that the reactions of others forces [*sic*] you to refine and perfect both historical and emotional accuracy. Obviously you're still searching and probing yourself and your material for meanings, personal meanings as well as historical and cultural ramifications."[26] When Haley stood at a lecture podium at Simpson College in Indianola, Indiana, or Virginia State College in Petersburg, Virginia, he could see immediately how audiences responded to his story. He could tell which aspects made people laugh or cry, which stories captured attention, and which anecdotes bored people. Haley honed his family story over the course of dozens of lectures before finishing the first chapter of his book.

Haley's lectures also gave him a chance to see firsthand how the story of his search for roots moved people across racial, regional, and national lines. "I have seen in arch-conservative Orange County, California, literally black-jacketed, beret-wearing Black Panthers and banker-dressed, suburbia-type male and female white people standing side by side, applauding, cheering," Haley wrote to a *Reader's Digest* editor. "And in Florida, and in Georgia, and in Alabama, and in Ohio, and in New York, and wherever."[27] Like an advertising executive adding up demographics or a political consultant counting constituencies, Haley defined success as reaching the largest possible audience. These responses made Haley even more certain of his book's tremendous cultural and commercial potential. *Before This Anger*, Haley predicted in 1969, "is going to do, in this present social problem we have, something comparable ... to what 'Uncle Tom's Cabin' did in another time—this book in [*sic*] an overwhelming healing direction through a vastly increased emotional effect upon black, upon white alike. About the world; you watch!"[28] Early in

1964, Haley published a nuanced essay in the *New York Times* on Harriet Beecher Stowe's novel and the lasting influence of the "Uncle Tom" image that illuminates why he wanted to compare *Before This Anger* to Stowe's book. Haley noted the "global renown" Stowe's work had achieved and admired "the novel's indisputable historical role" in fostering antislavery sentiments. "It is a deep irony that, a century later, the very name of Mrs. Stowe's hero is the worst insult the slaves' descendants can hurl at one another out of their frustrations in seeking what all other Americans take for granted," Haley wrote. Haley argued that *Uncle Tom* took on negative connotations after Stowe's story had been "vulgarized" in "terribly caricatured" theatrical performances. "For generations, hundreds of 'Tom' companies played and replayed every American city and hamlet outside the South," Haley observed. "Translations by the dozen thrived no less in the homelands of countless future American immigrants. When finally, in the nineteen-twenties, automobiles and movies killed history's most successful theatrical venture, some 70 years of repetition had infected the Western world with an incalculably poisonous 'Topsy' and 'Uncle Tom' image of the American Negro." The lesson Haley took from *Uncle Tom's Cabin* was that popular culture had real power to shape images of black people and that once stories became part of mass culture the meanings of these stories could change for good or ill. On the mass culture reach of *Uncle Tom's Cabin*, Haley could have quoted novelist Henry James, who called Stowe's novel a "wonderful 'leaping' fish" that "could naturally fly anywhere." "If the amount of life represented in such a work is measurable by the ease with which representation is taken up and carried further, carried even violently to the furthest," James wrote, "the fate of Mrs. Stowe's picture was conclusive: it simply sat down wherever it lighted and made itself, so to speak, at home."[29] Haley might also have noted how his friend James Baldwin used *Uncle Tom's Cabin* to critique the idea that protest novels could change society. "The 'protest' novel, so far from being disturbing, is an accepted and comforting aspect of the American scene, ramifying that framework we believe to be so necessary," Baldwin wrote. "Whatever unsettling questions are raised are evanescent, titillating; remote, for this has nothing to do with us, it is safely ensconced in the social arena, where, indeed, it has nothing to do with anyone, so that finally we receive a very definite thrill of virtue from the fact that we are reading such a book at all."[30] Like James and Baldwin, Haley saw clearly that popular culture was powerful and dangerous terrain and optimistically believed his family history could do important and positive work in this regard.[31]

Haley had always been skilled at selling his story by speaking directly to people. He pitched *Before This Anger* to Doubleday in 1964 over a lunch meeting and captivated television producers David Wolper and Stan Margulies at a similar meeting a decade later. Haley described a particularly memorable lunch with *Reader's Digest* editors. "Over the soup, I stood up and began walking about the room," Haley recalled. "I didn't feel like eating. I began describing my researching already. And without myself realizing it, I became impassioned, exhorting and gesticulating. My feeling was that these editors had to see, to feel, to understand what I did. They had to understand what might be possible, for the first time in the history of the Negroes, who were one-tenth of America's population."[32] Pacing about the room, Haley started acting out Chicken George and other characters from the book. By this point the editors had stopped eating and the cook and waiters were standing at the kitchen door listening intently. "We were all startled when I stopped," Haley wrote. "I had been exhorting for three and one half hours. I felt drained, empty—and suddenly I didn't care if the editors had understood or not."[33] As always, Haley's storytelling was successful, and *Reader's Digest* agreed to give him the travel money he needed. Similarly, after the film deal with Elia Kazan fell through, Haley's entertainment lawyer Lou Blau arranged a new deal with Columbia Pictures and invited the Columbia executives to hear Haley speak at Beverly Hills High School in 1968. Haley's lecture helped persuade the executives to option the film rights to *Before This Anger* for $50,000.[34]

When Doubleday pressured Haley to finish the book, he encouraged the editors and executives to attend one of his lectures at New York University law school. "I think it would be most effective if they could see, and hear, a sophisticated, packed, metropolitan audience response to the inherent content, the inherent everybody-identification, the inherent emotion of this book," Haley wrote to Reynolds.[35] Haley wanted Doubleday to see that, on his own initiative, he had generated in advance "a *huge* market for a book. By now I have spoken of this book literally across this nation, back and forth and again, to collectively about three-quarters of a million people.... It is, indeed, a book born of talk."[36] Haley wrote to Reynolds again after the NYU lecture to say that he hoped Doubleday now had "some visual and aural appreciation of the way that by now literally hundreds of thousands of people (in audiences for three years) across the country [are] awaiting this book—and you can project what that is going to be mean in terms of a virtual instant *explosion* of sales ... of the hardcover!"[37] Haley's speaking engagements across the country amounted to one of the largest advance publicity campaigns in the history of publishing or television.

Haley predicted that his would be the first hardcover book to sell one million copies, a bold prediction that proved accurate.

"With Doubleday's HELP, we can do it," he told Reynolds. "Though I will tell you right now, I intend to do all possible of the promotion MYSELF—the surest way!"[38] Reynolds praised Haley's speaking skills but as usual wanted to see Haley actually write *Before This Anger*. "You were perfectly magnificent as a speaker," Reynolds wrote. "I once heard Clarence Darrow speak and he spoke over two hours and held his audience. I thought he was the only man in the world who could do that. Now I've met a second one who could. However, I'm a man for writing rather than speaking. So on with the completion of the book."[39] When Reynolds offered these words of encouragement, Haley's book was still five years away from being completed. Haley's family saga, however, was starting to come into focus.

In early 1972, Haley changed the working title of his book from *Before This Anger* to *Roots*. "Have changed the title to one I like better ... as nearly everyone does: 'Roots,'" Haley wrote to a friend. "Numerous good reasons. One, primarily, the more I have written, the more it has impressed itself upon me that there is so much more to the black saga than the topical 'Anger.' And that new title, 'Roots,' is more generic among mankind, and I see this book, really, as kind of the black slice of the human saga."[40] Shortly thereafter Haley landed a cover story in the *New York Times Magazine* titled "My Furthest Back Person—'The African,'" that put in print the story he had been telling in lectures over the past several years.[41] The *Wall Street Journal* ran a front-page story, "Black Genealogy," that focused on Haley's newly titled *Roots*. "In recent years growing numbers of black Americans—many of them inspired by Mr. Haley's success—have begun digging into family Bibles, marriage and property records and other sources, attempting to reconstruct their family trees," the article informed readers.[42] An old friend from Hamilton

College wrote to rib Haley about his extensive media exposure in 1972: "Alex has a cover on the TIMES Mag ... Alex is front pg in the Wall Street Journal ... Alex is in Africa sailing up a river with Humphrey Bogart and Katie Hepburn ... I have a feeling you are turning into a goddam myth somehow."[43] This choice of words was apt. As *Roots* received more attention through the 1970s, Haley and his family story took on mythic qualities. By tracing his family's history back to eighteenth-century Gambia, Haley seemed to have accomplished the impossible. In doing so he came to embody new possibilities for black history and new potentials for thinking about the place of individuals and families in history. These mythic qualities made it possible for *Roots* to challenge earlier historical myths, like *Birth of a Nation* and *Gone with the Wind*, but they also put immense pressure on Haley.

Haley received over four thousand letters in response to the *New York Times Magazine* article. "I was fascinated with the story in the *New York Times Magazine* about your root tracing," one reader wrote. "As a young black adult I would really like to delve into my own family heritage. I have knowledge to go on collected from elderly aunts and uncles. This past year at school I sent for information from the census bureau to verify my family tree, but became discouraged when I remembered I came from slaves. This is why I was so excited after reading your article. It was quite moving."[44] An older white reader from New Haven wrote, "I can now understand why Black students at colleges are demanding courses in colleges in Black Studies; they should be proud of their ancestry and their background."[45] "I've still got tears in my eyes," another reader told Haley.[46] Many readers said they were eager to read more of Haley's book. "I just finished reading your delightful article 'The African' in to-day's New

York Sunday Times," a reader wrote. "How I would like to have read another two hundred pages of this colossal narrative."[47]

Haley also appeared on several television shows, including two appearances on the *David Frost Show*, which broadcast on Westinghouse Corporation "Group W" stations across the country. On the second visit, Haley presented Frost with a detailed report on the host's genealogy, a gesture Haley repeated for Johnny Carson in 1977 when he appeared on the *Tonight Show*. These appearances also generated positive responses from viewers. "Alex Haley is just terrific," wrote a viewer from Tucson, Arizona. "What a story teller and what marvelous history of his family tree. I could have listened to him all afternoon."[48] "I can't really tell you how thrilled I was with … the story of your search," a woman from New York wrote. "Thrilled to the point of tears, joyous tears.… Even thinking about it now I find myself filling up. What you have been able to do has been the dream of so many of us that know we have our roots in Africa."[49] "I'm watching your guest talk about his ancestry Roots in Africa," another viewer wrote to David Frost. "I've been here at my breakfast table absolutely glued to my chair. It is by far one of the most exciting interesting things I've heard on TV in a long long time."[50] Another viewer was fascinated by Haley's story even if he could not remember the author's name. "I am very interested in getting the name and mailing address of the gentleman you had last Tuesday," this viewer wrote to Frost. "He is the Black man who was able to trace his history back to Africa. Being Black myself I was very interested in his quest and eventual success."[51] Haley replied to a surprising number of these letters. "I appreciate your letter forwarded by the David Frost Show," Haley wrote to one viewer. "The great number of people who responded really build my motivation for finishing the long, tough job of writing the book."[52]

Haley found black audiences especially excited about his research. "Each time I have seen you on TV ... and all throughout my five readings of the *Times* feature, I have wept unashamedly," a woman from New York wrote. "One can just imagine what the actual experience must have done to and for you. You have made so many of us proud of not only you but of ourselves and most certainly of our forefathers about whom we knew so little until you. What can we ever do to repay you—or even just to say God Bless you and Thanks."[53] A professor at Albany State University, a historically black institution in Georgia, wrote to tell Haley that he was assigning Haley's *New York Times* article in his class and asked Haley to keep the history departments at black colleges apprised of his progress on *Roots.*[54] A librarian at the National Portrait Gallery expressed admiration for Haley's research but wondered if *Roots* would ever be published. "Of course we Black sisters and brothers feel like gathering up our little stories and tracing ourselves the way you did," she wrote, "but it is taking you so long to get that book out I am beginning to think it is a fairy tale."[55] After visiting the University of Wisconsin-Madison, Haley wrote to Charles Anderson, a former Tuskegee airman and a professor of African American studies, "Every time I have a new chance to share the adventure that is to become a book the response of those who hear it thrills me all over again."[56] He also wrote to sociologist Harry Edwards at University of California, Berkeley, to thank him for a warm welcome in the Bay Area. "One of these fine days [my book] will be out there on the stands," Haley wrote, "and I am working hard as I know how to make it a book which genuinely will make a positive difference in both black and white audiences concerning what really *is* the richness and beauty of Blackness!"[57]

As Haley and *Roots* garnered increasing publicity through the early 1970s, Haley's relationship to black scholars and cultural institutions grew more complicated. "We used to sit in the history department at Howard and wonder when the book was coming out because he was still doing the speech," musician and scholar Bernice Reagon recalled. "And we would hear stories so we thought it was going to be a history book, an academic book. I remember when the word started going around that it wasn't going to be a story of his research, it was going to be a reconstructed story and I can remember the disappointment. Because we wanted a book of his research, and we were very disappointed that that was not going to happen."[58] With the buzz generated by *Roots,* Haley received offers from publishers to write books on black history, African history, and black genealogy, areas in which he had no academic training. Simon and Schuster, for example, offered Haley a $5,000 advance to write a history of Africa in 1967, just months after Haley had made his first trip to the continent.[59] After a Carnegie Corporation executive heard Haley's lecture, the author was invited to the Carnegie office in New York. "All the executives were assembled," Haley wrote. "Told them the story. They proposed to me that I head up bringing into being a Black Genealogical Library!"[60] Haley's rising stature as an expert on black history opened many doors for him, but it was disconcerting to many professionals in the field. When Haley received the Carnegie grant to start a black genealogical project, for example, it strained his relationship with the Schomburg library, a black culture center in Harlem where George Sims and Haley had gathered research materials for *Roots.* "If I sound emotional in regards to your relationship with the Schomburg, it is only because I long for the kind of support which you are able to obtain for your new project to be available to the Schomburg," library chief Jean Blackwell Hutson wrote to Haley. "Your name has come up so often during this period because nearly every white person to whom we have appealed for support have [*sic*] said, 'Where are some prominent Black people who have used the Collection and who know its value,' and since you are in the news so much these days, it has often been asked, 'Why isn't Haley helping you,' and of course, all I can say is, 'He is busy doing his own thing.'"[61] This rift remained after *Roots* was published to acclaim. "I have been disappointed not to find Schomburg included in the promotion of 'Roots,'" Blackwell Hutson wrote to Haley in 1977. "You were so very enthusiastic about helping Schomburg in the early days of your research." Blackwell Hutson described the library as being "in a very bad state so far as acquisitions are concerned" and asked Haley to donate a 16 mm copy of *Roots* because the $5,400 cost to purchase the film was prohibitive.[62] As Haley became a national focal point for black history, his success seemed to come at the expense of cultural institutions like the Schomburg that had made his research possible.

Haley fit somewhat awkwardly with the intellectual and political directions of black studies in this era. The demand for Haley as a speaker on college campuses had much to do the Black Power movement and the associated growth of black studies programs in the late 1960s and early 1970s. Students demanded more black speakers, and Haley had established himself as one of the top lecturers in the country. Haley shared many affinities with students and faculty who developed black studies; he believed in affirming black culture, appreciating black history, and fostering black pride. But he also believed that all of these should be pursued with the least possible conflict or confrontation. He was, after all, a writer who had pitched an idea for a book called *How to Co-exist with Negroes,* and the sensibilities of white audiences always figured prominently in his thinking. This made him the rare speaker who could appeal to both black students and white administrators.

Haley also did not make any attempt to situate himself in the tradition of black artists and intellectuals who had looked to Africa or written about slavery before *Roots*. If Haley read Carter G. Woodson, Langston Hughes, W. E. B. DuBois, Pauli Murray, Richard Wright, or Waters Turpin, he very seldom mentioned these or other black writers to his lecture audiences or correspondents. C. Eric Lincoln, a longtime friend of Haley's and one of his most prominent academic backers, recalled that when the eminent black historian John Hope Franklin asked to meet Haley, Haley replied "John Hope who?" Around black academics, Lincoln recalled, Haley "often belittled himself and stayed out of their way and so on because he was so sensitive to the fact that he was not a college graduate."[63] Haley described his work as a professional writer in terms of academic credentials. He was elated when his father told him he considered the publication of *The Autobiography of Malcolm X* as the "equivalent to getting your Ph.D.," and after anthropologist Jan Vansina praised Haley's work in the Gambia Haley said, "I felt as if he had passed me as a Doctoral Candidate."[64]

Being outside academia made it possible for Haley to see *Roots* as something wholly unprecedented. This is the "first really collated, organized, documented and (most importantly) *humanized* Black History!" Haley wrote to his *Reader's Digest* editor when he sent the chapter of his book. Haley described how his lectures had taken him into the "'lion's dens' of black militancy: Cornell, San Francisco State, San Jose State," where "I am not generally championed at all, as an individual." "I have gone into these places, where people are clamoring about 'Black History,'" Haley continued, "and up there on the stages I have gone into really but smatterings, but sketches, of what this book is to have between its covers. And I have had the pleasure that I have not known one single instance when, at the end, there was not quite literally an ovation, generally a standing one. I do not feel this for *me,* but for the material I have been able to gather, giving us all new insight into Black History, documented, humanized!"[65] Haley, of course, did not write the first black history. Carter G. Woodson founded the Association for the Study of African American Life and History in 1915 and popularized Negro History Week (later Black History Month) in 1926. John Hope Franklin's *From Slavery to Freedom: A History of African Americans* (1947) was already decades old when Haley started lecturing on his search for roots. Novelist Margaret Walker's *Jubilee* (1966), a story of a slave family in the Civil War era based on stories she had heard from her grandmother, brought black family history to popular audiences (Walker later accused Haley of copyright infringement, but a judge dismissed the case). African histories and cultures were also more familiar to many black Americans than Haley supposed. Among other works, black readers enjoyed Eslanda Goode Robeson's *African Journey* (1945) and *Ebony* editor Era Bell Thompson's *Africa: Land of Fathers* (1954) years before *Roots* was published. Haley's unique contribution was to bring his historical fiction to the mass market, first through lectures and later through the book and television miniseries versions of *Roots.* While Haley did not write the first black history, he made black history available to more people and interesting to more people than anyone had before.

The increased attention *Roots* garnered in the early 1970s was both flattering and daunting for Haley. His busy lecture schedule generated lots of interest in his family saga but left him with little writing time. Every lecture sold more readers on a book he was in danger of never finishing. Many of the admirers who wrote to Haley asked after the publication date of his book, which he had promised to finish every year since 1964. "I feel almost guilty about the time the book is taking, as so many people express, as you do, deep and genuine anticipation of it," Haley wrote to a librarian in Los Angeles. "But it hopes to be a book to realize its promise and that demands this unusual long exacting care in the writing."[66] Haley saw the avalanche of letters piled on his desk after the *New York Times Magazine* article as "another barometer as to the reception awaiting the book.... I am certain that other authors have been as pressured as I feel know—to *finish,* but I don't know if many have had as much advance receptivity for the book yet in the typewriter. It's kind of a deep responsibility feeling."[67]

Before Haley had completed a full draft of *Roots* he had given over one hundred paid lectures on his family research, sold the rights to the hardcover and paperback editions of the book, contracted to condense his story for *Reader's Digest,* and sold the film rights twice, first to Columbia Pictures and later to David Wolper. It is difficult to think of any work in progress that was so commercially successful and eagerly anticipated, much less one by a black author.

Why did so many people want to hear Haley's story? In 1969, Haley tried to answer this question for a local newspaper in Utica, New York. "Essentially what motivates this steadily-mounting pre-publication interest in my book simply is that it will offer a ground-breaking saga of Black History and Black Heritage, in which, now, there is an intense international interest," Haley wrote. "Black history or heritage held virtually no interest for whites, and woefully little interest for blacks until quite recent times. But the last twenty years, say, have seen us all become acutely racially sensitized. Today, a sharply increased awareness of black history and black heritage have [*sic*] come to be recognized as a vital primary requisite if we are to ameliorate the racial problem which qualifies easily today as America's greatest domestic crisis."[68]

If Haley benefited from a growing interest in black history, his storytelling abilities made this history something that audiences could feel intimately. Author Frank Chin captured this best in describing Haley as a "medium" whose voice allowed people to touch the past. "You've aroused a kind of unsuspected madness in all the people I watched listen to you," Chin told Haley. "Yours is a story people want to possess personally and cherish in secret to enlarge with their own lives.... Your story all but arouses superstition in your listeners, a certain fright a gentle terror of bringing the past, the voices of grandmothers we've somehow betrayed in our failing memory, rooms we've abandoned and are afraid to enter again because they've grown dark and some hostile to us ... and you seem to come from those places." Chin described how Haley had an uncanny ability to make each person in a large lecture audience feel personally invested in his story. "It's amazing how after you've gone everyone becomes private," Chin wrote, "as if they've just seen a loved one die and how, for a few moments, everyone is both excited and little irritable, unwilling to let you out of them. Everyone, in his own way feels an expert on what they've heard, if not in terms of the facts, then in terms of feelings, and is unwilling to corrupt or pollute their understanding, their personal experience of your story with anyone else's."[69] Haley had a remarkable ability to speak to a large audience and have each person come away feeling as if he was talking to them individually.

These haunting qualities of Haley's lectures are not immediately evident in *Roots*. The characters in the book and the television miniseries are tasked primarily with surviving and advancing the family story from Kunta Kinte in the 1760s to Alex Haley in the 1970s. Neither Haley nor the television screenwriters allowed the characters much space for thoughts, dreams, feelings, or fears that did not fit this steady historical trajectory. In his lectures, Haley told his story in flashbacks, moving between his research in the 1960s and 1970s and his ancestors in the eighteenth and nineteenth centuries. He relayed memories of hearing his family elders talk on the front porch and these voices intertwined with his own recollections of traveling to the Gambia and various research archives. While Haley always expressed more curiosity about his characters' actions than their feelings, his lectures presented his own feelings—as a writer, researcher, family member, and black American—vividly. Readers and television audiences described reading and watching *Roots* in visceral terms, whereas lecture audiences more often described hearing Haley speak in affective terms. The haunting qualities Chin identified in Haley's lectures were largely excised when the book and television series became chronological narratives that emphasized the characters' march through history rather than Haley's reflections on what this history meant.

Haley's lectures, even more than the book or the television versions of *Roots*, made audiences feel personally invested in his research for his family's history. Critics who obsessed over which parts of Haley's story were true and which parts were fabricated misunderstood what made the work a cultural phenomenon. People were drawn to Haley's story because it was compelling and persuasive, not because every part of the story was factually accurate. By speaking about *Roots*, Haley encouraged people to see history and themselves in new ways.

Gil Noble, for example, interviewed Haley in 1972 on *Like it Is*, a black public affairs television program that broadcast in New

York City. "Filming my jazz doc took me to Jamaica to examine the genesis of African music there, into today's Calypso music," Noble wrote to Haley after the broadcast. "It turned out to be an emotional trip for me, because I went for the 1st time to ... a small town, where my father was born. I saw the house in which he was raised ... the same house where his father was raised ... and back even, to my great-grandfather.... I met people who knew my family (hardly any are left) and they told me a lot about my blood line, that I didn't know." Like millions of other listeners, readers, and viewers, Haley's story made Noble see his own family's history with new eyes. "I think you should know, that our short meeting and interview played a large role in my behavior in Jamaica ... the 1st step of my African bloodline. Again, thank you."[70]

CHAPTER FOUR

Writing *Roots*

"I'm *so* much anticipating when I can afford to quit the regular lecturing circuit, which eats up time I'd far rather spend writing," Alex Haley wrote to a *Reader's Digest* editor at the end of 1973. "It's not that the lectures are without regard, though: by now, I have spoken of this book to more than 1.5 million people in live audience, who are out there awaiting it."[1] Each day brought more mail from people eager to buy and read *Roots*, but Alex Haley still had to write the book.

Haley had established the basic story line for his family saga by the summer of 1969. He mailed the first chapter to his editor at *Reader's Digest* and felt compelled to explain why a single chapter ran over two hundred pages. "I have not had it in me to leave out a single item that all the years of research turned up of what, truly, *was* the African culture of the mid-1700s," Haley wrote. "You will see, clinically, the immense problem I faced. It could *not* be, all of this, in any way simply some rhetorical listing of items of that culture. That would be a book for students, scholars. People, by the many millions, need to know, almost by an osmosis, this culture." Haley's job, as he understood it, was "to weave [this] culture about the growing-up of the boy, Kunta Kinte. The chapter opens with his being born. It will end when he is a young man of about 16."[2] Haley later described the structure of *Roots*'s first section as echoing *The Autobiography of Malcolm X.* "I did not editorialize," Haley said of the Malcolm X book, "but simply started with the subject as a child—as a fetus, actually—and related, in a very low-key way, successively, what happened to him, from childhood to adulthood. And I used that same technique with Kunta Kinte. It taught me to let the readers write their own editorial; I don't do it for them."[3]

Haley explained that the book's vision of Kunta Kinte's childhood as a free person was "the tree's trunk." Once readers identified with Kunta as a child, the horrors of his enslavement would be more vivid. "Everything that subsequently happens in the book derives at least part of its emotional power out of the reader's knowing, for themselves, in an impact way, the delineated life and culture in which that infant, boy, young man Kunta Kinte grew up in Juffure Village, Gambia, West Africa," Haley wrote. "Having grown up with this boy there, then when he goes into that stinking, fetid slaveship hold, in chains, in pains, the readers are going to experience that hold with him." Haley had an abiding faith in the power of words to convey feelings, and he did not distinguish between the types of sentiments *Roots* might engender. Haley invited readers to empathize with Kunta as a child so that, chapters later, they would be more deeply traumatized by Kunta's enslavement. "When on [Kunta's] fourth escape his foot is cut in half (across the arch) for punishment, I am going to make a reader's foot hurt," Haley wrote. Haley said, "The foot-cutting is going to be three paragraphs I want no one ever to forget," and he conducted specific research to make this scene of brutality come alive for readers. "I have been … to a physicist," Haley wrote, "I have in cold abstract physics terms what happens when a six-foot man raises an axe with a three-foot handle and a four-pound head, and pulls it suddenly down toward a target—I have it in terms of foot-pounds, velocity, things like that … I have a surgeon's cold, clinical description of every single successive thing that axe's blade severs, epidermis through sole." Haley concluded by promising, "I have worked, Tony. Ain't nobody— nobody, nobody, nobody, who reads it going to be unaffected by this book."[4]

Haley wrote and revised chapters of *Roots* regularly from 1967 to 1975. He preferred to start writing after dinner: "All the effort to massage a synthesis of my research into myself is planned for the late night moments when it flows out of me from as close to my subconscious as I can free myself to give."[5] Often, Haley would speak into a dictation machine from which a typist would later prepare a chapter draft. Haley liked to write and revise while he traveled, and he described working on planes "as if they were my office."[6] In handwritten jottings Haley marked time in the many months he worked on *Roots:*

July 20, 1969: Earlier this afternoon, man landed on the moon. Listened to broadcast in dining car of train California Zephyr.

August 20, 1973: Dad died this morning, 82. Finally he is back with mama, the wife he loved.

October 3, 1973: 5:15 a.m.—wow! Must get *some* sleep; must catch 8 a.m. flight to enter lecture tour.

October 4, 1973: Braniff #237 from St. Paul/Minneapolis to Kansas City. After lecture last night, slept 11 hours; needed! Feel great!!

August 11, 1975: Happy birthday to me! 54! Wow! Where'd those years go?[7]

Epochal events, personal moments, and quotidian details ran together amid the sea of manuscript pages that threatened to engulf him. Haley preferred goldenrod paper and green felt pens (which he described as his "two major fetishes"), and many of the thousands of archived pages of his drafts are so marked up that they practically bleed green ink.[8] It took Haley a long time to finish *Roots*, but it was not for a lack of effort. He wrote, revised, and wrangled his prose for years to create his family history.

While it is clear that *Roots* is Haley's story, it is equally clear that the book would not have been finished without the assistance of his friend and editor Murray Fisher, the pressure applied by Doubleday, or the financial incentive of the television deal with David Wolper and ABC. Haley had a vision for how "Kunta Kinte's descendants [would] fall into the 260-year pageantry" of American history, but he needed help to turn this vision into *Roots*.[9] "Murray Fisher had been my editor for years at *Playboy* magazine when I solicited his clinical expertise to help me structure this book from a seeming impassable maze of researched materials," Haley wrote in the acknowledgments to *Roots*. "After we had established *Roots*' pattern of chapters, next the story line was developed, which he then shepherded throughout. Finally, in the book's pressurized completion phase, he even drafted some of *Roots*' scenes, and his brilliant editing pen steadily tightened the book's great length."[10] The six years of work between Haley and Fisher that preceded these three sentences were productive and at time contentious. This relationship between author and editor reveals a great deal about the pressure Haley faced as he wrote *Roots*.

Murray Fisher was twelve years younger than Haley and came to their relationship with more worldly experience. Fisher grew up in Asia—first in China, where his parents were American missionaries, and then in Tokyo, Japan, where his father was assigned for *Reader's Digest*. Fisher worked as a war correspondent in South Korea and for NBC before being hired by Hugh Hefner at *Playboy*. At *Playboy*'s office in Chicago, Fisher developed and edited the monthly celebrity interview feature, which debuted in 1962 with Haley's interview of Miles Davis. Fisher helped edit *The Autobiography of Malcolm X* and left *Playboy* in 1974 to work full time with Haley on finishing *Roots*.[11] After working together closely for several years, Haley told Fisher that their relationship was evidence that "friendships can thrive between sharply diverse personalities." "You're brilliant, mercurial, cosmopolitan; you decide/act almost by reflex," Haley said. "I'm really deeply of Henning: slower, methodic, pray nightly; innately I listen, observe, saying nothing until I can sufficiently playback, mull over, finally decide. This pattern, in fact, is why Roots exists— one decade of this pattern.... I despise any unnecessary confrontations—as I think most are; I've engaged in two angry, shouting confrontations, the last in 1947."[12]

Haley and Fisher talked on the telephone about drafts of the book for a couple of hours nearly every day in 1970. Haley was living in San Francisco after divorcing his second wife, Julie, and it would be three years before he would see the couple's young daughter, Cindy, again.[13] "'Before This Anger' really now is happening," Haley wrote to his agent Paul Reynolds at the end of the year. "My best writing happens in thrusts," Haley told Reynolds, noting that he was "working about 18 hours each day, sleeping in short takes." Haley tried to avoid distractions and accepted telephone calls from only a handful of people, such as Fisher. "When Murray has done his thing, editing, at which he is magnificent, sometimes he is enough overcome by the steadily building sheer overwhelming drama of the book being done now that he will telephone and read the last take of it over the phone," Haley said.[14]

Fisher could be a harsh editor. He often returned drafts to Haley with barbed comments in the margins: "What the hell is this?"; "Enough of this already—blah, blah, blah"; "Pretty dull stuff"; "This is history not story"; and the writing workshop standard, "Show, don't tell."[15] Haley considered Fisher a "brilliant editor at cutting and condensing," and he responded remarkably well to these criticisms of his work.[16] While Haley had a sizable ego, he also recognized, rightly, that he needed an editor to rein in his story. Left to his own devices, Haley gathered more and more research material and continuously revised his chapter drafts. The top of one draft includes Haley's handwritten note: "A further rewrite not originally intended, but I began doodling, then it demanded eventually full rewrite."[17] Haley's creative process required him to continually iterate, and this made an editor indispensable to the development of *Roots*.

Haley's favorite place to write was at sea, and he frequently booked trips on freighters to work on his book. The summer of 1971 found Haley on a ship that sailed around Mexico, South America, and the Caribbean before returning to San Francisco.[18] "I am working better than ever in any other locale," Haley wrote to Reynolds as the ship pulled away from Buenos Aires. "Tomorrow I will write Chapter 31 ... in which Kunta Kinte, 16, is captured. By Rio, ten days from now, I hope to have him across the Atlantic and in Colonial Annapolis. Then I am going to have about another 40 days, living and eating and sleeping with Kinte and his descendants across ante-bellum slavery, and the Civil War, Emancipation and my birth." Haley was optimistic that the writing would go more quickly once Kunta had reached America. "It will go appreciably faster once Kinte is in the Colonial

US—because then there is natural forward movement," Haley wrote. "It has been agonizingly hard to create movement, steadily, in the static situation of 31 chapters whose primary purpose is to instill deeply into readers an awareness of what was African culture. But I know I have done it. No one ever will read this book and again think of a no-culture Africa."[19] Haley also reminded Reynolds that he intended to be one of his most successful clients. "The next time you chance to be talking to Irving Wallace," Haley said, referring to the best-selling novelist, "mention to him that I said you cannot go into a South America bookstore without his titles all over! The guy's sales must be utterly incredible! (Although I am going to show him something, with 'Before This Anger,' to be sure!)"[20]

Haley's desire to introduce readers to African culture led him to gather pages and pages of research notes. "I've invested so much time and work collecting all of the items I have of the 1750s-1760s *authentic* Mandinka (Mandingo) village culture, from which Kunta was taken (and, symbolically, all slaves)—that at this stage, I want *every* item woven into the rough manuscript, so that culling necessary can be done from that total material.... I feel it momentously important," Haley wrote. "One, this *is,* genuinely, Black History which is being so-clamored for. Lecturing across this country, North, East, South, West, sharing with audiences, mixed black-and-white, really only bits and pieces of what is to be in the book, I have witnessed emotional responses actually often to the point of tears (including my own). So that's another reason I'm including here even the unused-as-yet, for you to appraise for potential weaving-in: the book is pre-tested in its effect."[21] Haley sent Fisher fifty single-spaced pages of notes on topics ranging from Gambian folktales and traditional fishing methods to kingdoms in Mali and the practices of Nigerian elephant hunters.[22] In one of his notebooks,

Haley wrote that he wanted the book to have "enough details to make the story live and real—but not a history lesson (i.e., don't know how many *pounds* of beeswax)."[23] Haley's research impulses ran toward the collecting of minute details as though he needed to gather pages of historical facts to balance the fictional parts of his story. Haley later told Reynolds, "Sometimes, even *I* can't understand why had it taken *so* long [to finish *Roots*]. I mean apart from all of the lecturing, and so forth. I think that I did the thing called 'over-researching,' in fact I know I did, for I find myself not using whole blocks of this or that which took weeks, or even months to get into my notebooks."[24] Fashioning this material into a narrative quickly grew unwieldy, which is one of the reasons Fisher took on such an important role as an editor.

Fisher came to play such an crucial role in developing *Roots* that Haley gave him 10 percent of the book's literary rights and 5 percent of the motion picture rights. Haley wrote to Reynolds in the spring of 1973, asking him to draw up the paperwork. "My reason for this derives from the special mammoth nature of ROOTS, and the fact that Murray is investing, as my friend, a really singular job of editing which will contribute much to ROOTS' success, which will be also singular," Haley explained. Haley said that he valued the "intensiveness, expertness and otherwise overall caliber of editing of ROOTS that Murray Fisher is doing" and felt this work was worthy of significant monetary compensation.[25] Haley's agreement with Fisher was also motivated by Haley's recognition that *Roots* overwhelmed him. "I'll never again work as hard as this, at least for as *long* as this, on another book," Haley told Reynolds. "I feel as if I'm climbing up a waterfall. It is really like writing four books."[26]

Money problems continued to trail Haley, making it more difficult to complete his epic book. The IRS put a tax lien on Haley's bank account in the summer of 1973, and at times Haley could not afford the xeroxing fees to send copies of drafts to Fisher, *Reader's Digest,* or Doubleday.[27] "You surely know that I'm so characteristic of so many of my craft, who have no ability in properly managing their finances," Haley wrote to Reynolds. "Indeed, that's a good part of why 'Roots' isn't in bookstores now; for lack of proper managing otherwise, my chief income is from lecturing, which although it pays well still has eaten up all kinds of time that should have been spent with my typewriter and editing pen."[28] Haley's busy and lucrative lecture schedule proved to be a double-edged sword. On the one hand, lectures brought Haley much-needed money and built a robust advance audience for *Roots.* On the other hand, every day Haley traveled to deliver a lecture was a day he was not writing his book. "I have got to become able to quit lecturing until after 'Roots' is delivered," Haley concluded.[29]

Haley's financial problems were compounded in August 1973 when his ex-wife Julie was committed to a psychiatric hospital for severe depression. Haley was in Negril, Jamaica, when he received the news. "Of course I'm sorry for Julie, who had dropped her insurance," Haley wrote to Reynolds, before reflecting on what this meant for his daughter. "Immediately my problem is Cindy, without a functional mother. [Julie's mother] says someone can be hired fulltime, or she herself will quit work if I can reimburse. My child support's not quite half enough to handle all this."[30] Haley wrote to Lisa Drew at Doubleday to ask for a $10,000 advance to cover these unexpected expenses. Reynolds told Haley not to be too optimistic on this front. "Remember, they signed a contract for this book in Aug. 1964," Reynolds reminded him. "I don't think they're going to write out a check for $10,000 now." The solution, Reynolds argued in his familiar refrain, was to finish the book. "Of course you must try to help

Julie and Cindy, but Cindy will not starve if you can't help her and finishing Roots will mean that you can help her in the future," Reynolds wrote.

> If you help her now and as a result cannot finish Roots, you will be incapable of helping her six months or a year from now when she'll need your help just as much. Your whole career so depends on your finishing Roots.... As far as I can predict, Roots should solve your financial problems. Nothing else that I know of will. What I'm trying to say is that I think you'll be doing more for Cindy and Julie for the long pull by finishing Roots and not helping them than you will by not finishing Roots because of immediate help to them.[31]

The failures of Haley's first two marriages and his shortcomings as a father did not make him unique among celebrities and career-oriented men of his generation, but they are noteworthy since he wrote the most famous family chronicle in American history. This is less paradoxical than it may seem. Haley described his search for roots as a detective story, and the project, with international travel and regular speaking engagements, suited his wanderlust and fulfilled his need to meet and woo new people. *Roots* allowed Haley to engage with the idea of family on his terms in a way that day-to-day life as a husband and father did not.

Haley took Reynolds's coldly pragmatic financial advice and rededicated himself in the fall of 1973 to finishing *Roots*. Haley said that he recognized that "the biggest negative presently in my career is that my years of delay with ROOTS understandably has [*sic*] lowered my credibility among publishers."[32] Still, Haley sent Reynolds an ambitious three-year work schedule in which he planned to finish not only *Roots* but also a how-to book on black genealogy and a book on the Great Migration titled *Booker*. He expected to cap off this remarkable stretch of productivity with the film version of *Roots* coming out during the bicentennial in 1976. "It is almost as if Roots was written for that timing, through we know it wasn't," Haley said.[33] By this time Haley projected that *Roots* would be over sixteen hundred pages, and Fisher was busy cutting and condensing Haley's drafts.[34] With every passing month, Haley's optimism about finishing *Roots* seemed increasingly unwarranted. The book that had established him as a writer, *The Autobiography of Malcolm X,* was almost a decade old. He had missed dozens of book deadlines. And the racial tensions of the 1960s that had inspired Haley's desire to move "beyond this anger" were no longer front-page news.

When *Reader's Digest* published the first excerpt from *Roots* in 1974, no one was happier than Haley. "I am having the good, warm feeling of being vindicated," Haley wrote upon hearing that his *Digest* editor liked the piece. "As you know, literally for years I have been dropping notes, saying I'm in this or that process with the book, until I know that it was starting to sound almost mythical."[35] While Haley's story of his search for roots had already circulated widely via lectures, television talk show appearances, and articles in the *New York Times, Wall Street Journal,* and other newspapers and magazines, the *Reader's Digest* piece was the first time readers saw the narrative of Kunta Kinte that Haley had written and Fisher had polished. In *Reader's Digest* Haley found a perfect venue to launch *Roots.* Haley had published his first national magazine article in *Reader's Digest* in 1954, he had spoken several times at the *Digest*-affiliated World Press Institute in St. Paul, Minnesota, and the magazine had supported Haley's family history project since 1966, providing much-needed travel and research funds. Each month the magazine delivered accessible, interesting, and educational stories to a hundred million readers across thirty countries. *Reader's*

Digest's goal was to bring culture to mass audiences, which was also what Haley hoped to achieve with *Roots*. Haley's description of what he hoped to accomplish through his writing could have been the mission statement for *Reader's Digest*. "I want and hope merely to try and write what I do in such a way that it will evoke such response as comes from the great bulk of my readers, 'I had not realized _____,' 'I didn't know _____,' 'I feel that I better understand _____' and so forth," Haley wrote in 1974. "Stated another way, if I can be a cause of an increased genuine awareness, and understanding, among we collective creatures of The Maker here upon this earth, then I will be happy."[36]

Millions of people read Haley's *Roots* preview in *Reader's Digest*, and thousands wrote to tell him how much the work moved them. "As I finished tears streaked down my face," a woman from Columbus, Ohio, wrote. "I found your [two-part condensed] book the most touching truthful work of our heritage. Thank you for this. I hope to someday see this as a permanent part of Black History in our public school system."[37] A public school official from New York told Haley that his efforts to make readers feel as though they were part of the story were successful. "I was alongside of Kunta from Juffure to Virginia," she wrote. "Roots was the best thing I have ever read in my whole entire life."[38] A *Philadelphia Daily News* editor told Haley, "The joy of seeing it in Reader's Digest is that it will reach its largest audience. Largest, that is, until TV does it. That will be The Event." This editor also told Haley that he liked the book's blend of fact and fiction. "Roots is one of the great mystery novels of our time," he wrote. "Don't let it get Dewey-Decimal-ed into sociology!"[39] Haley was thrilled at the outpouring of admiration for the condensed version of *Roots*. "One of the most meaningful things for me is that it's seeming to have quite as much intrigue for whites as for blacks," he wrote. "The whites predominantly writing that Roots evokes in them the want to know more of whence they came. It reinforces my feeling that what Roots actually does is present the black facet of the humankind saga."[40]

Producers David Wolper and Stan Margulies had the most important responses to the *Reader's Digest* article. Originally from New York City, Wolper had studied film and journalism at the University of Southern California and had cofounded a television distribution company in his early twenties. By the early 1960s he had established Wolper Productions, which developed and sold dozens of documentaries to the broadcast networks. Stan Margulies, who joined Wolper Productions in 1968, recalled that he and Wolper had sold ABC in 1972 on two shows about generations of family. One focused on Native Americans in the Pacific Northwest, while the other focused on four generations of police officers. Neither show was produced, but Wolper and Margulies remained interested in the idea of bringing generational stories to television.[41] They found the story they were looking for in *Roots*. "In the current (May) issue of Reader's Digest there is an excerpt from a forthcoming book, Roots, by Alex Haley," Wolper wrote to Margulies. "He is an American Negro who painstakingly traces his family back to its original roots in Africa. Using stories handed down in his family, plus his education and historical museums and associations, he manages finally to locate the actual African village where his family began. It is an incredible mystery-suspense tale, spanning three continents and seven generations."[42] Actress and civil rights activist Ruby Dee had told Wolper about Haley's story in 1972, but at the time Columbia Pictures had an option on the film rights. By 1974, however, the book still had not been published,

Figure 7. Stan Margulies and David Wolper celebrate their Emmy win for *Roots*, 1977. Nate Cutler/Globe Photos Inc.

so Columbia elected not to extend their option.[43] Wolper told Margulies that he expected *Roots* to be "next season's biggest and most prestigious project" and said they should make an offer for the rights.

Haley's agents, entertainment lawyer Lou Blau in Los Angeles and literary agent Paul Reynolds in New York, were also busy cultivating potential bidders for the film/television rights to *Roots*. "I suspect that across the next two months, as the *Reader's Digest* condensation runs, we are going to collect some motpix/TV bids of great interest," Haley wrote.[44] Haley was also eager to capitalize on *Roots's* marketing potential. "Unlike most motion picture properties, this one involves two valuable subsidiary aspects that we should … participate in to a major degree," Haley wrote. "*Very* valuable will be the academic markets for any documentary film of *My Search for Roots,* as evidenced by the perennial heavy demand for my merely lecturing about it. And anticible is a coming market for 'Roots' or 'Kinte' oriented products, such as sweatshirts, jigsaw puzzles of African villages, sundry models of applicable things."[45] While some critics blamed the television production for commercializing *Roots,* it is important to acknowledge that Haley was always eager for his work to achieve its full commercial potential. The success of the *Reader's Digest* preview made Haley more ambitious about the promotional possibilities. Haley initially planned to follow Reynolds's advice to wait until *Roots* was finished to sell the film/TV rights, when there would be "a very maximum *seller's* market."[46] Lou Blau, however, was eager to make a deal. With producer David Merrick and Warner Brothers studio also showing interest in *Roots,* Blau negotiated a deal with Wolper.[47] Wolper paid Haley $50,000 for the film/television option to *Roots,* with another $200,000 promised when Haley finished the book. The payment went to the Kinte Corporation, a tax shelter Haley set up on advice of Lou Blau.[48] In Haley's decade of work before finishing *Roots,* Doubleday paid him $77,000.[49] These payments went toward Haley's tax debts and child support obligations, and Haley always felt as if Doubleday did not value the epic book he was writing. The deal with Wolper was the windfall

Haley had hoped to achieve with his project from the outset. While Haley had missed dozens of deadlines with his publisher, the television deal gave him the financial incentive and pressure he needed to finish writing *Roots*.

Like his previous pitches to Doubleday and *Reader's Digest,* Haley's spoken presentation of *Roots* over lunch at the Beverley Hills Tennis Club wowed Wolper and Margulies. "What I didn't know there but learned later was that what Alex did at lunch was basically to give us his university lecture, which is dynamite, but over a lunch table it is double-dynamite," Margulies remembered. "We sat there and our mouths dropped open 14 feet and we told Alex on the basis of that we were interested." Margulies and Wolper also persuaded Haley that television, rather than film, was the best medium for *Roots*. "Alex was interested in communicating with the greatest number of people and we said one night on television is the equivalent to ten years of a movie run," Margulies said. "If you really want to reach America, it's called television and at the end of the luncheon we had a feeling that Alex was for it." Once they had the television rights to *Roots,* Wolper and Margulies sold the project to ABC by having Haley give his presentation to ABC executives in a private room at the Beverly Hills Hotel.[50]

The television deal gave Haley some much-needed cash, but it also meant he now had both Doubleday and Wolper/ABC waiting for him to finish *Roots*. Reynolds worried that Haley was spending too much time in Los Angeles talking with Wolper about the television production. "This is 'Dr. Reynolds, the slave driver' talking," Reynolds wrote to Haley, referencing one of the white characters in *Roots*. "Delighted as I am with your deal with Wolper ... unless Roots is completely finished you should not go back to California, you should not do a stroke of work for Wolper ... regardless of the contract. The book is the vital thing.… With no book, your whole house of cards would fall to pieces."[51] Reynolds had reason to worry. As the head screenwriter Bill Blinn was starting a treatment of the first television episode of *Roots* in December 1974, Haley missed yet another deadline with Doubleday.[52] "I completely understand their dubiousness where I'm concerned," Haley told Reynolds regarding Doubleday. "Ten years is a long time for any book. (I wager that will be one of the chief things advertised.)"[53]

Lisa Drew, Haley's editor at Doubleday, had not heard from Haley for weeks before the missed deadline and learned from a newspaper article that Wolper had made a deal with ABC to broadcast *Roots*.[54] "Somebody has given me a clipping from the Durham, North Carolina *Morning Herald* which says that Alex Haley's ROOTS is being developed as a film for ABC," Drew wrote to Reynolds. "Is this correct? If so, could you please give me an idea as to when they plan to use it on television? Do you have any further word on when the rest of the book is coming in to me?"[55] Working on opposite coasts, Drew and Margulies talked regularly on the telephone trying to stay abreast of Haley's progress. Drew recalled that "Stan would call me up and say, 'We're up to the point where Tom has run off and done this and what happens next?' and I'd say, 'Why are you asking me? You guys are ahead of me.'"[56] While the schedule of ABC's production was not yet determined, it was clear to Drew and her colleagues at Doubleday that "it was going to be a big deal" and that "there was going to be extremely serious extended publicity of our publication."[57]

ABC initially planned to air *Roots* in March 1976, and Wolper feared that Haley would not get his manuscript to Doubleday in time for the book to be published before the series broadcast.[58] Screenwriters Bill Blinn and Ernest Kinoy had completed treatments of *Roots* episodes 2 and 3, but neither they nor Wolper knew how Haley's story would conclude. "Alex, we are running out of time," Lou Blau told Haley in August 1975. "David Wolper is most apprehensive that ABC might very well walk away from the project if they were aware of the fact that all of the material has not yet been submitted to Wolper. Wolper emphasized that what you have submitted so far is not enough for his purposes, and you must submit your complete manuscript. It would indeed be a tragedy if the ABC deal goes down the drain."[59] Haley, working in Jamaica at the time, replied that even with Fisher's editing assistance, *Roots* was too much for him. "Right now, this room is so inundated with *Roots,* not to mention my head, that I feel I don't know if I'm coming or going," Haley told Blau. "I understand Wolper's concern, Doubleday's concern, I'm working to finish the utterfastest I know how, like about 19 hours spent between editing pen or at this machine since this time yesterday; and I have the Faith that we'll see sundry records and precedents set when *Roots* gets out there next year."[60] Haley had written Reynolds and Stan Margulies days earlier, telling them that Lisa Drew and Murray Fisher had both joined him in Jamaica and that the place had been a "beehive of work" as the three worked to finish the book.[61] "We've arrived at a kind of rough schedule where all work pretty much through the day," Haley wrote. "After dinner, Lisa works until 10:30 or so, and Murray to midnight or one a.m. I sleep for awhile after dinner until Murray's ready to turn in, when he wakes me, and I take the swing shift until day, in the quiet, working ahead of them."[62] Haley said that all three got along very well but that Fisher had asked Drew not to say anything about the hands-on role he was playing in the completion of *Roots.*[63]

Haley knew that if he did not finish *Roots* by November 1975 Wolper would choose not to exercise the option on the television rights. This would cost Haley $200,000 plus all of the exposure that a nationally broadcast series would bring to him and his book. The pressure of making this all-important deadline exposed simmering tensions in Haley's relationship with Fisher. The two had worked so closely for so many years on *Roots* that Fisher began to feel possessive of the story. While Haley desperately needed an editor's assistance, he bristled at Fisher's domineering manner. Just before *Reader's Digest* published the first excerpt from the book in 1974, Fisher called Reynolds and said he was furious that he had not seen the final version of the chapter before it went to the magazine.[64] For his part, Haley was upset that Fisher had phoned Reynolds. "I do *not* want him calling you or anyone else involved in handling *Roots*," Haley wrote. "That is not his role. *I* am the author. He is an invited editor. Murray is a good friend; he is a brilliant editor, I think. He possesses an aggressive, dominating type of personality, which I regard as fine for his own life, but don't thrust it upon *me!* I feel so strongly about these overstepping-of-role tendencies of his that if I find that he continues to exhibit them, considering that it's *my* book, *my* career, then I have quietly determined that he simply will never see the manuscript of the book's latter half."[65] Later in the same letter, though, Haley told Reynolds he hoped to patch things up with Fisher and then "press him to catch up" on editing the drafts.

These tensions reemerged in September 1975 when Stan Margulies hosted a dinner with Haley, Fisher, and screenwriter Bill Blinn. As the dinner guests talked about the *Roots* project, Haley grew annoyed that Fisher repeatedly interrupted him to finish stories about characters and events in the book. Haley felt upstaged and retreated to a balcony to collect his thoughts. Back in Jamaica, Haley wrote Fisher a lengthy letter.

"I'm taking *Roots* from here in without your editing," Haley told Fisher, promising that the editor would still receive the agreed-upon percentage of the book and television rights. "The arrangement I volunteered makes it clear how much I both respect and solicit expert editing," Haley continued. "During our working month, cumulatively I came to feel that you all but personify intransigence, that you consider that once the manuscript's in your hands, who dares intrude? The author who would long sustain a cooperativeness with that perspective *inevitably* sustains a subjective sense of being professionally reduced, diminished; of self-doubt; of dribbling out his pebbles of self-confidence as a writer. Murray, I hope you can understand that it was scary, for awhile after I returned here, to write, uncertain inside if what was on the pages was going to *survive*. I'm too fond of me for that, my friend!"[66] Haley told Fisher he was angry that the editor had directed a typist to put "Edited by Murray Fisher" on the title page of an earlier manuscript draft. Haley said he considered this akin to giving Fisher "co-credit" for writing *Roots*. "That is absurd Murray," Haley wrote. "For my friend to perform his technical expertise, in appreciation I volunteered a generosity that's far as I know, without precedent in the authorship business."[67] Haley also worried that Fisher was telling too many people about their work together on *Roots*. "This information dropped, seeded, in enough places, it can become the sort of titillating tidbit that can outgrow weeds and outlast dye," Haley wrote. "Gaining dimension as it goes, in time it's heard in cocktail parties in Idaho 'Look, I happen to know he didn't really write it.' … I have got to avert any occasion for any 'secret' attaching to *Roots*."[68]

As Haley navigated his relationship with his editor and rushed to finish *Roots* before the television deadline, he was stalked, as always, by money problems. "In a nutshell, my money situation is I've next to no income until I finish the long, long book, which I contractually *must* by Nov 30," Haley wrote explaining why he did not have $760 to pay for his Master Charge account. Haley told the assistant manager at San Francisco's Crocker National Bank that his money woes would soon be over. "In the first half of December I'll receive $200,000 as a first payment on the TV rights," he wrote. "The first day after that first sum's deposited I plan to spend writing checks." Haley even had to apologize to Flying Finger Manuscript Service for failing to pay a bill for typing a draft of *Roots*.[69] Haley was philosophical about his constant money trouble. The "irony was that as long as I kept on those incredible lecturing itineraries you know I used to keep, earning the $50–80,000 a year I did at times . . . I could never possibly find the time to finish my book," Haley wrote. "Or put another way, I was solvent, I was 'secure,' but I could not remain that and gamble on myself on the BIG one, you know? There's something metaphysical about that."[70]

Haley also felt the accumulated pressure of a decade of missed deadlines. "All I know is that I feel ready to cry when now or then someone writes, or says, 'Aren't you finished *yet?*'" Haley wrote to sociologist and University of California Santa Cruz administrator Herman Blake.[71] "I have written about 18 hours every day, seven days a week all the summer, finishing Roots which absorbs work like a sponge," Haley wrote to another friend. "Now I have about five weeks left to make a deadline on whose making hangs publication in early August 1976, followed by a long television series (14 hours) to open in Sept. It is *so* pressured that I am sending increments to the film people, whose writers are doing scripts from that, as they get it."[72] Haley said he felt "like a steamroller was chasing" him.[73]

With the television deadline looming, Haley wrote to Fisher to mend fences. Haley started the letter at four in the morning; he had been up late working with an ear infection, fever, and sore throat. "I think that we have the very real potential to work together in achieving some of the most formidable literature that has come down the line; and of visual products that will rank with the best as well," Haley wrote to Fisher.[74] Haley told Fisher that he still needed him as an editor, "our new understanding being that simply I will follow you to make sure it feels right, is right, to me."

Over a ranging five-page letter, Haley wrote openly about what it meant to him to achieve success as a black author and the slights he continued to face. "I have heard I suppose two or three hundred of us [black artists, scholars, and celebrities] testify that in countless ways we have perceived how the average white people tend to underestimate us; to see us and so often to deal with us in ways which like as not they are themselves unconscious, as of lesser capacities for thinking, for discerning," Haley wrote. Haley had interviewed and socialized with enough black celebrities to know that success did not eliminate racism and could heighten jealousy and distrust. "What all of this has to do with you and me and *Roots* is that *Roots* aspires to be a very symbol of black people's bidding via the immensely powerful route of literature to be taken into the mainstream of acceptance of groups of people on par with each other.... For a book to achieve this for a historically maligned group would amount to a very staggering human contribution."[75] Haley recognized that *Roots* was going to lead to an intense level of scrutiny of him. "It is clearly imperative that I be worthy to sustain that image," Haley wrote. "I have got to be able to stand under the spotlight of the scrutiny that will come, first curiously, then as the book grows bigger, increasingly critically.... It doesn't go on forever, this scrutiny of critical bent; if a period of it can be weathered without the object of it springing any serious leaks, then okay, then it relents, and all's okay."[76]

For Haley, he and Fisher had to make it clear that *Roots* was an authentically black book. Haley believed that black celebrities like Motown Records founder Berry Gordy and actor Sammy Davis Jr. were victims of "black rejection phenomena." To cut down successful black people, Haley felt, the media "subtly discover and reveal that in fact they're somehow the product of, or controlled by, or contained by, white people. That seems to satisfy white people that all's well; among black people the nice hopeful hero is virtually dumped with infuriation, or with disdain."[77] Haley asked Fisher to help him navigate this danger. "You and I have both got to be fully aware of the potentials of threats to what's at stake," Haley advised. "By *no* means does this intend to suggest you're obscured from sight.... I *want* your editor role to be known. My only concern now is the *context* in which we do this.... You present the writer who faced the staggering organizational and presentation problems, which you as a trained, fresh eye and editing brain sought to help ... and we're homefree."[78] Haley described having already been visited in Jamaica by a representative of a civil rights organization who pressed the author to demand more black writers and production staff on the television series. Haley brushed away these concerns. "It seems of little moment that *I* am black, that *Roots* projects to pioneer in its area for black interests at large," Haley wrote. "I can hear now some shrill [critics], black, 'didn't you know any *black* editors?' I can deal with that. The thing I cannot deal with is the slightest innuendo that I am a product, or controlled, or contained, or any variation of such, however untrue; the point is it cannot be let to start."[79]

Haley was much less worried about the response of black critics to *Roots* or the lack of black screenwriters or directors on the television series than he was with meeting the deadline for

Wolper. Haley told Fisher he looked forward to hosting him in Jamaica to make a final push to the deadline. He promised that My Lewis, a recent PhD graduate from Ohio State University who had sought out Haley as a mentor, would be on hand to type up the revised manuscript. Lewis, whom Haley described as "diminutive, black, cute, quiet, sensitive, [and] very, very sharp," later became Haley's third wife.[80] "We have GOT to make this deadline," Haley wrote as he wrapped up the letter at 5:30 a.m. "Wolper Inc., must have it, in time to read, as their option has to be lifted by November 30, which means money, the start of it. I do not think I mentioned previously that in the way the Good Lord works His wonders, the new TV format is that they'll premiere it (after early August book publication) with a September night's full prime-time three-hour show, to be followed by weekly one-hour shows. *That* ought to sell *over* a million books in hardcover, don't you think?"[81]

CHAPTER FIVE

Producing *Roots*

"Alex Haley has completed the manuscript for the book Roots," producer Stan Margulies wrote to ABC's Lou Rudolph after Thanksgiving in 1975. "Now that you have got this, don't expect anything else in your Christmas stocking."[1] By the time Haley finished his epic book, Margulies and head screenwriter Bill Blinn had been working for over a year to adapt the story for television. For much of this time they were working to develop story lines, scenes, and characters that Haley had not yet committed to paper. Soon after Blinn joined the project in the fall of 1974 he attended several of Haley's lectures to get a handle on the story. Haley and Blinn got along well, and he thought the series of lectures would show the screenwriter how diverse audiences responded to *Roots*. "I couldn't have planned a much better succession of audiences for the accompanying scriptwriter to share a wide range of responses to my 'narrating,' in effect, the Roots researching adventure," Haley wrote to Margulies. "Commonwealth [College]'s an open enrollment college. W. Maryland's a church college. After a banquet of professional librarians we'll have an audience of very

conservative Mennonites. Winston-Salem State is a Black university. Finally, World Press Institute is an annual assembly of foreign
professional journalists sponsored by Reader's Digest."[2] Like
almost all of Haley's lecture audiences, Blinn was captivated by
Haley. "It was mesmerizing to watch Haley tell his story," Blinn
recalled. "He was a fascinating storyteller. He talked quietly, he
talked with almost no histrionics, no role playing.... You could not
look away, you could not not listen to what he was saying. He was
hypnotic."[3]

Blinn and Margulies wrote the early treatments for the *Roots*
television series using flashbacks that moved between Haley's
research process in the 1960s and 1970s and Haley's ancestors in
the eighteenth and nineteenth centuries. "I felt very strongly that
the story needed a twentieth-century identification," Margulies
recalled. "I felt that we would all be better off if we could tell the
story through the person of a sophisticated, intelligent, worldly
citizen of the US of America in 1977—that we'd understand him
in a minute because he is obviously one of us, and if we liked him
we could then go into his story."[4] One version started with Haley
asking African delegates at the United Nations for help identify-
ing the Mandinka words that Haley said he had heard from his
elders. Another draft opened with the assassination of Malcolm
X in 1965 as the event that sparked Haley's quest.

Blinn and Margulies spent months tinkering with different
flashback versions of the story. "We went around and around, and
finally I went to Stan and I said, 'This is a lecture—very boring,'"
Blinn said. "I understand all of the good intentions but I don't think
we are going to keep an audience."[5] Margulies shared Blinn's concerns. "We finally, one day, looked at each other and said, 'It's terrible—just fucking awful,'" Margulies recalled. "And in the course
of that day we said, 'What would happen if we took Alex out of the

story,' and what happened was suddenly the story became crystal clear.... The strength of the story in terms of television was the Kunta Kinte story ... which had never been seen nor ever been done."[6] Margulies and Blinn described being "seduced" by Haley's storytelling and not realizing until Haley submitted more chapters that his book's narrative was chronological and did not use flashbacks.[7] "The minute we dropped Alex," Margulies concluded, "the thing took off like a rocket."[8] Margulies still had to explain this decision to Haley, who had expected to play a significant role as a character and narrator when *Roots* came to the screen. "The reason we are dropping you is that you just can't stand up to Kunta Kinte," Margulies told Haley. "Kinte is bigger than you are. And anytime we take away from Kunta Kinte is lost time."[9]

This decision made the casting of Kunta Kinte crucial to the success of *Roots*. Veteran casting director Lynn Stalmaster sought out young Hollywood talent and contacted New York University, Northwestern University, the University of Southern California, the University of California at Los Angeles, and other top theater programs to find an actor to portray Haley's ancestor. "We wanted the audience to completely become involved with Kunta Kinte, as someone they didn't know, a brand-new experience," Stalmaster recalled.[10] This description echoed Haley's desire for readers to identify with Kunta as a baby and follow his life as a free young man before being enslaved. The crucial difference for the television production, however, was that this identification would have to be mapped onto a specific actor. Before audiences could meet Kunta Kinte, Stalmaster had to find an actor that could get the approval of Wolper, Margulies, director David Greene, and various ABC executives. Stalmaster auditioned dozens of young actors for the role but struggled to find someone on whom all of the decision makers could agree.

LeVar Burton heard the casting announcement in class as a sophomore at the University of Southern California (USC). Burton was born in 1957 in West Germany, where his father was stationed as a photographer in the US Army. He moved to Sacramento, California, with his mother after his parents separated when he was three. In his early teens Burton planned to become a priest and entered a Catholic seminary. After deciding that his passion was to be an actor, he left the seminary and earned a drama scholarship to USC.

Burton and two other actors, Hilly Hicks and Ernest Thomas, were called back for screen tests in March 1976.[11] Hicks and Thomas were several years older than Burton and had more professional acting experience. The nineteen-year-old Burton's largest role was in a campus production of *Oklahoma!*, where he played Ali Hakim, the Persian peddler. Burton had never been on a sound stage or performed in front of a film camera, but if he was nervous in his *Roots* audition it did not show. He was the "coolest cat I have ever seen in my life," Margulies recalled. "I mean, first we thought well maybe he is stoned, maybe he doesn't understand that he is testing for the part. We couldn't understand how anybody could be that calm and collected. But that's LeVar."[12] As Burton's audition tape went back and forth between ABC executives in New York and Los Angeles, network executives were nervous about taking a chance on the young and inexperienced black actor. Margulies said ABC worried that Burton looked "too African." "We wanted someone who is physically more attractive," the network told Margulies regarding Burton. "He's got those thick African lips."[13] This speaks to the challenge of casting *Roots* in an industry and a country where racist ideals of beauty were deeply ingrained. Margulies, Wolper, and ABC executives agreed that *Roots* had the potential to be commercially successful, but they also shared concerns about finding black actors who would not make white audiences or themselves uncomfortable.

Margulies and Wolper arranged for Burton to meet with ABC executives in person to try to overcome their concerns. "I had seen LeVar's test, which I didn't like very much," ABC's Brandon Stoddard said. "He looked great, but the test was not very good.... He came into my office with David and Stan ... and he was just so impressive in person. He was so Kunta Kinte—the energy, the feeling, the power, the positiveness of LeVar—that we said ok."[14] Everyone recognized that Burton's performance as Kunta Kinte would be critical to the success of *Roots*. "If the audiences did not like and sympathize with Kunta Kinte, you could throw the rest of the series out the window because nobody was going to be watching," Margulies said.[15] David Greene, who was tapped to direct the opening episodes of *Roots* after a successful turn on the hit miniseries *Rich Man, Poor Man* (1976), was confident he could help Burton deliver a good performance but reflected that "the graveyard is built with directors who said they can make a star of this kid."[16]

To ensure that white viewers would watch *Roots,* the producers and network sought out established television stars to cast in the white roles. "The problem with *Roots* was that there had never been a successful black drama in the history of television," Stoddard recalled. "I was terrified. I thought what we'll do is we'll get big heavyweight white actors and build around them.... We were scared no one would come to the party."[17] Casting director Lynn Stalmaster initially lobbied to cast less famous actors but came around to see the logic of looking for television names. "I generally prefer to cast actors who are not well known ... specifically in a project like this where you have a certain

Figure 8. LeVar Burton with director David Greene on the set of *Roots*. ABC Photo Archives/Getty Images.

truth and you don't want any distractions," Stalmaster said. "I totally empathize with the network wanting to have some people to publicize, so that an audience ... might say, 'Oh, I want to see Chuck Conners, I want to see Lorne Greene' and then discover that they are caught up in this original concept and perhaps learning something in the process."[18] Writer Bill Blinn felt these familiar white actors would help white viewers work through a range of emotions, "not just unrelenting white guilt, we were dealing with white insecurity, white problems, white flaws." Blinn argued that without these points of identification "it would be too easy for the white guy sitting in his chair at home to say, 'I'd never do that, I'd never be that mean to another human being. I wouldn't be [the overseer character] Vic Morrow beating that kid to death just to say a new name. I'd never do that.' Fine, would you be the Robert Reed character? Would you be the Sandy Duncan character? ... Well, in that case you would have been part of the problem."[19] A viewer from Placerville, California, was among those who found this casting strategy successful. "I think it was particularly effective to have had these characters played by usually well liked and well known actors," she wrote. "Some of my favorites were among them, but for eight days they were intolerable to me."[20]

In discussing the casting for *Roots,* the producers were explicit in stating that the series had to appeal to white viewers in order to be a commercial success. Whereas the book version of *Roots* has no major white characters, this was never seriously considered as an option for the television series. David Wolper argued that having white "television names" in *Roots* was the only way to ensure that it would not be pigeonholed as a black show. "If people perceive Roots to be a black history show—nobody is going to watch it," Wolper said. "If they say, 'Let me see, there are no names in it, a lot of black actors and there are no whites' … it looks like it's going to be a black journal, it's all going to be blacks telling about their history, if it was perceived like that, *Roots* would have been a disaster from a ratings standpoint."[21] A similar logic extended to the casting of black roles. "It was very important that we used black actors that are not perceived to be artsy-craftsy," Wolper said. "We tried to get black actors that are more accepted to the white audience.… Leslie Uggams is safe, Richard Roundtree is safe, Ben Vereen is safe, so all are safe."[22] For Wolper and the network, these casting decisions were simple arithmetic. "Remember the television audience is only 10 percent black and 90 percent white," Wolper said after *Roots*'s record-breaking run. "So if we do the show for blacks and every black in America watches, it is a disaster—a total disaster."[23] Wolper was a television veteran who had pitched and developed programs for two decades before *Roots*. He understood the logics of race and demographics that governed Hollywood as well as anyone. There was never a possibility that *Roots* would be broadcast on one of the three networks while being marketed primarily to black audiences. Haley also shared these commercial aspirations of his family story and always intended for his project to be marketed to the largest possible audience. Rather than arguing over whether Wolper and ABC whitewashed *Roots,* as some critics charged, it is more productive to see *Roots* in the context of the racial realities of network television in this era.

However much the producers geared *Roots* to the perceived preferences of white viewers, the series still promised to be a once-in-a-generation opportunity for black actors. The *Roots* casting call created a buzz among black performers in the spring of 1976, leaving casting director Lynn Stalmaster with an overflowing folder of headshots and résumés. After casting Burton as the young Kunta Kinte, the producers looked for black actors whom audiences would recognize. The producers' wish list featured dozens of prominent black actors and celebrities (mostly men), including Muhammad Ali, Bill Cosby, Sammy Davis Jr., Redd Foxx, Isaac Hayes, Sidney Poitier, Richard Pryor, Diana Ross, Billy Dee Williams, and Flip Wilson.[24] The actors who earned the major roles in *Roots* each had impressive acting credits. Louis Gossett Jr., who played Fiddler, a character who mentors Kunta Kinte, was a veteran of New York's esteemed Negro Ensemble Company and had a number of Broadway, television, and film credits.[25] John Amos, who played the older Kunta Kinte, had starred as the father on *Good Times* before quitting the Norman Lear–produced show when it started focusing on the character J.J. and his catchphrase, "Dy-no-mite."[26] Jamaican-born actress Madge Sinclair, who played Belle, a character who marries Kunta Kinte and gives birth to Kizzy, had appeared in the

Figure 9. Louis Gosset Jr. and LeVar Burton filming a scene from *Roots* in Savannah, Georgia. ABC Photo Archives/Getty Images.

film *Leadbelly* (1976) and had had small roles in several television series. Leslie Uggams, who played Kizzy, had won a Tony Award for her role in *Hallelujah, Baby!* (1968) and had hosted her own television variety show, *The Leslie Uggams Show,* in 1969. Richard Roundtree, who portrayed Kizzy's love interest, was famous from the *Shaft* films and television series (1971–74), while Ben Vereen, who played Kizzy's son Chicken George, was a Broadway star and Tony Award winner for *Pippin* (1973).

Roots was more than just another acting credit and paycheck for these actors. The series gave them an opportunity to represent black history in ways that had been missing in their own school experiences. "It gave us a sense of pride," Leslie Uggams said. "The way we had been depicted. We were just slaves on a plantation. No one knew where we came from and how did we get there. Alex wrote this story of people who were kings and queens and had a beautiful life ... [and were] taken away to another country, denied speaking their own language, names."[27] Ben Vereen recalled, "When I was growing up, there was only a paragraph [in school textbooks]. You were slaves and Lincoln freed you."[28] John Amos, who was one of the first students to integrate schools in East Orange, New Jersey, also remembered his school textbooks being derogatory about Africa and Africans. "The only reference made to Africa in my childhood history books was that it was shaped like a pork chop and inhabited by savages," Amos said. "So it was a tremendous vindication for me to play that character and help to rectify some of those stereotypes."[29] Burton felt *Roots* exposed a new side of the history of slavery. "In every history unit I ever had in school, slavery was always referred to as an economic institution," Burton said. "It was an economic engine, upon which this country was built. The human cost was never part of that module in school. We got schooled through *Roots* of the human cost of that equation."[30] While the black freedom struggle made the histories of African Americans and Africa more visible on college campuses, it took years for new scholarship to trickle down to high school textbooks.[31]

When the cast and crew traveled to Savannah, Georgia, to film the first episode in April 1976, they knew *Roots* had the potential to be groundbreaking television. Alex Haley's frequent presence on the set contributed to the sense that *Roots* would be a special job. The producers arranged for Haley to talk about *Roots* to the cast and crew at their hotel the night before filming began. Haley's *Roots* would not be published for another four months, so for many of the cast and crew this was their first time hearing Haley tell his story. "Alex brought such validity to what we were doing, this was his family story," Burton recalled.[32] Georg

Stanford Brown, who played Haley's great-grandfather Tom Hardy, said, "We sat around Haley like children, he was our father."[33] Haley was well suited for this role of on-set mentor, sage, and consultant. Several actors sought Haley out to ask questions about different characters. "He was able to tell us little details to help us in performance," Brown remembered. "We always had Alex to turn to."[34] Ebou Manga, the Gambian student who had facilitated Haley's successful research trips to Africa, was also on the set to offer the actors tips on Mandinka language and culture.[35] In addition to answering questions about the characters, Haley shared galley copies of *Roots* with some actors. "Alex came to my hotel room and he brought me a galleys copy [of *Roots*], and he had placed a bookmark in the section of the book that began Kunta Kinte's Middle Passage," Burton recalled. "That was the first time I had a chance to read any of the novel.... It was perfect, it was just what I needed to go into those days' filming."[36] While several aspects of Haley's family genealogy did not stand up to the scrutiny of journalists and academics, his skill as a storyteller gave the *Roots* cast and crew a sense they were bringing a powerful story to television. This sense of seriousness, commitment, and purpose was ultimately more important than historical accuracy in creating a memorable television miniseries.

Bringing Haley's book to the screen presented the producers with several challenges. The first was how to make the opening scenes, set in the Gambia in the 1760s, appear realistic. The series' budget of over $6 million was large by television standards but small compared to a film's. In designing the sets and costumes the producers tried to avoid stereotyped images of Africa in films like *Tarzan* or National Geographic–style documentaries. To portray an image of Africa that would be true to Haley's book,

Figure 10. Alex Haley holds a galleys copy of *Roots* on the set in Savannah, Georgia. ABC Photo Archives/Getty Images.

the producers relied on the author's research on eighteenth-century village life and photographs from his recent trips to the Gambia. While searching out potential filming locations, the producers unexpectedly found the Oyotunji African Village near Savannah (the Oyotunji African Village later moved to Sheldon, South Carolina). Dozens of African Americans who were interested in learning, practicing, and teaching West African culture lived in the village. "They knew a lot because they had studied a lot," director David Greene said. "So we brought them to Savannah and put them up with us in the Ramada Inn." Several members of the Oyotunji African Village appeared as dancers or served as consultants for the Africa section of *Roots*. "We were so lucky, we fell into all of this really authentic African information, which we used," Greene said.[37] As the Oyotunji African Village

Figure 11. LeVar Burton and Alex Haley. ABC Photo
Archives/Getty Images.

suggests, many black Americans had been interested in connecting with African culture and history long before *Roots* and did not
see the book or the television miniseries as educational in the
way that Haley supposed.[38]

As producers tried to bring an "authentic" version of Gambian
village life to television, their biggest challenge was whether
actresses could be shown with bare breasts. When ABC reviewed
the scripts for the African and slave ship sections of *Roots,* Tom
Kersey, director of the network's office of Standards and Practices,
explained that his office was granting *Roots* greater liberties than

other ABC programs. "In the interest of maximizing a sense of authenticity that we expect to contribute meaningfully to the dramatic and historical value of this unique project, we will permit certain exceptions to our general policies," Kersey wrote. "Surely all parties involved share the conviction that nothing about this production should appear exploitative, particularly with regard to the handling of sex and nudity. Through careful handling this sensitive material will be judged not as sensational programming for television, but as a necessary and appropriate ingredient to the story we are telling. Much will depend upon the actual direction and execution of the scenes." Kersey emphasized that the producers would have to walk a fine line between authenticity and what could be shown on television. "You have told us that Mandinka women were at least partially nude in their customary mode of attire," Kersey told Margulies. "In the interest of authenticity, portrayal of breast nudity among women will be allowed in scenes occurring in Africa and on the slave ship, subject to certain conditions." The Standards and Practices director went on to offer specific suggestions regarding camera positioning and casting to ensure compliance. "In the African locales, please limit the exposure of nude breasts to long-range shots," Kersey wrote. "Close-ups must be shot from the shoulder level or above. In casting these scenes, we ask that you not employ actresses whose physical presence would make them a distracting feature in themselves."[39] The *Roots* producers heeded these suggestions. "The women can be bare breasted [but] we must observe the long shot convention," Margulies reported to Wolper after consulting with Standards and Practices. "The question of bare breasts also relates to the actress. We should not use an obvious sex symbol— a Lola Falana—as one of our nude ladies.... When Fanta is being chased about the deck, we must be careful to avoid any unnecessary bobbing of the bare breasts. Since [the character] is a 16-year-old-girl, we should cast someone with small, firm bosoms. Again, the bare breast status is okay as long as it isn't the main purpose of the scene."[40] ABC's Brandon Stoddard later joked that at some points there were four men in a room debating the issue before the network reviewer, who finally said, "We'll compromise and you can have an A bra, no closer than 30 feet."[41]

After reviewing the preliminary film footage, ABC's Standards and Practices reviewers were satisfied with how the producers had handled the nudity. "The young women, all extras, appear as background," an ABC official wrote. "There is no camera emphasis on breast nudity and no attempt to sensationalize or sexualize it." The ABC representative continued, "This will not be the first time that bare breasts have been seen on television. We have viewed, and allowed our children to view, similar scenes in episodes of 'Wild Kingdom' and on National Geographic specials. They are depicted as authentic background, and in their very naturalness do not arouse any more attention than a flock of hens would in the background of a farm scene."[42] This ABC official's comparison of black actresses to "a flock of hens" makes it clear that there were aspects of representation beyond the purview of Standards and Practices. However much *Roots*'s producers were committed to portraying Haley's characters in a positive light, they were working against decades of racist and sexist portrayals of black people and Africa in film, television, and visual culture. This meant that the same production decisions regarding casting, costuming, and set design that might earn praise as "authentic" representations of historical village life could also lead viewers, like the Standards and Practices officials, to draw racist and sexist comparisons of black characters to farm animals.

Roots's producers and directors walked a tightrope by asking black actors to portray enslaved people. Each black actor brought his or her own family history and personal experiences with racism to the set. When these memories and experiences mingled with the historical weight of the Haley's story, they created a combustible mixture of emotions. John Amos, who played the older Kunta Kinte, described having an experience while filming *Roots* where he felt that his enslaved ancestors were speaking to him. During filming at Hunter's Ranch in Southern California, Amos fell to the ground and started shouting. Amos, who had no history of seizures, could hear dozens of voices and felt emotionally overwhelmed. "I felt like I had become totally taken by the spirit of my ancestors ... and those millions who had died on the ships on the way over here as slaves," Amos recalled.[43] "I know for a fact that I had more than fifty people talking to me at one time and I could hear every one of their conversations."[44] When he recovered, Amos understood the episode to be a call for him to be a conduit for the voices of his enslaved ancestors. "'Now you will be our voice, you will speak,'" Amos recalled. "'You will not break as we did not break. You will not break Kunta Kinte.' And that's what I carried through the rest of the project."[45] Amos described this as the most challenging acting role of his career because "it was impossible for me to emotionally separate myself from slavery and the traumas of being a slave and then to come home."[46] After *Roots,* Amos said he took a role in the short-lived science fiction television series *Future Cop* because "I needed something to help erase the scar tissue from Kunta Kinte."[47]

Roots was emotionally taxing for other black actors because it required them to assume subservient roles. Richard Roundtree, well known in the 1970s for his title role as a private detective in the *Shaft* films, had a particularly difficult time with a scene that called for him to grovel before George Hamilton's character. "When you're doing something like Roots with its historical significance it's magical," Roundtree said. "It was never ever work with the exception of the scene I had with George Hamilton. I said, 'We are going to do this in one take and one take only.'"[48] Marvin Chomsky, who directed the episode, recalled how he pushed Roundtree in this scene. "When [Richard Roundtree] had to crawl on his knees and had to say, 'Massa, I'm sorry, Master George Hamilton,' it was a brutal moment," Chomsky said. "Because Richard is the kind of man who is proud of being a black man, who has come to where he is in life as a fulfilled individual, and when he had to play crawling on his knees it was something that so physically revolted Richard that he couldn't do it. He couldn't—until I said, 'God damn it, get on your fucking knees—you're an actor, if you can't do it I'll kick you in the balls.'" Chomsky felt that challenging the six-foot-two-inch Roundtree was essential to the scene's success. "I had to beat Richard down," Chomsky said. "Richard wept, Richard was marvelous, Richard was brilliant, but it went beyond what I would [normally] have to do or what I would expect from an actor, it was a tough thing for him to do and he did it because Richard is pure professional and he had to rise above his own dignity to do it."[49] Screenwriter Bill Blinn recalled this scene as the tensest racial moment on the set. "This character was embodying everything [Richard Roundtree] fought against all of his entire professional life," Blinn said. "It was bringing him emotionally to a really bad place.... It quickly became clear that no white director, or white producer, or white anybody would be able to help Richard through this. The other black cast and crew rallied around him."[50] Though *Roots* producers and directors engaged in extensive correspondence and discussions regarding the appropriate way to film bare-breasted extras, they did not spend much time talking about what it meant to ask black performers to play slaves. Black actors had to rely on each other and themselves to navigate the emotions that *Roots* evoked.

While *Roots* boasted one of the largest collections of black acting talent in television history, civil rights advocates called attention to the lack of black writers and directors working on the series. Woodie King, a producer and director who had founded the New Federal Theater in New York to stage black-themed productions, led this campaign. In May 1976, near the end of the first month of filming *Roots,* King wrote to Wolper and Margulies to demand that the series employ more black professionals behind the camera. King sent copies of his letter to the *Hollywood Reporter, Variety,* the National Association for the Advancement of Colored People, the Congress of Racial Equality, and all three television broadcast networks to put pressure on *Roots*'s producers. "I must write this letter because of a grave injustice and a complete lack of insight from a major Hollywood producer," King wrote. "Not one Black director or Producer or script writer has been hired to work on Roots. This is 1976: One cannot deal with that old argument about there being no qualified Blacks; nor can one remain silent when it happens." King questioned how an all-white production staff could do justice to Haley's story. "We do understand the great backlash in Hollywood to Black projects of intellect and maturity and we do laud the producers," King wrote. "Yet Wolper pictures and Stan Margulies will tell our history from their point of view to some twenty five million Americans with no input from Black Americans. The director of photography will even be white! I don't believe that any other nationality in the world would let this happen: the recording of one's history *forever* by another race of people; people who have been historically our oppressors, our slave masters." King praised Haley as a talented writer but expressed frustration that the author did not push harder for black writers or directors. "We all respect Dr. Haley but that respect wanes when one realizes the man spent over two years with Malcolm X," King wrote, "Did he understand any of the things Malcolm related to him?" King concluded with a threat. "If the producers continue to ignore Black professionals in this industry, Blacks have no other recourse but to let their feelings be known to the networks and the sponsors."[51]

King's protest pushed the producers to seek out two talented black film professionals, director Gilbert Moses and director of photography Joseph Wilcots. Originally from Cleveland, Ohio, Gilbert Moses moved to Jackson, Mississippi, in the early 1960s, where he cofounded the Free Southern Theater, a radical black theater company with connections to the Student Nonviolent Coordinating Committee. Moses directed Amiri Baraka's play *Slave Ship*, first in the South and then in New York City.[52] He won an Obie award for *Slave Ship* and directed Melvin Van Peebles's *Ain't Supposed to Die a Natural Death* and several other plays in the 1970s. The *New York Times* described Moses in 1972 as "among the most highly respected and busiest black directors on the scene." "My whole thing is working on developing a black audience," Moses told the *Times*. "We blacks are starved for images of ourselves all over this country."[53] Moses first heard Alex Haley tell his *Roots* story at Crenshaw High School in west Los Angeles in the late 1960s and teased Wolper when the producer boasted that he had known about *Roots* since 1972, saying, "Niggers knew about that in '68."[54]

Margulies recalled that ABC initially balked at hiring Moses to direct an episode of *Roots* because he did not yet have any

Figure 12. Director Gilbert Moses, at right with hat, watches over filming. Director of photography Joe Wilcots is obscured behind camera. ABC Photo Archives/Getty Images.

filmmaking experience. There were "no black directors outside of Gordon Parks and Michael Schultz" that ABC would consider for a two-hour television movie, Margulies recalled, "much less something as important as this."[55] Moses knew that he had not been the producers' first choice and did not initially hit it off with Margulies. "I think it was obligatory and sort of condescending that they ... had this checklist of black directors," Moses said. "When I went in for an interview with Stan Margulies I was pretty dissatisfied—I was disappointed ... because Margulies really didn't know who I was [or] any of the credits I had amassed in the theater."[56] Still, Moses felt that once he was hired "Margulies supported me all the way through," even though there were "endless" technical problems as Moses directed his first television show.[57] "I think Margulies was really happy about how he not only gave me an opportunity," Moses said, "but I think

I came through in a way that was surprising and gave another kind of texture to the film."[58] Margulies agreed that hiring Moses "made such a difference to the actors."[59]

Actors were also happy to see director of photography Joe Wilcots behind the camera. As a child in Des Moines, Iowa, Wilcots built his own darkroom in his family's house. His first film job was making slides and reediting films for the state department in Iowa. He broke into Hollywood and got his union card at Joe Westheimer's optical effects studio.[60] Wilcots became the first black member of the International Cinematographers Guild in 1967, and a colleague described him as the "Jackie Robinson of cinematography."[61] Wilcots was the second assistant cameraman on Gordon Parks's film *The Learning Tree* (1969) before working his way up to the director of photography on Parks's *Leadbelly* (1976).

Wolper learned about Wilcots from one of the black cameramen the producer had hired to work on *Wattstax*, a 1973 documentary film on a huge music festival in Watts. Wilcots, who shot eight of the twelve hours of *Roots*, was particularly skilled at lighting scenes so that darker-skinned actors would be visible. "[Since childhood] I have seen a number of pictures where I was totally disappointed in the way black people were lit," Wilcots explained. "I was tired of having black people on the screen and not being able to see them."[62] In describing his camera and lighting techniques, Wilcots explained that too many of his white counterparts did not give black actors equal visibility in films. "The same consideration that you would give a can—a dark can and a light can in a commercial—must be given to people," Wilcots said. "In the past I think, too often, cameramen neglected to give that equal consideration to black people in the scene and therefore the black person was lost in the scene. Not because he didn't know his craft, but because of lack of consideration for the value of that person in the scene."[63] As the director of photography, Wilcots managed the camera crew (which included two black assistant cameramen), grips, and electricians. Gilbert Moses felt that a sense of community developed among the black cast and crew. "We were doing something, one of the few times that was relevant to us," Moses said. "We were making a view together out of our own history and our own identity and we were doing it well and that is … what we trained for."[64] Wilcots agreed and approached Haley on the set one day to thank him. "All of these people have been hired by you, because you dared to put pencil on paper," Wilcots told Haley.[65]

While Woodie King's complaint pushed the producers to find and hire Moses and Wilcots, the screenwriters remained all white. Wolper and Margulies's response to the call for black writers on *Roots* was simple. "We felt that we did have a black writer … named Alex Haley," Margulies said.[66] Head writer Bill Blinn said the first question he asked Wolper and Margulies was "Do you want a black guy to do this?" To which the producers replied, "Alex is black enough for any one of us."[67] For his part, Haley encouraged the producers to take this position. While he was in Jamaica working to finish *Roots* in 1975, Haley described being visited by someone from a "pretty potent black organization," who pressed the author regarding black participation in the *Roots* television series and book promotion. This "virtual interrogation" frustrated Haley. "It seems of little moment that *I* am black," Haley wrote.[68] When Haley signed the television deal with Wolper he advised the producers to look for the most experienced television writers, without regard to race. Haley viewed *Roots* as the symbolic story of all black Americans, but he wanted to be the only black writer associated with series.

In the months while the cast and crew were busy filming *Roots,* ABC network executives and the producers were carefully crafting a marketing plan for the series. No network had ever broadcast a twelve-hour miniseries, much less a story in which enslaved black people were the protagonists. To market *Roots,* Wolper and ABC decided they would emphasize "family" as the series' universal theme. Wolper recalled that when Ruby Dee had told him about Haley's *Roots* in 1972, he immediately recognized that the project already had a *TV Guide*–ready one-sentence pitch: "seven generations of a black family from Africa to today." "I didn't even know the story," Wolper recalled. "I didn't have to. The concept was there from that first night."[69] ABC gave *Roots* the subtitle "The Triumph of an American Family." This small but important tweak to the book's subtitle, "The Saga of an American Family," promised viewers that Haley's ancestors would weather the horrors of slavery and emerge triumphantly as Americans.

In addition to emphasizing the universality of *Roots* as a family story, Wolper and ABC stressed that *Roots* was a major television event. Here *Roots* fit into ABC's new slate of "Novels for Television." The network's first miniseries, *Rich Man, Poor Man,* based on a 1969 novel by Irvin Shaw, was a commercial success and formed the basis for part of the network's marketing campaign for *Roots.* "Roots has many of the same elements that 'Rich Man, Poor Man' had, and that we know the public will respond to, principally, a continuing story with maturing characters who experience every kind of emotion," ABC's Carole Stevens wrote to her colleagues. The key difference, Stevens continued, was that "Roots is based on a non-fiction book that will be published only three months prior to air, and that Roots, as a book, will have more prestige and significance beyond that of the novel

'Rich Man, Poor Man.' We must begin now to create an audience for Roots and whet their appetites for a project that they know will be 'in the tradition of Rich Man, Poor Man' plus."[70] As Stevens noted, a key difference between *Roots* and *Rich Man, Poor Man* was that *Roots* would broadcast very shortly after the publication of the book. Wolper worked with ABC and Doubleday to coordinate the publication and promotion of the book with the television series. "The network could put only so much promotion into *Roots*," Wolper recalled. "It had eighty other things to promote.... I had the feeling that if you release a book three or four months before the show goes on the air, then all the book's advertising and promotion flows into the TV promotion.... For four months people would be hearing about *Roots*."[71]

For ABC, calling *Roots* a "novel" signified that it was a large-scale story, not that it was fiction. Doubleday worried that promoting *Roots* as a "Novel for Television" would confuse the publisher's sales staff and readers. "This is the second notice I have seen of ABC announcing Roots as an adaptation of a novel," Doubleday's Lisa Drew wrote to Margulies. "The book is absolutely *not* a novel; it is nonfiction, and totally accurate American history. The thing that disturbs me about this is that Doubleday is selling it as nonfiction and this is going to be very confusing to our salesmen to keep seeing references to it as a novel. Would you please make it clear to ABC's publicity and advertising departments that this book is completely nonfiction and is being sold as such by Doubleday."[72] Ken McCormick later said that he considered *Roots* fiction but deferred to Drew, who had taken over as Haley's editor at Doubleday. Drew said she opted to call *Roots* "nonfiction" because she "was terribly afraid if we called this book fiction, although it had fiction elements in it, the people who are not sympathetic to the viewpoint of the book would use that as an excuse to say … this is fiction and it is all made up and didn't happen that way."[73] For their part, neither ABC nor Wolper worried about the contradiction of referring to *Roots* as both "nonfiction" and a "novel." They were invested in making *Roots* an epic television event, not in debating literary genres.

This coordinated marketing effort had its tensions. Wolper expressed frustration that ABC and Doubleday were producing promotional material that did not mention his name. "When you put out the ads for the book, be sure, when you say to the effect, 'Soon to be a major ABC Television Program' also say, 'A David L. Wolper Production,'" Wolper wrote to Lisa Drew. "There are two reasons for this. One, it is good for me; and two, it will indicate to the people who read the ad that this is going to be a first-class production."[74] After *Newsweek* ran an article profiling *Roots* in June 1976, Wolper wrote a strongly worded letter to ABC. "I have just finished reading the wonderful article in Newsweek," Wolper wrote. "I think it was absolutely terrific, except that I am extremely upset by the fact that, in all the references throughout the article, it was referred to as 'ABC's production of Haley's epic,' 'ABC has signed LeVar Burton,' and 'An ABC film crew wrapped up Savannah shooting.' All three of those statements are simply not true. The name of WOLPER should have been inserted for ABC." Wolper continued, "In the future, I expect the ABC executives, and the ABC Press and Public Relations Departments to make a more-than-routine effort, in all releases and in all conversations regarding ROOTS, to see that 'DAVID L WOLPER, EXECUTIVE PRODUCER' or 'A DAVID L. WOLPER PRODUCTION' is mentioned."[75]

Wolper's demand for due credit is a useful reminder that in addition to being a history-making book and television series, *Roots* was above all else a commercial property. Its potential to expose millions of viewers and readers to the history of slavery was tied directly to the ability of ABC, Doubleday, Wolper, Haley, and other interests to profit from its commercial success. ABC's marketing guide for their affiliate station promotion managers was unabashedly titled "'Roots' Exploitation Opportunities." "We cannot overemphasize the importance of this series and need and encourage your support on this project," the ABC guide read. "Roots offers you an extraordinary opportunity to enhance your station's stature in your community as well as provide your viewers with a superlative and deeply moving entertainment." The network advised stations to contact "bookstores, department stores, libraries [which] all have a vested interest in Alex Haley's best seller—take advantage of it and contact them with your tie-in ideas for posters, point-of-purchase cards, etc. Remind them of the 'Rich Man, Poor Man' bonanza."[76] ABC told local affiliates that Los Angeles mayor Tom Bradley had already agreed to declare January 23–30, 1977, as "'Roots' Week" and encouraged more stations to work with their local mayor to do the same. (Over two dozen cities eventually declared "*Roots* Week" at ABC's suggestion.)[77]

All of this marketing effort was designed to get viewers to tune in for the first episode. "When you are doing a miniseries, so much of it is about the promotion, publicity, and advertising, because you have one night to get them in the house ... if you don't get them into the tent on the opening night, you are dead," ABC's Brandon Stoddard said. "We developed a war room ... where we would meet with publicity, promotion, advertising, and on-air people once a week, and we would break it out and plan for something breaking on *Roots* for sixth months in advance ... we planned out every story."[78] Critic Lawrence Laurent wrote in the *Washington Post* that the "heavy load of advance material for the telecast of 'Roots' brings back memories of a buildup for a Hollywood movie in the 1930s."[79] This extensive marketing campaign was in support of a series that promised to foreground black history in ways that had never been seen before on television.

In light of this massive promotional effort, it is remarkable that ABC was still scared that *Roots* would not attract an audience. In November 1976, Fred Silverman, ABC's director of programming, announced that ABC would take the unusual step of airing *Roots* on eight consecutive nights. In the press release, Silverman framed this scheduling decision as a way to capture *Roots*'s emotional intensity. "We are taking this unprecedented approach to airing a 'Novel for Television' to insure maximum impact and continuity for what has already proven to be one of the most important dramatic stories of our time," Silverman said. "By creating an 'eight-day-week' for this unique presentation we can provide the same kind of story concentration that is the very nature of a novel. A work this exceptional, this eagerly awaited, not only allows but requires exceptional treatment."[80] Silverman and his colleagues later acknowledged that ABC aired *Roots* in an unprecedented "eight-day-week" to limit the damage if the series did not catch on with television audiences. Brandon Stoddard, who championed *Roots* at ABC and reported to Silverman, said he knew his boss was "terrified" of *Roots* and figured, "We're going to run it in a block in January" so that the network would only have "one bad week."[81] Silverman said he "loved the property" but was "nervous as can be" about airing it. Silverman was especially nervous about broadcasting any part of *Roots* during the crucial February sweeps period that helped set local advertising rates for the next period. "Maybe the best thing to do is back into January and do it all in one week,"

Silverman concluded. *Roots* "tapped a chord that I didn't call," Silverman later admitted. "I would have put it in February. As it is we got seventy shares in January, which didn't do us a hell of a lot of good in the sweeps. And I never heard the end of it from the affiliates."[82]

By the time the first episode of *Roots* aired on January 23, 1977, Alex Haley's book had sold over a million copies in hardcover, ABC had invested over $6 million in the production and marketing of *Roots,* and *Roots*'s producers had cast several white television stars to make white audiences comfortable watching a series about a black family in slavery. Despite all of this, there was still no guarantee that *Roots* would be a commercially successful television series. Wolper, Margulies, Stoddard, and Silverman bet that *Roots* could be a lucrative property, but on the night of the first broadcast all they could do was hope that Americans would tune in to watch *Roots.*

CHAPTER SIX

Reading *Roots*

Alex Haley's *Roots* is three stories in one book. The first quarter of the book describes Kunta Kinte's childhood in the Gambia, his capture, and his forced journey to America aboard the *Lord Ligonier.* This story of an African Eden and forced exile from it is followed by four hundred pages of family history, stretching across seven generations from Kunta Kinte's arrival in America in 1767 to Haley's birth in 1921. Finally, the book's last twenty pages tell the story of Haley's search for his roots, a story he told hundreds of times in lectures. *Roots* is a long and uneven book, but these three stories gave readers and critics plenty to enjoy, analyze, and debate.

Roots made Kunta Kinte the most famous African in American history. The long first section of Haley's epic family history takes place in the small Gambian village of Juffure, where Kunta Kinte was born and lived as a free person for sixteen years. "The reason I devoted the first 126 pages of the book to Kunta's life in Africa, which some critics found both long and boring, was that so little has been known up to now in the West, by white or black, about the depth and richness of African culture, which I happen to think we can all learn something from," Haley said.[1] Creating this vision of Kunta's childhood in Africa became an overwhelming obsession for Haley. "I spent two years just researching and digging out actual facts of African cultural life—ceremonies, implements, etc., everything I could find on the subject," Haley said. "But, when I finished, I had this unwieldy mass of material and I had to come up with some way of organizing it. I made a notebook for each of the 16 years that Kunta had spent in Africa, then separated the information I had gathered in terms of the age at which Kunta would have been exposed to it. This ordered the material and gave the early part of the book a feeling of authenticity, validity."[2]

Some reviewers criticized Haley for idealizing life in eighteenth-century Juffure, Gambia, and Africa. "That the real Juffure of two hundred years ago was anything like the pastoral village Haley describes is not possible," historian Willie Lee Rose wrote in the *New York Review of Books*. "Whatever bucolic character Juffure may have today, it was in the eighteenth century a busy trading center, inhabited by possibly as many as 3,000 people."[3] The Gambian officials who facilitated Haley's research in the country told the author about this colonial history, but the author chose to portray the Gambia as an African Eden. "I, we, need a place called Eden," Haley said. "My people need a Plymouth Rock."[4] Haley wanted Kunta Kinte's childhood in Juffure to serve as a symbolic beginning for all African Americans. "In the case of blacks, there just simply hasn't been anything like a valid history of the family culture, love and compassion," Haley said. "History talked about the slaves amorphously, as a body of people who endured this and that.... [My hope is] that this story of our people can help alleviate the legacies of the fact that preponderantly the histories have been written by the winner."[5]

In creating an idyllic image of Kunta Kinte's life in Juffure, Haley hoped to displace the racist images of Africa he had seen in his youth. "I thought of Africa as being pretty much the way it had been depicted in the movies," Haley said. "My far-off relatives were there, dancing and waving spears and raising hell while Johnny Weissmuller swung through the trees."[6] Like millions of filmgoers, Haley learned about Africa from the *Tarzan* and *Jungle Jim* films, which starred former Olympic swimming champion Johnny Weissmuller. "All of us, black and white, who are over 20 years of age thought of *Tarzan* or *Jungle Jim* as our concept of Africa," Haley argued.[7] Haley carried these childhood movie memories into adulthood and saw his book as an opportunity to tell a different story about Africa. After *Roots* had broken publishing and television ratings records, Haley said, "The thing I am proudest of is that [*Roots*] helped replace the prevailing African image of Tarzan with that of Kunta Kinte, which is more appropriate and accurate."[8] Roger Wilkins, a black civil rights activist, journalist, and historian, welcomed this new view of Africa. "My parents, as typical college-educated Americans, did not know enough of Africa or of slavery to protect me from the overwhelming shame that I felt because of the misinformation that washed over this culture," Wilkins wrote. "Just as the revolution in black consciousness removed many of those shackles in the late sixties, the story of Kunta Kinte filled blacks at all levels with great pride and chased the shame."[9] Acclaimed writer Maya Angelou agreed that *Roots* challenged long-held stereotypes of Africa. "For centuries, we (all Americans) were led to believe that Africa was a country belonging to wild animals, where naked, primitive human beings spent their time either climbing trees, leading safaris, or eating each other; and, although we denied the teaching publicly, we at least half-believed the description," Angelou wrote. "Then Alex Haley's 'Roots' burst upon the national consciousness. Using the formidable work as lens, for the first time we were able to see Africans at home (on the continent) and abroad (three hundred years and thousands of miles removed to the United States, South America, the Caribbean, Nova Scotia) as simply human beings caught in the clutches of circumstances over which they had little and often no control."[10]

In addition to replacing racist popular culture's visions of Africa, Haley wanted readers to know Kunta Kinte as a free member of a family and community who loved him. "I wanted to plant Kunta's roots so deep, as I told the story of his life from birth to capture, that the wrench of his being torn from the soil of his homeland would be as heartbreaking for the reader as it was for me," Haley said.[11] Haley needed Kunta Kinte to be the patriarch for his family history, but the family story Haley heard in Gambia did not flesh out Kunta Kinte as a person. Gambian storyteller Kebba Fofana Kinte told Haley who Kunta Kinte's parents and siblings were and when he disappeared from the village, but for *Roots* to work Haley needed Kunta Kinte to be more than a name on a family tree.

In the lengthy Africa section of *Roots*, Haley asked readers to share his experience of creating Kunta Kinte. "The reader literally shared his birth. . . . We became beguiled by him as we shared his journey through life," Haley said. "When I say 'we,' I mean I was as beguiled as anyone else in recounting the story of his life. There were many times when I would catch myself at the typewriter or with pen in hand, feeling as though I were standing off somewhere at the edge of the village watching Kunta doing the things I was writing about at the time."[12] Haley described writing about Kunta's enslavement in similar terms. "When [Kunta] finally was captured, I felt as though I had been hit in the head with a two-by-four," Haley said. "In fact, I was so broken up over his capture, that I quit writing for several weeks."[13] With Kunta's capture, Haley said, "slavery ceased to be impersonal. Indeed, it became highly personal to millions of readers who identified with him in human terms, very much as I did."[14]

By devoting the first third of *Roots* to Kunta Kinte's life, Haley achieved the difficult task of making his book work as a specific story about one family's journey through slavery, as a representative story about black enslavement and survival, and, most broadly, as a generalizable story about coming to America. Doubleday's advertising for *Roots* emphasized this mix of specific black experiences and universal themes. "Twelve years ago, Alex Haley went searching for answers to questions we all ask," a book advertisement read. "Who am I? Where did I come from? Who were my ancestors? The quest was more difficult for him than it would be for most Americans: his ancestors arrived in this country neither on the Mayflower nor in steerage, but in chains."[15] Doubleday and Haley welcomed readers to see *Roots* as a generalizable story of a family's journey to America. "Searching for his roots, Alex Haley helps us discover our own," Doubleday's advertising promised. Indeed, *Roots* benefited from and contributed to a groundswell in interest in genealogy in the 1970s. How-to genealogy books like Ethel Williams's *Know Your Ancestors* (1968), Gilbert Doane's *Searching for Your Ancestors* (1973), Val Greenwood's *The Researcher's Guide to American Genealogy* (1974), and Suzanne Hilton's *Who Do You Think You Are? Digging for Your Family Roots* (1976) preceded Haley's, while Dan Rottenberg's *Finding Our Father: A Guidebook to Jewish Genealogy* (1977) and Charles Blockson's *Black Genealogy* (1977) came out shortly after

Roots. Literary scholar Louis Rubin described *Roots* as producing "a kind of national vogue for root-grubbing." Rubin joked, "I have no doubt that a minimum of one dozen New York publishing houses have since commissioned journalists to return to the jungles of such faraway places as Esthonia, the Orkney Islands, and the Schwartzwald and search out the peregrinations and former penal conditions of their forebears."[16] *Newsweek*'s July 4, 1977, cover picked up this theme with the headline "Everybody's Search for Roots." While Doubleday and Haley pitched *Roots* as a universal family story, everyone who picked up *Roots* knew that Haley's farthest-back person would be captured and transported to United States on a slave ship. While readers could enjoy Haley's "Saga of an American Family" without grappling with the horrible magnitude of slavery, *Roots* made it clear that the process of becoming American for black people was categorically different from that for European immigrants.

While Haley was not the first author to root the history of black Americans in Africa or to tell an uplifting story of a family's survival during and after slavery, *Roots* had far more support from the commercial publishing industry (and later television) than previous works of black history. Doubleday's extensive promotion of Haley's book and the book's physical size (it is 587 pages long) helped establish *Roots* as an important work that should be on the bookshelf in every black home. "For the first time in our history, there is a perfect gift for every child past the age of 10 years," Jim Cleaver wrote in the *Los Angeles Sentinel,* a leading black newspaper, just before Christmas in 1976. "Of course, the 'perfect gift' to which we refer is a book entitled 'Roots.'"[17] Cleaver continued, "The past several years have seen this society evolve into a newly discovered kind of consciousness about blackness. There have been all kinds of groups formed that relate to the 'black awareness' aspect of our community. But never before has such a chronicle about the evolution of the African from freeman to slave to freeman been written."[18] A reviewer in the *Atlanta Daily World,* the city's largest black newspaper, praised *Roots* in similar terms. "Haley's book 'Roots' adds some dignity to our existence in America," Charles Price wrote. "This is not because of the skillfulness of his writing or the novelty of the events that he writes about, but rather because he has taken the time to treat the experiences of blacks as human experiences."[19] Chuck Stone, a black journalist and scholar, looked to classical history to find an adequate comparison for Haley's epic work. "For its literary gracefulness, Roots, the book, will stand in solitary preeminence, distinguished by its narrative sweep, historical detail, and eloquent craftsmanship," Stone wrote. "Alex Haley is the Thucydides of our day, interpreting the Black Diaspora as majestically as the Greek historian catalogues the Peloponnesian War."[20]

Roots also became part of ongoing debates about black families, much closer at hand than ancient Greece. The year after Haley signed the contract for *Before This Anger,* Daniel Patrick Moynihan, assistant secretary of labor in the Johnson administration, wrote the government report *The Black Family: A Case for National Action* (1965). Moynihan argued that black urban families were deeply troubled. "There is no one Negro problem," Moynihan wrote. "There is no one solution. Nonetheless, at the center of the tangle of pathology is the weakness of the family structure. Once or twice removed, it will be found to be the principal source of most of the aberrant, inadequate, or antisocial behavior that did not establish, but now serves to perpetuate the cycle of poverty and deprivation." Moynihan argued that this black family instability started in slavery: "It was by destroying the

Negro family under slavery that white America broke the will of the Negro people."[21] The Moynihan Report influenced political and scholarly debates regarding black families for decades and prompted historian Herbert Gutman to research and write *The Black Family in Slavery and Freedom, 1750–1925* (1976), which argued that slave marriages and two-parent households were much more common than Moynihan or previous scholars of slavery had suggested.[22]

Haley never explicitly discussed the Moynihan Report, but in his lectures and interviews before and after the publication of *Roots* Haley argued that American families of all races were not as strong as they once had been. "It seems that this country today is afflicted by rootlessness," Haley said. "We are a young country, brash, we have all this technology and it seems we are rapidly drawing away from our sense of heritage. We're drawing away from old people. Since the '60s, it has come to be fashionable to be irreverent toward older people."[23] Haley blamed television and other media for much of this detachment, even as he was busy consulting on the television adaptation of *Roots*. "It used to be, before television and radio, families' entertainment tended to be gathering in the home and listening to the old people talk," Haley said. "Now kids don't have time to listen to old people say 'boo.' ... Television came along and there was no more talking."[24] While Haley had lived in New York, San Francisco, and Los Angeles and traveled broadly, Henning, Tennessee, remained his frame of reference for the golden age of family and community life. "In the 40 or so years since I grew up in Henning, the family has been shrinking and drifting apart," Haley said in an interview with *Playboy*. "As America has moved from the country to the city, from huge, messy old homes echoing with the noise of three generations to closet-sized, $400-a-month apartments for swinging singles eating TV dinners alone in 600-unit high-rises; from sitting on front porches, listening to grandmothers tell family stories like the ones I heard, to sitting in suburban rec rooms with baby sitters while Mom and Dad go out." Haley said he did not want to "run down" urban and suburban America or "romanticize" the rural past but argued that "there's no question that somewhere along the way between then and now, we've lost something very precious: a sense of community, which is nothing more than a congregation of *families*."[25] Haley advocated a traditional view of family that would have resonated with supporters of the Moynihan Report. Like Gutman's book, though, Haley's *Roots* looked to the era of slavery to find an example of a stable black family.

In the process of celebrating the strength and resilience of black families, *Roots* also unsettled long-held myths about benevolent plantation "families" where slave masters supposedly cared for their slaves like children. Among the thousands of letters Haley received, some came from whites who tried to reconcile their own family histories and views of slavery with *Roots*. "I think we all needed to be told what the slaves suffered during these inhuman years," a white reader from suburban Seattle wrote. "I am 41 years old and just a year ago, I found, in tracing my own roots that my great, great, great grandfather, Nathaniel Owens of Green Co., Kentucky, had slaves on his plantation. In the year 1830, he had 29 slaves. I discussed this with my father, and was told Nathaniel Owens was good to his slaves, and when they were freed, they didn't want to leave him." After asking Haley if the sprinter and Olympic gold medalist Jesse Owens was a descendant of Nathaniel Owens, the reader confessed that she was still trying to come to terms with slavery as part of her family's history. "Mr. Haley, I want to tell you I was shocked that any ancestors of mine had slaves," she wrote. "None of your ancestors were involved with mine, but the slaves belonging to Nathaniel must've suffered the same things before he bought them. I hope he was good to them, as I've been told. Just the same I would humbly like to apologize to those people for whatever they suffered. So to those people, I now, 148 years later say, I am sorry."[26] Many reviewers attributed the success of *Roots* to "white guilt," but this and similar letters speak to more interesting and complicated feelings. If *Roots* gave black Americans a vision of a black family's history they could find empowering and inspiring, the book encouraged some white Americans to see slavery as part of their own family's history. These engagements were messy, though they could be productive. Nathaniel Owens's descendant, for example, clung to the idea of a benevolent slave master even as she apologized.

Haley understood that most white Americans held distorted views of slavery shaped by a powerful mix of popular culture fables like *Birth of a Nation* and *Gone with the Wind,* history textbooks that downplayed slavery or romanticized the antebellum South, and family stories. A reader from Shreveport, for example, wrote to Haley to say that she and her husband felt "real compassion with the slaves" in his book but were "deeply disturbed" that all the slave owners were depicted "as cruel and viewing their slaves as little more than cattle." In contrast, she wrote, "Our family owned a plantation in Florien, Louisiana from the 1700's through the time of the Civil War. In the cemetery is the grave of the original owner. At his feet is the grave of a negro slave. The slave requested to be buried at his master's feet."[27] Haley encountered these anecdotes rationalizing slavery over and over again. "People had such a mythological view of slavery and what it involved," Haley said. "Those who offer that argument seek to defend the long-prevailing image of benevolent masters. But no matter how good the master may have been it did not change the status of his slaves."[28] More than just upsetting the view of benevolent plantation families, Haley made it clear that slave owners populate the family trees of many white Americans. *Roots,* more than other books during the 1970s genealogy renaissance, made it clear that family histories are not always celebratory.

Roots attacked the mythological view of slavery with "faction" rather than footnotes. "Since I wasn't yet around when most of the story occurred," Haley wrote in *Roots,* "by far most of the dialogue and most of the incidents are of necessity a novelized amalgam of what I *know* took place together with what my researching led me to plausibly *feel* took place."[29] Elsewhere Haley said, "Call it 'faction,' if you like, or heightened history, or fiction based on the lives of real people."[30]

Haley's approach to writing "faction" made many critics uneasy. "*Roots* is a hybrid work," literary critic Arnold Rampersad wrote. "It links the detective skills of a superior investigative reporter to the powers of a would-be fiction writer, and the product is a work of extremely uneven texture but unquestionable final success." Rampersad argued that Haley simply did not possess the creative writing skills to do justice to the fictional potential of *Roots.* "The solemnity of the basic theme of *Roots* also cannot obscure the fact that the Afro-American novel is too accomplished in its basic skills for *Roots* to pass as a well wrought novel or romance," Rampersad argued. "Technically, the work is so innocent of fictive ingenuity that it seldom surpasses the standards of the most popular of historical romances."[31] Historian Willie Lee Rose raised similar concerns from a different disciplinary perspective. "The problem of characterizing the individual people of so many generations, of making more than a score of persons come alive in the special circumstances of two vastly different cultures, and over a span of two centuries, challenges Haley the artist, and taxes Haley the historian," Rose wrote. "There are long sections in the book that will cause the historian to call *Roots* fiction, when literary critics may prefer to call it history rather than judge it as art. For *Roots* is long and ambitious, and all of its parts are not as good as the best parts."[32] *New York Times* reviewer Christopher Lehmann-Haupt argued that despite Haley's attempt to mix fact and fiction, *Roots* "all reads like fiction, and very conventional fiction at that."[33] Lehmann-Haupt described the last section of *Roots,* where Haley details his search for his ancestors, as the book's most remarkable passage. "It is here that we are finally convinced that the dramatic family-chronicle Mr. Haley has told is not the novel that it appears, but actual history," Lehmann-Haupt wrote, before suggesting that Haley would have been better served by writing an autobiography about his search rather than a novelized history. "By writing 'Roots' Mr. Haley has done something merely ordinary," Lehmann-Haupt argued, "whereas by laying the groundwork to write it—by tracing his heritage back to its African roots and thereby providing a concrete example to those millions of American blacks whose true names remain unknown—he has done something extraordinary."[34]

Haley's blend of fact and fiction received more attention after the *London Times* published a story in April 1977 by travel journalist Mark Ottaway raising questions about Haley's research in the Gambia. Ottaway visited the Gambia, spoke with Gambian archivist and historian Bakari Sidibe, and wrote that "the vital link in Haley's claim to have traced his ancestry to Kunta Kinte and Juffure was provided by a man of notorious unreliability who knew in advance what Haley wanted to hear and who subsequently gave a totally different version of the tale."[35] Ottaway noted several other inconsistencies with Haley's research, and his story received international attention.

The *New York Times* asked a number of prominent historians to weigh in on the *Roots* controversy. Many were unmoved by the issues with Haley's research but were careful to note that *Roots* was not the work of a professional historian. "It's a work of fiction," Harvard historian Bernard Baylin said. "And its importance is as a work of fiction and a very powerful one. I don't think its importance rests on whether or not such and such a ship was in such and such a place. I don't give a damn if they don't find the ship he names. It's a powerful book for other reasons altogether. This account is the author's perception of the meaning of slavery, and the account is one of sensibility. I don't think it turns on details. It turns on a state of mind, and there's no documentation of that." Yale's Edmund Morgan, whose 1975 book *American Slavery, American Freedom* influenced a generation of scholarship, argued that "errors about the location of the village are not very important—nobody will deny there was a slave trade." Ultimately, Morgan suggested, *Roots* is "a statement of someone's search for an identity. It would seem to me to retain a good deal of impact no matter how many mistakes the man has made. In any genealogy there are bound to be a number of mistakes.... If they can prove willful mistakes, I guess I wouldn't draw very many conclusions, because I don't think the book will have a great impact on historians anyway." Robert Fogel, author of *Time on the Cross,* a controversial economic history of slavery, also offered qualified praise of Haley. "I thought *Roots* was the best historical novel ever written on slavery, and I say that not to demean it, because a first-rate historical novel can frequently give you a better sense of historical knowledge than carefully researched history," Fogel said. "I never applied to it the standards I would have if it had been written by C. Vann Woodward or Oscar Handlin." Harvard's Oscar Handlin thought his fellow historians were being too easy on Haley and *Roots*. "A fraud's a fraud," Handlin said. "Most historians are cowardly about reviewing history books. The whole idea of being factual about material has gone out the window. Historians are reluctant—cowardly—about calling attention to factual errors when the general theme is in the right direction. That goes for foreign policy, for race and for this book. I think it's a disgrace."[36]

Other scholars argued that myth had always been a part of historical storytelling. "The problem is we all need certain myths about the past, and one must remember how much in the myths about the Pilgrims or the immigrants coming here has been reversed," Yale's David Davis said.[37] Warren Roberts, director of the Museum of African Art, was more vociferous in his defense of Haley, comparing *Roots* favorably to Arnold Toynbee's twelve-volume *A Study of History* (1934–61). "If Haley's source for the African part of his history 'was,' as Ottaway writes, 'a man of notorious unreliability who probably knew beforehand what Haley wanted to hear,' the result is far less inaccurate than Toynbee's with his gigantic omissions of entire eras and civilizations," Roberts wrote. "If some of Haley's roots are myths ('working hypotheses'), they are far more valuable for purposes of achieving human understanding at this transient stage of history-writing than the myths they are supplanting."[38]

C. Eric Lincoln, a black scholar and friend of Haley, said he had heard other academics put down *Roots* "because it's not history" but suggested that Haley's skill was in capturing a larger "cultural truth." Haley was "a genius in having the imagination which enabled him to create characters that make the truth live," Lincoln argued. "Here you have this vast expanse of history, this vast experience that nobody thought important enough to record, and Alex is able to take the outlines, which is all that is available to him, and to give those outlines meaning by the creation of characters ... by the creation of situations which makes of a blank period of American history a living experience."[39] *Washington Post* reviewer Robert Maynard agreed that *Roots* had to be evaluated as a story told to a mass commercial readership rather than by typical academic criteria. "I picked [*Roots*] up in suspicion and put it down so overcome by the power of the narrative that my first reaction was to wonder how much it mattered whether every detail of Haley's lineage had been precisely established," Maynard wrote. "I would have preferred a book loaded with footnotes and other documentation, but that is not this book.... What is surprising to me now is how much less important that documentation became as I moved through the story of seven generations of a family."[40] Thomas Lask, writing in the *New York Times,* concurred. "For those unnumbered readers who never touch a historical monograph or peruse the charts and statistics of an article in an abstruse journal," Lask wrote, "'Roots' will remain the most meaningful account of the black experience in America."[41] *Roots* reached hundreds of thousands more readers than academic treatments of slavery or black history, and C. Eric Lincoln suspected that academic critics of *Roots* were jealous of the book's success. "I don't care what the academics say," Lincoln concluded. "I challenge the academics to go out and to do as well."[42]

Award committees were also unsure how to categorize Haley's book. Both the Pulitzer Prize and National Book Award gave *Roots* special awards rather than putting the book in the fiction or nonfiction categories. "We didn't care whether it was history or fiction, or a personal confession," said Richard Baker, the head of the Pulitzer Prize Board. "It deserved a special award."[43] Ken McCormick, one of Haley's editors at Doubleday, wrote to congratulate the author on the National Book Award. McCormick described the award as "a very nice tribute to you" but noted, "I think there is something pretty sad in a set of categories that can't adjust itself to your extraordinary book."[44]

For his part, Haley spoke frequently about how he created his particular brand of "faction." "I wrote 'Roots' as a novel from the point of view of the characters," Haley said.[45] As Haley and his research assistant George Sims amassed boxes of research material on different historical periods and subjects, Haley tried to keep in mind that "there was so much that [the characters] couldn't know" about the eras in which they were living or how the nation's and family's histories would unfold. Haley liked to tell a story about jazz musician Miles Davis to illustrate what it meant to become engrossed in creative work. "Miles said he got so full of music that when he was on the subway to go from Julliard to downtown to play with [Charlie Parker], when the subway door would ... squeak, his mind involuntarily would catch the key, whatever note it squeaked in," Haley said. "And then his fingers would just involuntary twitch into that trumpet-key position, and all this would happen unconsciously with him." Haley said he felt a similar sense of creative embodiment with *Roots*. "I got that way with this book, in phases of it. Where I was writing parts, I WAS the people, I wasn't me, I WAS THEM."[46] As with so much of *Roots,* Haley also traced his storytelling techniques back to conversations with his family elders. Cousin Georgia "talked of the people on the porch as if they weren't dead, but just had gone off-stage behind the curtains," Haley said. "It was ambiguous and vague, yet supremely charging."[47]

Haley came to embrace the idea that history was a set of competing interpretations. In notes prepared in response to the Ottaway controversy, Haley's wrote, "There is no set, fixed history. History is—what A writes; what B writes; and what really happened—which will never be known."[48] Elsewhere, Haley jotted notes to remind interviewers and audiences that the Western canon was full of mythical characters created from real historical figures. "There was a real Hamlet, there was a real Johann Faust," Haley wrote in his notebook, "but the world knows Shakespeare's mythological Hamlet, Goethe's Faust."[49] Haley elaborated on his conception of history in a 1979 interview. "The popular concept is if a book is labeled history, it is supposed to be true solid substance material of what was," Haley said. "That's not true. It can't be true. How does somebody know what happened all that time.... You can go in any great library you want to go to and pick out five different books on the subject of the Battle of Manassas, the first battle of the Civil War, and you will get five variations or versions about that same battle. All this is saying is that history is not constant. How can it be?"[50]

Despite all of the hand-wringing over *Roots* as "faction," Haley's book was shaped less by his sense of how to write historical fiction than by his desire to make all the stories he gathered and created fit together neatly. While it is not always clear in *Roots* where Haley is drawing from archival documents, oral traditions, published secondary sources, or his imagination, the book never veers from the straight line it draws from Kunta Kinte's birth in 1750s' Gambia to Haley's researching of *Roots* in the 1970s. If Haley toyed with the boundaries between fact and fiction and came to see all history as interpretive, he was dogmatic about keeping the story going as steady as a heartbeat from generation to generation. Many readers loved the steadiness of

Figure 13. Haley signing copies of *Roots* at mall in Los Angeles, 1977. Bettmann/Corbis/AP Images.

Haley's narrative and found it moving, even when they knew in advance how the story would turn out. "I was deeply involved with your narrative," a reader from Arkansas wrote. "I remained dry-eyed throughout, until ... well, it was silly, really. I knew it was coming. I've read several of your interviews, and knew why I had bought the book, so you tell me why it happened.... Page 564, end of Chapter 117: 'The baby boy, six weeks old, was me.' I started to cry. He's done it! I practically shouted. He's really, actually gone and done it!"[51] Few authors have moved hundreds of thousands of readers to tears, and this emotional impact, more than a complex narrative or literary masterpiece, was what Haley sought to produce.

Haley's plentiful notes, letters, and drafts offer tantalizing hints of the people, incidents, and themes that did not fit his orderly vision for *Roots*. In his unpublished manuscript "My

Search for Roots," Haley described a woman, Old Sister Dinti, whom he had known as a boy in Henning, Tennessee. "She had actually *been* a slave, and to prove it she would let anybody, including us boys, push their hands up her bare back under her blouse to feel for themselves the hard raised welts that still remained from the beatings she had gotten as a young slave girl," Haley wrote.

> Old Sister Dinti liked having us feel her back as much as we were thrilled by the mystery of it, for it opened the door to her talking about what the slaves ate, what they wore, and how they were mistreated and in return would play tricks on their massas, mistresses, and overseers. I remember a kind of wonder at her presence. As I worked on *Roots* I began to feel on my own back the welts of her youth as the tactile memory of them returned to my fingers when I read of whipping after whipping and saw the early photographs of the skin of slaves, pictures where in brutal clarity I saw the crisscrossed scars raised as high above the smooth flesh as the whips had cut deep into it.[52]

This story is a more compelling meditation on the embodied nature of history and memory than anything that appears in *Roots*. Haley describes touching Old Sister Dinti's scars as a sensuous gateway to learning about slavery, both in terms of the physical brutality enslaved people endured and the everyday lives they led. This story paints an intimate image of history being written on, and told through, a woman's body. Haley's memory of Old Sister Dinti makes it even more frustrating that the female characters in *Roots* are so woefully underdeveloped.

Haley also recounted feeling haunted as he wrote *Roots*. "Sometimes I would feel as if I was going crazy or something," he wrote. "Not really ghosts, they seemed fleshed in some ephemeral way, but translucent." When he reached the later generations in his story, Haley recalled, "I began to experience the most eerie sensation that I was about to be born. Prior to this when I got to those whom I actually had known I had the feeling they were right there in the room with me, sitting in chairs watching, with no eye or face movements."[53] In public, Haley presented his journeys into the past as emotionally uplifting, but his private notes suggest that writing *Roots* was also emotionally troubling. James Baldwin sent Haley a letter in the late 1960s that noted, cryptically, "You and I have very different [writing] styles: mine has hysteria which can't be hidden, yours is the species of hysteria which must be hidden."[54] What I think Baldwin meant is that Haley, in his public persona and writing style, studiously avoided going off message or delving into the darker and more unsettling aspects of his story. Haley presented genealogy and history as sources of uplift and nourishment for black people and all Americans. He knew that the past could also be a scary place, but he kept these unnerving aspects hidden.

Other traces in Haley's archives talk of death, murder, and suicide in ways that are not represented in *Roots*. "Sometimes my Grandma would stand my hair on end, telling in a hushed voice of the revenge that angry slaves would take on their masters," Haley wrote in "My Search for Roots." "I learned how embittered old black mammy nurses stuck long darning needles into the heads of massa's infants, and then wailed louder than anyone else beside the small graves during the funerals." Haley retold a lot of stories from his grandmother in his lectures and interviews, but never this one. His notes include a quotation from slave ship captain Thomas Phillips about slaves jumping overboard into the ocean and a page labeled "Suicidal Slaves" that cited a story from a plantation overseer about slaves who, "setting their faces toward Africa, would march down into the water, singing as they marched, till recalled to their senses only by the drowning of some of the party."[55] The theme of *Roots* was the strength of Haley's ancestors to survive in America, but the lives and deaths of other enslaved people haunt the margins of *Roots*. What happened to the other 139 Africans who unwillingly boarded the *Lord Ligonier* at Fort James en route to America? The shipping records showed Haley that forty-two enslaved people died on the voyage, but what were their stories? And what were the stories of those who survived?

If Haley were a different kind of writer he could have made these numerous gaps, erasures, and hauntings part of his story. This probably would have improved the long-term critical reputation of *Roots* and made it easier to take the work seriously alongside books like *Kindred* (1979), *Beloved* (1987), and *Middle Passage* (1990) that told stories about slavery while also reflecting on the challenges and implications of telling such stories. One can lament that Haley did not possess the literary talent and imagination of Octavia Butler, Toni Morrison, or Charles Johnson (few, of course, do), but we should not underestimate how difficult it was to write a book that millions of people wanted to buy and read, especially a book about slavery. Haley's sense of the mass market was as keen as any writer's, and this, combined with his own desire to fashion a neat and linear narrative, determined the composition of *Roots*.

Two great figures in American and African American letters, Maya Angelou and James Baldwin, viewed *Roots* as more of an open-ended and challenging story. "The book and television dramatization of it clarify how America's largest minority came to these shores," Angelou wrote. "In the face of today's racial and class strife, I don't believe that any modern black writer would work 12 years only to answer the perennial questions 'Why am

I here?' and 'How did I come so lonely to this place?' I believe, rather, that Haley has given us the subsequent question: 'Admitting all that has gone before, admitting our duplicity, our complicity and our greed, what do we, all Americans, do next?'"[56] Baldwin also saw *Roots* as a story whose ending had yet to be written. After Kunta Kinte is kidnapped and brought to America, Baldwin wrote, "It can be said that we know the rest of the story—how it turned out, so to speak, but frankly, I don't think that we do know the rest of the story. It *hasn't* turned out yet, which is the rage and pain and danger of this country. Alex Haley's taking us back through time to the village of his ancestors is an act of faith and courage, but this book is also an act of love, and it is this which makes it haunting."[57]

CHAPTER SEVEN

Watching *Roots*

Roots started with a birthing mother's cry. After months of promotion by ABC, millions of Americans tuned in to watch the opening night of the television adaptation of Alex Haley's best-selling family story. The first thing television viewers heard and saw after the opening credits was Binta Kinte giving birth to a baby boy. Binta can be heard moaning from inside of a thatched hut in Savannah, Georgia, on a film set designed to stand in for eighteenth-century Gambia. Binta is squatting and holding onto the large wooden pole at the center of the dwelling. Binta, shown from the shoulders up, is assisted by two midwives, while her husband Omoro paces anxiously outside. An infant's cry punctuates the birthing scene, and moments later the audience learns the baby's name. Holding the baby up toward a star-filled sky, Omoro says, "Kunta Kinte, behold the only thing greater than yourself."

Opening the series with this birthing scene was strategic. Part of the strategy was to foreground some of the series' prominent actors. Cicely Tyson, who played Binta, was an award-winning actress and, along with Ed Asner, the most famous and highest-paid actor in the cast. (Tyson had enough clout to request and receive a credit for her hairdresser, Omar.) Maya Angelou, an actress and author well known for her autobiography *I Know Why the Caged Bird Sings* (1969), played one of the midwives, while Thalmus Rasulala, recognizable from blaxploitation films and various television roles, played Omoro. The scene was also was strategic because the producers hoped starting with a birth would help the series appeal to viewers across demographic lines. Haley described a similar motivation for starting his book with Kunta's birth and childhood. "I hope," Haley noted, the audience will be "intrigued with a disarming baby—for babies are universal."[1] While they wanted to start with a baby, the producers approached this scene cautiously. "The birth sequence should be beautiful, and we should be very careful of groans and seeing Binta squat to give birth," Stan Margulies wrote to David Wolper. "It is not a question of being authentic—but simply that too graphic a depiction of a birth in the first few minutes of the show might destroy everything that is to come."[2] The televised birthing scene closely resembled the opening of Haley's book. "Early in the spring of 1750, in the village of Juffure, four days upriver from the coast of The Gambia, West Africa, a manchild was born to Omoro and Binta Kinte," Haley wrote to open *Roots*. "Forcing forth from Binta's strong young body, he was as black as she was, flecked and slippery with Binta's blood, and he was bawling. The two wrinkled midwives, old Nyo Boto and the baby's Grandmother Yaisa, saw that it was a boy and laughed with joy."[3] David Greene, who directed the first episode of *Roots*, described the first page of Haley's *Roots* as "poetry" and remembers thinking, "How can I live up to that?"[4]

Despite Greene's concerns, the twelve-hour television series lived up to and productively transformed Haley's *Roots*. The

Figure 14. Binta Kinte (Cicely Tyson) and midwife Nyo Boto (Maya Angelou) show baby Kunta to Omoro and viewers.

Figure 15. Omoro Kinte (Thalmus Rasulala) holds baby Kunta skyward.

televised *Roots* made the events described in the book visible to millions of viewers and aligned the book's characters with flesh-and-blood actors. While similar claims can be made for almost all screen adaptations, the stakes for *Roots*, as a popular history of slavery, were higher. *Roots* televised scenes of brutality, such as captured Africans being transported across the ocean on a slave ship, Kunta Kinte being whipped on the Waller plantation, and sexual violence against enslaved women. But *Roots* also broadcast scenes of caring among black families and enslaved people. *Roots* mixed the emotional pull of a melodrama, the seriousness and scope of a historical drama, and some of the violence, sex, and humor of an exploitation film. This combination of genre characteristics made some critics and viewers uneasy. Writing in *Time*, for example, Richard Schickel criticized *Roots* as "Middlebrow Mandingo," referring to the 1975 film *Mandingo*, an antebellum melodrama that titillated viewers with interracial sex. Schickel compared *Roots* unfavorably to a BBC series, *The Fight against Slavery* (1975, syndicated in the United States on PBS in 1976–77), that he found to be a "more subtle and mature work."[5] David Wolper and ABC, however, proudly designed *Roots* as middle-brow entertainment to tell a story about slavery that would appeal to a large mass audience. This mass audience, *Los Angeles Times* critic Mary Beth Crain argued, was crucial to *Roots*'s place in US culture and to the series' impact on the popular history of slavery. "The mass catharsis of 'Roots,'" Crain suggested, "has at last formulated a weapon equal in power to *Birth of a Nation*."[6] For eight nights in the winter of 1977, *Roots* walked a tightrope, appealing to universal themes of family and resilience while asking television audiences to identify with the lives, emotions, and struggles of a host of free and enslaved black characters. Over a hundred million Americans (and, later, millions more globally) were enthralled, horrified, and entertained by what they saw.

The television adaptation of *Roots* differed from the book in several key respects. Most controversially, the television production gave white characters much larger roles than in Haley's book. In Haley's book, the white slave catchers and slave ship crew are called *toubob*, and a white character with a proper name does not appear until Kunta learns the name of "Massa William Waller" at the end of chapter 51, over two hundred pages into the book. (Haley's archives include the draft of a chapter written from the perspective of Captain Davies, but the author decided it was not needed.)[7] In contrast, after opening with Kunta Kinte's birth in 1750 the television series jumps ahead fifteen years to a scene set in an Annapolis, Maryland, port where Captain Thomas Davies is preparing to sail the *Lord Ligonier* to the coast of the Gambia. The slave ship captain in Haley's book was unnamed and was described only from Kunta's perspective. The captain's personal history, motivations, and emotions were irrelevant for Haley's story. Ed Asner, famous for his role as Lou Grant on the *Mary Tyler Moore Show,* played Captain Davies in the televised version of *Roots,* and promotional material for the series featured Asner prominently. The Davies character, established by the screenwriters and embodied by Asner, was a religious man who was morally conflicted about taking part in his first slaving voyage. "The captain," Asner said, "created the good German, the person who goes along with evil."[8] Asner's Captain Davies looked virtuous in comparison to his first mate Mr. Slater, portrayed by Ralph Waite. Waite, also a familiar television star from his role as the father on *The Waltons,* played a veteran slave ship crew member who enjoyed brutalizing slaves.

Figure 16. Ed Asner received top billing in ABC's promotion of *Roots*. Asner's character, the slave ship captain Thomas Davies, played a much larger role in the television version of *Roots* than in Alex Haley's book. ABC Photo Archives/Getty Images.

The first episode of *Roots* cuts between Kunta's life as a young man in the Edenic village of Juffure and the *Lord Ligonier* steadily approaching the Gambian coast. Head screenwriter Bill Blinn said that he had struggled for months to figure out how to structure the opening episode of *Roots*. At one point, Blinn planned to start with the assassination of Malcolm X and feature Haley as a narrator. After deciding that Kunta Kinte needed to be the story's focal point, Blinn looked for a way to build narrative tension and to get white characters on screen early. Blinn found inspiration in the form of a 1962 Kirk Douglas star vehicle called *Lonely Are the Brave*. Blinn recalled that *Lonely Are the Brave* opened with the characters played by Douglas and Carroll O'Conner on a collision course. "You know they're going to meet," Blinn said. "You don't know why, you don't know how, you don't know what the connection is, but the storytelling has told us these two are gonna [connect]." This gave Blinn an idea for *Roots*. "Let's just start with the captain of the slave ship getting this assignment," Blinn said. "We could keep cutting back to that slave ship, and seeing what was going on with Ed Asner ... Because we know that over the horizon there was trouble. Once we got that construction we had a very solid footing to start the picture."[9]

While the series rushed to get Kunta out of Africa, *Roots* did not shy away from Kunta's traumatic voyage to America in the hold of a slave ship. The Middle Passage scene in *Roots* was crucial to depicting the transition between freedom in Africa and slavery in the new world. *Roots* was a story about coming to America, but it was not an immigrant story. The horrors of the Middle Passage cannot be adequately represented in any medium, and before *Roots* the journey had been depicted rarely in films and never on television.

In a warehouse on the outskirts of Savannah, production designer Jan Scott and her team designed and built the set for the first televised representation of the Middle Passage. Scott navigated several technical challenges in creating a realistic cargo hold film set on dry land. Scott monitored the color value of the wood to ensure that the black actors could be lit properly. She measured the walkway between the racks to make it small enough to appear cramped but large enough to accommodate a film camera. And she rigged lights to swing above the cargo hold, creating the impression that the ship was rocking with the ocean's waves. When Stan Margulies objected that the aisle planking looked too clean, Scott prepared a mixture of corn-flakes, shredded wheat, and bran. She moistened the concoction, let it sit overnight, and applied it the next day so the floor of the set looked like it was covered in urine and feces. Scott recalled

Figure 17. The Middle Passage scene in *Roots* was crucial to depicting the transition between freedom in Africa and slavery in the new world.

that director David Greene walked onto the set and "stood at the bow looking down the aisle and all of the sudden he started to cry.... So he liked the set. I've never had a director walk in on a set and cry before."[10]

The human component of the Middle Passage scene was more complicated. LeVar Burton and Ji-Tu Cumbuka, who played a character called the Wrestler, were the only Hollywood actors in the cargo hold for the Middle Passage scene. All of the other enslaved characters were young black extras recruited from Savannah. The local casting consultants stopped young people at gas stations, shopping centers, and on their way to and from school. Each prospective extra was photographed and described on an index card in terms of sex, height, weight, and age (many were students from Savannah State University). The index cards also included a section where the casting consultants described the young people's skin complexion in a variety of terms, such as "Negro," "black," "dark," "pecan," "mahogany," "dark brown," medium dark brown," and "medium brown." This array calls to mind artists like Nella Larsen who were keenly aware of the tremendous diversity of black people. "For the hundredth time she marveled at the gradations within this oppressed race of hers," Larsen wrote of Helga Crane, the protagonist in her novel *Quicksand* (1928), watching a "swirling mass" of black dancers. "A dozen shades slid by. There was sooty black, shiny black, taupe, mahogany, bronze, copper, gold, orange, yellow, peach, ivory, pinky white, pastry white."[11] Larsen made it clear that these gradations of blackness told their own stories about history and genealogy, pointing to "Africa, Europe, perhaps with a pinch of Asia." The casting consultants used language similar to Larsen's, but their task was more narrowly defined. They were looking for extras to portray recently captured Africans, so the note "may be too light" meant the person was unlikely to be hired. This logic was in contrast to the preference Hollywood usually showed for light-skinned black actors.

The producers needed dozens of extras to fill the cargo hold set, and those that were selected were paid about thirty dollars a day.[12] "I had the problem of teaching them to be actors, Africans, they had no idea," director David Greene said. "I'm giving these young men a lecture about their history, then chained their ankles, then put oatmeal on their bodies."[13] Screenwriter Bill Blinn described being moved by the realism of the Middle Passage scene. "All of the stuff in the slave ship was as good as we could have imagined," Blinn said. "The [film] dailies were difficult to watch, because the reality of being in that hold was horrific.... All of [the actors and extras] knew it was true. Between the lines I think most of them knew that someone with whom

Figure 18. The local casting consultant for *Roots* looked for young black people around Savannah, like these two students from Savannah State University, to serve as extras during the Middle Passage scene.

they had a blood relationship went through this dreadful, awful life. And that they owed it to them to portray it as well as they could."[14] In the *Washington Post*, Sander Vanocur singled out the Middle Passage scene in praising *Roots*. "The scenes on the ship, with the slaves chained together, stacked alongside one another, lying in their vomit and excrement, … are something we have never seen before," Vanocur wrote. "We have read about slavery. But we have never seen it, never in such painstaking detail and never being experienced with such excruciating pain." Vanocur described *Roots* as reintroducing a "sense of wonder" to television. "Television, when it sets out to portray reality, usually distorts it or just nibbles at it," Vanocur argued. "I am at a loss for the proper word to use to describe what television has done with Alex Haley's imagined reality.... All you know is that what you have seen leaves you with a terrible and transcending anguish."[15] *Newsweek* reviewer Harry Waters agreed: "The scenes in the hold, where 140 shackled slaves writhe in anguish, may be the most harrowing ever to enter our living rooms."[16] Many audience letters also pointed to this scene, including a viewer from Skokie, Illinois. "When I was fourteen years old and in the eighth grade, I learned about the history of the Black people," he wrote. "All the text book reading in the world, though, could not have made the same impression on me as did scenes from *Roots* (e.g. the episodes which took place on the slave ship)."[17]

While everyone agreed that the recreation of the slave ship's voyage made for frighteningly realistic television, none of the *Roots* production team gave much thought to what shooting this scene would mean for the black performers involved. After lying on wooden planks for several hours, being shackled to the person next to them, and being covered with simulated vomit and excrement, most of the extras did not return for a second day of filming. Recreating the conditions by which their ancestors came to the United States was difficult and traumatic work, especially at an extra's daily pay rate.

The case of Rebecca Bess is the most glaring example in this regard. Credited as "girl on ship," Bess appears near the end of the first episode as an enslaved woman delivered to Captain Davies's room as a "bellywarmer." In the scene the sixteen-year-old Bess, who had never acted professionally, stares with terror at Asner's character, her arms covering her bare breasts. While Captain Davies says he "does not approve of fornication," it is implied that he rapes the young girl, signaling that this Christian character has too been debased by the slave trade. The next day (at the start of the second episode of the series), the young girl (still topless) climbs the rigging of the ship and jumps into the ocean to drown. In a series structured around the will of Haley's ancestors to survive, Bess's "girl on ship" stands out as the only character to choose death over the horrors of slavery.

Bess came to *Roots* via Eddie Smith, a local black stunt coordinator in Savannah. She received $187 for diving from the ship into the ocean, which she had to do twice because the camera failed on the first shot. Bess did not know how to swim, so the stunt coordinator gave her lessons in the pool at the Ramada Inn where the cast was staying. Director David Greene recalled that Bess was eager to earn the money to help her parents because her mother was in the hospital. "She was a very quiet girl and she did that dive," Greene said. "Oh we had people in wet suits, we had crews on the ship to jump overboard and save her. We had a boat right off the end.... She touched all our hearts and there she was topless, climbing up on the rigging and jumping over and that was only one of many occasions when we stood there and looked and just saw history and knew that it had happened and it is just astonishing." Greene described shooting the scenes with Bess as a "deeply moving experience." "How do you think I felt when a genuine sixteen-year-old southern girl jumped off the rigging of that ship and committed suicide? You can hardly bear to watch it, and I could hardly bear to say 'action.'"[18] Greene's slippage here between Bess (a "genuine sixteen-year-old southern girl") and the historical character and incident she portrayed is revealing. Greene and the *Roots* production team wanted audiences to see this television drama in similarly realistic terms. Audiences described watching *Roots* as a physically and emotionally wrenching experience, but creating these realistic representations of slavery often came at the expense of black performers.

Rebecca Bess, for example, told a different and less celebratory story about her work on *Roots*. She filed a lawsuit against David Wolper in 1984, claiming that she had been promised a screen actors' guild stunt contract. While it is not clear how Bess's case was resolved, the terms in which she described her teenage role in *Roots* are telling. "During the filming I was required to go topless which I was not told I would have to do until we were on the set and getting ready to film," Bess wrote. "I was required to drop my top approximately ten times.... I would be required to go topless once more as I would be taken to Ed Asner as a belly warmer by Ralph Waite. It would appear as though Ed Asner had sex with me that night and the next day I would run up on the deck trying to escape, climb up the mast, and jump overboard into the ocean.... During the filming I was required to jump off the ship twice. The reason being that during the first jump there was camera failure."[19] In all of the discussions among *Roots* producers and ABC's Standards and Practices officials about how bare breasts could be shown on television, these white men never considered what it would mean for young black women to play these roles. For most of these performers, like Bess, *Roots* would be their first and only time appearing on television. While reviewers and audiences praised the harrowing realism of the slave ship scenes, the young black performers deserve much of the credit.

Even Burton, *Roots*'s breakout star, was overwhelmed with emotion during the filming of this Middle Passage scene. "I don't remember very much [about the Middle Passage shooting] till this day," Burton said later. "It's as if I was transported. We shot that sequence in two or three days, and I have vague memories of the morning of day one.... I feel like I completely disappeared and something else came forward, someone else."[20] Burton described the Middle Passage shooting as "brutal." "All of my ancestors, those people that I am spiritually and genetically connected to, came forward and really held me up during that day," Burton said. "LeVar left and somebody else came in.... That's how I survived it."[21] ABC's official press release for Burton glossed this experience differently: "It's a long and unlikely trip from the stately halls of the University of Southern California to the sadistic hell of a slaveship hold, but LeVar Burton, not yet out of his teens, made that trip for his role as Kunta Kinta."[22] For ABC Burton's experience playing an enslaved person was promotional fodder, but for Burton and other black actors and extras it was an experience freighted with trauma and history.

Roots's most iconic scene forced Burton to work through similar emotions. After Kunta Kinte arrives in Annapolis, Maryland, he is purchased by John Waller and transported to the Waller plantation in Spotsylvania County, Virginia. The plantation overseer, played by Vic Morrow, tasks Fiddler, played by Louis Gossett Jr., with teaching Kunta how to be a slave. Kunta refuses to accept this unfreedom or to answer to his assigned slave name, Toby. He runs away but is captured and returned to the plantation. In the climatic scene, the overseer commands a black man to whip Kunta, over and over again, in front of the other enslaved people. "When the master gives something, you take," the overseer says. "He gave you a name. It's a nice name. It's Toby. And it's going to be yours until the day you die. Now I know you understand me and I want to hear it." Every time Kunta repeats his birth name he is whipped again. The beating continues until Kunta finally says, "My name is Toby."[23]

"They were beating LeVar Burton and Kunta Kinte as one," Burton later said of the scene.[24] "I was really uncomfortable with the idea of being whipped," Burton remembered. While makeup artists created the appearance of lacerations on his back, the

Figure 19. Kunta Kinte (LeVar Burton) is whipped until he accepts his slave name, "Toby."

whip was real. Burton had to stand, with his hands tied to scaffolding above his head, while a bullwhip struck him. On the first day of shooting the scene, Burton flinched every time the whipped cracked, so director John Erman postponed the scene for a couple of days. The young actor spent a day with the stunt expert who handled the bullwhip. Burton watched the stunt expert do tricks with the whip until Burton was comfortable that the expert could control the tip of the whip (traveling up to 120 miles an hour) so that it would wrap around the actor's body without breaking the skin. The second shooting was successful, and Burton considered the scene one of the most powerful in the series. "Kunta was a warrior," Burton said, "and he maintained that aspect of his identity throughout his entire life, he never surrendered who he was.... It was the indomitability of his human spirit, his warrior spirit, that prevented him from accepting that name, and that's what that scene is about. I control who I am."[25]

John Erman, who directed the episode, described it as a "devastating scene." "The whole episode is about the fact that somebody is trying to break this young man's spirit, and that's what slavery was all about," Erman said. Erman remembered that ABC sent the producers a note warning against scenes with whipping or blood. "The welts on the back is not the power of the scene," Erman argued. "The power of the scene is what's on that boy's face and how he struggles to hold on to his identity and finally, finally, says, 'My name is Toby.' That's the thing you react to, not the whip."[26]

Burton, Morrow, Asner, and other cast members appeared on television talk shows like *Good Morning America* and *Dinah!* to promote *Roots* and to show that the black and white actors held no animosity toward each other, despite the racism and brutality they had depicted on screen. These interviews helped persuade at least one viewer that she could watch the series. "I could not watch Roots until the final episode," she wrote to Haley. "I had seen you on TV before Roots and realized I *could not* watch it. Too horrible. My family did watch. But for me, it was like the movie Jaws ... I had to read *all* the background into the filming of Jaws before seeing it. This is the same. Now that I have heard that they called in a whip expert (a whip—expert???) and that LeVar and Vic are *friends* and that Vic did not handle the whip, etc. Then I can see Roots."[27] Like this elementary school teacher from Fairfax, Virginia, many viewers interpreted *Roots* in relation to the vast array of promotional material and interviews about the series that circulated across different print and broadcast media. Knowing "how the scenes were filmed and that it's not really happening," as this viewer put it, gave audiences more to think about and talk in relation to *Roots*. Viewers had different levels of investment in seeing *Roots* as real or fictional, and these personal interpretations and the discussions and debates that often followed helped *Roots* become a cultural phenomenon.

While the whipping of Kunta Kinte/Toby is the series' most iconic and referenced moment, the scene was only five minutes of a twelve-hour series and is a misleading way to remember *Roots*. *Roots* did not linger on whippings and physical brutality but instead featured a range of relationships and emotions. The series, for example, features several scenes of the enslaved characters interacting in their own spaces, out of sight of the white characters. These scenes gave viewers a sense of the interior lives of the black characters. Haley's *Roots* devoted dozens of pages to these slave quarters' conversations. Haley said he was inspired by interviews with formerly enslaved people conducted by the Works Progress Administration in the 1930s. "The fact is that most slaves were innately as smart as their masters," Haley said. "There wasn't a single slave who wasn't smart enough to lull white folks into thinking he was ignorant.... What whites seldom realized was that through a highly effective grapevine, nearly every slave out in the cotton fields learned in minutes just about everything that went on in the 'big house,' even behind closed doors.... Yet their masters knew next to nothing about *them*."[28] The scenes were important to showing enslaved characters experience emotions beyond pain and suffering. Describing a courting scene between Kunta and Belle, John Amos said the scene "gave us a chance to refute, not just stereotypes about men and women who were in the institution as slaves, but it also made the audiences appreciate this relationship and the pressures of it, which this man and woman tried to have some sense of normalcy in their lives."[29]

These scenes in the slave quarters also offered some moments of wry humor. Viewers heard about American colonists defeating the British through a dinner conversation among Belle, Fiddler, and Kunta:

> BELLE: I've never seen white folks carrying on so. They all so happy, they can't believe it. They keep saying over and over, "The British have surrendered. The war is over, the war is over. Freedom is won."
>
> FIDDLER: Ain't that just fine, though? White folks be free. I've been worrying and tossing at night about them getting their freedom, been the mostest thing on my mind. Sure is one happy nigger now. Don't have to worry about them poor white folks no more.[30]

This brief exchange unsettles the usual chronology of American history, marking the nation's independence day as just one of the thousands of days before and after the Revolutionary War that black people were held in bondage. This scene calls to mind Frederick Douglass's "What to a Slave Is the Fourth of July?," where Douglass told an audience of New York abolitionists in 1852, "This Fourth of July is yours, not mine. You may rejoice. I must mourn."[31] *Roots* is an American story, but it is organized around the dates that are important for Haley's generational story, not the usual dates found in US history textbooks.

Director David Greene described *Roots* as a soap opera, and like any good melodrama, *Roots* involved a lot of talking. Some of the best lines came from Kunta's daughter Kizzy. In Haley's *Roots*, Kizzy and the other female characters were underdeveloped. Haley tried to inhabit the characters in his book, but he admitted this creative process worked better for the male characters. "If you feel the emotions of the characters as you are writing about them you can better deal with them, you can sort of sense what they are, what makes them tick," Haley said. "When I was writing Kunta Kinte, I was Kunta Kinte during the various stages of his life. There were times when I was Chicken George and so forth.... I didn't tell myself to identify. I simply identified on the basis of what I was writing." Reflecting on characters like Binta, Belle, and Kizzy, Haley said, "I found more difficulty trying to feel what the women felt who were characterized in my book. Obviously, I identify more with male characters because I am a man, and for that reason I guess it was more difficult for me to feel the emotions of the female characters."[32] Haley also viewed his genealogical story in decidedly patriarchal terms, despite the important role his Cousin Georgia and other female elders played in passing down the family history. In Haley's typed notes, for example, he described envisioning the millions of Africans who endured the Middle Passage, and "among them, one human grain of sand, my own great-great-great-great-grandfather, Kunta Kinty [*sic*]; his testes containing the rest of us."[33] Indeed, Kizzy does not appear in Haley's early versions of his family history, and when she does show up in later drafts she is little more than a generational bridge to get from Kunta Kinte to Chicken George.

There were no women writers or directors on the *Roots* television series, and the male production team was not necessarily more attuned than Haley to creating credible female characters. What the television series had on its side were several talented black actresses, such as Cicely Tyson, Madge Sinclair, and Leslie Uggams. Uggams, who played Kizzy, had the largest and most demanding role. Whereas LeVar Burton and John Amos shared the role of Kunta Kinte, the producers used makeup and state-of-the-art prosthetics to allow the thirty-three-year-old Uggams to play Kizzy from a teenager into her seventies. Uggams also had to portray a wider range of emotions than any other character. Over the course of three episodes, Kizzy learns the family history from her father, Kunta; is sold away and separated from her family; is raped by her new master, Tom Lea; gives birth to the son produced by this rape, Chicken George; and becomes the matriarch for a community of enslaved people. Uggams, who was best known for performing in musicals and variety shows, said, "A lot of people were shocked, they didn't expect that I was capable of portraying something that heavy." Like her black cast mates, Uggams found *Roots* rewarding but emotionally challenging. "I would come home [after filming] very, very angry," Uggams recalled. "I made a lot of phone calls to my mother and father and talking about my grandmother and great-grandmother and how could they put up with this."[34]

Uggams's best scenes come opposite Sandy Duncan, who played Missy Anne Reynolds, the niece of Dr. William Reynolds, who owned Kizzy and Kunta. In one scene, Kizzy helps Missy Anne select clothes for dinner and Missy Anne confides in Kizzy about her romantic involvement with a distant cousin. The characters talk almost as friends, and viewers learn that Missy Anne taught Kizzy to read, a secret they need to keep from Dr. Reynolds. "You keep my secrets and I'll keep yours," Missy Anne tells Kizzy. "I'll protect you, Kizzy, I'll always protect you."[35] Moments later, over a picnic in a meadow, Missy Anne tells Kizzy that her uncle is planning to gift Kizzy to her. "You'll be my slave, Kizzy, we'll be together for ever. And you'll never have to be afraid again, because I'll protect you, Kizzy." Kizzy gently protests, "There seems just so much happening all of the sudden." The exchange that follows is one of the most didactic moments in the series.

> MISSY ANNE: It will be better than ever for you and me, Kizzy. And it will be legal. You hear me, Kizzy? Legal.

KIZZY: Don't know nothing about legal.

MISSY ANNE: Well, legal is ... it's just the law. Black people are slaves and white people own them. That's just the way it is.

KIZZY: I know. Just don't understand it, I guess.

MISSY ANNE: Well, think of it this way, Kizzy. It's the natural way of things. I suppose it's because white folks are just naturally smarter than niggers. Like men are smarter than women. Now, everyone knows that for heaven's sake.

KIZZY: You mean that's the way God made it?

MISSY ANNE: Exactly. So if it wasn't right, now he'd change it wouldn't he?[36]

Producer Stan Margulies described this episode as the "one out-and-out woman's show in the series," and as in a melodramatic soap opera, this scene works because Uggams and Duncan wring additional emotion and meaning out of the script.[37] Duncan is upbeat as she delivers her lines, giggling and smiling while explaining the naturalness of slavery and patriarchy. Uggams's face registers confusion, but also a sort of wiliness as Kizzy draws Missy Anne out. Missy Anne is repeating rationales for slavery that outlived the peculiar institution and propped up romantic visions of plantation life. *Roots* undermines these views by pushing the idea of childhood friendship between slaves and masters to a ludicrous extreme. "Kizzy, don't you want to be my slave?" Missy Anne says near the end of their conversation, slightly offended. "Aren't you my friend?"[38]

In the television series Kizzy has a character arc, and a chance for a small measure of revenge, that she is denied in the book. Decades after she is sold away from the Reynolds plantation, a horse-drawn carriage arrives at the Lea plantation with a familiar passenger, Missy Anne. Kizzy recognizes Missy Anne, but Missy Anne pretends not to remember her old "friend." When

Figure 20. Kizzy Kinte (Leslie Uggams) talks with Missy Anne Reynolds (Sandy Duncan).

Kizzy goes to get Missy Anne water, she spits in the cup before delivering it to her. This was not initially in the script, but Uggams and director Gilbert Moses talked about how to conclude Kizzy's storyline. "Something had to happen to put a button on this relationship," Uggams said.[39] It was a small victory. Kizzy remained the property of the man who had raped her and fathered her son, Chicken George. Still, *Roots* asked viewers to see Kizzy as more than just a bridge connecting the male members in Haley's family history.

The eight episodes of *Roots* are uneven. The producers spent much of the budget on filming in Savannah, hoping the opening episodes would hook the audience. Back in Hollywood, *Roots* filmed at the Hunter film ranch near where *Planet of the Apes* and dozens of others films and television shows were filmed. The plantation house was just a facade created by the production designer, and the producers were constantly asking ABC for more money to hire "extra extras" so that the plantation scenes did not look too sparsely populated.[40] Writer Bill Blinn lamented the lack of budget for the later episodes, which he described as looking "like *Bonanza* with a lot of black actors."[41]

Television audiences did not seem to mind. When the ratings came after the last episode aired on January 30, 1977, *Roots* was the most watched television series of all time, displacing *Gone with the Wind*. Over one hundred million people saw the final episode, and *Roots* held seven of the top ten spots on the list of the most viewed shows of all time.

In letters and newspaper accounts, viewers described the experience of watching *Roots* in vivid detail. Watching *Roots* "hurt at physical and psychic levels in [the] most excruciating ways," civil rights activist and FCC commissioner Benjamin Hooks said. "It gagged at the throat, throbbed at the temples, burned behind the eyeballs, ripped at the gut, tugged at the chest. At times, I would have to shut off the set and walk out of the room, ears burning, knees wobbly. But back I would come for more, enthralled at the television rendering of this emotionally searing drama."[42] A black public relations director in Nashville said, "My children and I just sat there, crying. We couldn't talk. We just cried." A white secretary in New York responded similarly: "It's so powerful, it's so distressful, I just feel awful, but I'm glad my children are watching."[43] For black artist James William Donaldson, *Roots* also resonated with his present-day family. "I was watching 'Roots,' the episode where Kizzy is taken from her parents … and all of a sudden I felt this welling up of emotion," Donaldson said. "I went to my daughter's bedroom and kissed her, thankful that she was with me and could not be

Figure 21. Patrons watching *Roots* at a bar in Harlem. John Sotomayor/The New York Times/Redux.

taken away like Kizzy."[44] Other viewers interpreted *Roots* in the context of US race relations in the late 1970s, seeing the show offering support for policies like affirmative action or busing. For many viewers *Roots* was both intensely personal and very public, with audiences gathering to watch *Roots* at bars, community centers, and libraries and talking about *Roots* at offices, schools, and churches.

Everyone had an opinion on *Roots*. Ronald Reagan, former governor of California and future president of the United States, was not a fan of the show. "Very frankly, I thought the bias of all the good people being one color and all the bad people being another was rather destructive," Reagan argued.[45] The opinions of people less famous than Reagan were published as letters to the editors of newspapers across the country. These letters make it clear that viewers found very different meanings in the miniseries. Many saw the series as casting new light on black identity. "After viewing the movie and reading the novel, I shall never be the same," a woman wrote to the *Los Angeles Sentinel*. "It gave me a sense of pride and dignity. I cried with the characters, I laughed with them, I felt their lashes, understood their agony. The outstanding thing about 'Roots' is that it was written by a black man, about a black man and his courage and determination to hold onto his true identity."[46] A viewer in South Carolina wrote, "I viewed the movie 'Roots' in its entirety and can truly say it has opened my eyes and the eyes of many others to our black ancestry. I have been told and have read many versions of the past from which the black race descended but could never actually visualize how our ancestors struggled for freedom, therefore, the past has been meaningless."[47] Dozens of other letter writers approached *Roots* in terms of white guilt and innocence with regards to slavery. "Should we be punished for the sins of our fathers?" a viewer from Seattle asked. "I feel that what happened wasn't something the white race did to the black race. Not all black people were involved and not all white people were involved. I don't feel we should look at it today as 'something I did to you,' because 'we' did not exist then."[48] A viewer from Indiana was more direct: "Inasmuch as my own foreign born granddaddy didn't have lots of spare time for oppressing black folks while struggling with a new language and working in Chicago's stockyards; my own personal guilt is rather low."[49] In Pasadena, a "Seething Southerner" wrote a letter describing her worries about what children might learn from *Roots*. "My family and I have just sat in front of our TV screen watching 'Roots,'" she wrote. "I'm seething.... If there was ever a distorted piece of propaganda 'Roots' is it. I'm not saying any of that didn't happen: what I am saying is that anything which pictures every white as vicious and heartless, and every black as sweet, good and a help-less victim, is an out-and-out lie. The thing I hate in this is that children are going to believe the lie."[50] This opinion prompted a reply by a writer who signed her letter "Kizzy": "Why doesn't 'Seething Southerner' read books on slavery. Why not come to Northwest Pasadena or Altadena and talk to old people who came out of the South, whose mothers were the 'Massa's' chil-dren, like my mother."[51] In newspapers across the United States viewers debated, praised, and criticized *Roots,* making connec-tions among the television miniseries, what they believed about slavery, and their own family histories. All of this amounted to one of the first national conversations on race, with all of the hope, ambiguity, and futility that this Clinton-era phrase evokes.

Critics wrestled with what it meant that millions of Ameri-cans had read and watched *Roots* and were suddenly talking about race and slavery. "The essence of the racial struggle in America has not been physical, or legal, or even spiritual," Roger Wilkins wrote in the *New York Times.* "It has been existential, about truth and falsehood, reality and illusion. The ABC televi-sion series offered one black man's vision of historical reality— more or less shared by millions of his black countrymen—and spread it large before the American people. In that sense, 'Roots' may have been the most significant civil rights event since the Selma to Montgomery march of 1965."[52] Texas congress-woman Barbara Jordan argued that *Roots* benefited from a qui-eter period in race relations. "Everything converged—the right time, the right story and the right form," Jordan said. "The country, I feel, was ready for it. At some other time I don't feel it would have had that kind of widespread acceptance and atten-tion—specifically in the '60s. Then it might have spawned resentments and apprehensions the country couldn't have taken." Jordan's Congressional Black Congress colleagues Charles Rangel and John Conyers noted both that *Roots* could be enlightening and that it would not change the social and economic standing of black Americans. Rangel stated, "It helps people identify and gets conversations started, but I can't see any lasting effect." Conyers argued, "It doesn't cure unemployment or take people out of the ghetto. But it's a democratic statement as eloquent as any that's ever been devised."[53]

Television stations in over fifty nations broadcast *Roots* during the next two years, including stations in West Germany, Japan, and Nigeria. These global viewers watched the show in varied local and national contexts. In West Germany, *Roots* provoked some of the first discussions of the Holocaust in German broadcasting.[54] In Japan, Asahi National Broadcasting Company director Naohiro Nakamura admitted, "Japanese audiences usually prefer something about white people [in foreign films], and we were not very interested at first." Asahi eventually bought rights to show *Roots* from Warner Brothers after deciding the series was "high quality" drama that was "not too artists, not too high-brow" for Japanese audiences."[55] In Nigeria, *Roots* prompted public discussions on slavery and fueled government demands for reparations a decade later. Broadcasters and political interests in South Africa and Brazil, in contrast, refused to import *Roots* for fear it would support black freedom struggles in those nations, while US diplomats in each country organized private screenings of the series. Warner Brothers, in selling *Roots* to global broadcasters, billed the series as "the world's most-watched television drama."[56]

If *Roots* had a critical flaw, it was that it made the history of slavery about people and their feelings rather than about systems of power and capital. In *Time*'s cover story "Why 'Roots' Hit Home," the magazine noted that *Roots* had "sensitized" people to black history but wondered, "Sensitized in what way? How long do white Americans need to feel guilty about the evils committed by their ancestors? Is there a statute of limitations on guilt?" *Roots*'s emotional appeal reached millions of people, but it also invited viewers to make the series about their own emotional needs. Black journalist Chuck Stone described *Roots* as "an electronic orgy in white guilt successfully hustled by white TV literary minstrels."[57] Producer David Wolper probably would have objected to being called a "white TV literary minstrel," but he would have agreed that *Roots* catered to the desires of white viewers. "Remember, the television audience is only 10 percent black and 90 percent white," Wolper said after *Roots*'s record-breaking run. "So if we do the show for blacks and every black in America watches, it is a disaster—a total disaster."[58]

Roots was pitched to white audiences, but so was nearly every other show in US television history. What made *Roots* unique was that it asked television audiences to identify with the lives, emotions, and struggles of a host of free and enslaved black characters. This was groundbreaking in 1977, and the four decades since *Roots* have underscored how uncommon it is to have black actors, culture, and history featured in a mass commercial production.

CHAPTER EIGHT

A Troublesome Property

"A Troublesome Property" is the title of a chapter in Kenneth Stampp's *The Peculiar Institution* (1956) and the subtitle of Charles Burnett's PBS film *Nat Turner* (2003). Stampp's book challenged the view of benevolent slaveholders and described how enslaved blacks actively resisted slavery. Burnett's film mixes documentary and dramatization to explore the different versions of the story of slave revolt leader Nat Turner and the various emotional and economic investments motivating these divergent takes on history. These themes are at play in *Roots*, but Alex Haley's family story became a different sort of "troublesome property." In the decade he spent writing and speaking about *Roots*, Haley consistently promised his agents, editors, and himself that *Roots* would be a commercial success. The publication and broadcast of *Roots* in 1976–77 proved Haley correct, but the months after were consumed by struggles over who should reap these rewards. Haley sued Doubleday in a royalty dispute, while other authors brought plagiarism lawsuits against Haley claiming that *Roots* had copied from previously published works. The lawsuits over *Roots* were unseemly because, on some level, they were about who could profit from the history of slavery. Haley worked tirelessly to sell his family history, to transform his search for roots into property. *Roots*'s massive success was more troublesome than Haley could have imagined.

Roots made Haley a lot of money. A *New Times* article featured a cartoon illustration of Haley dressed like a farmer, holding a hoe and wearing denim overalls, a red and white checked shirt, and a straw hat. Haley is grinning as he pulls a fistful of dollars from a green field of money.[1] Other newspaper and magazine articles with headlines like "The Making of a Millionaire," "Alex Haley Finds 'Roots' Means Bucks," and "Writer Alex Haley's Slave Ancestors Help Him Make It Rich" marveled at the money Haley made from his family history.[2] "With the money he will make from the book and TV production, Haley would be able to purchase all the slaves in the country during that period, including Kunta," the *Cleveland Call and Post* suggested. "Grandpa Kunta would be proud of him now."[3]

Other commentators worried that *Roots* was becoming overly commercialized. The *Oakland Tribune* illustrated a story about *Roots*'s success with a picture of Haley on a US twenty-dollar bill. "The price for financial success," columnist Mary Ellen Ferry wrote, "is that both Haley and the story of his African ancestors are being fed into the maw of the insatiable American information and entertainment machine to be spit back out in records and films, in books, magazines and newspapers."[4] None of this should have surprised anyone who had been following the development of *Roots*. Since the 1960s Haley had been touting the commercial potential of his story, and two years before *Roots* was published he had already been anticipating the market for "'Roots' or 'Kinte' oriented products, such as sweatshirts, jigsaw puzzles of African villages, sundry models of applicable things."[5]

Among the licensing deals Haley signed after *Roots* was finished was a deal with Schlitz beer for a calendar featuring artistic renderings of scenes from the television series. The agreement paid Haley and David Wolper $25,000 each but proved challenging because the deal was signed before the actors gave permission to use their likenesses.[6] Two weeks after *Roots* broadcast, Wolper wrote to a dozen actors to belatedly ask for rights to their images. "The unprecedented success of *Roots* has overwhelmed us all," Wolper wrote. "Dozens of requests have already been received for licenses for many products based upon the programs. We are most concerned about preserving the important identity and stature of *Roots,* however, we also believe that we can continue to protect its social, educational, and humanitarian importance by granting carefully selected licenses.... I hope you will join with us in these activities."[7] Wolper continued to chase down permissions several months later, appealing to Georg Stanford Brown, who represented several other cast members in negotiations with the producer. "Taste and value—value to society—and to the people who watched *Roots* are the bench marks before we approve any item," Wolper said, without mentioning what value the Schlitz calendar might serve. "Everything done in *Roots* merchandising has an educational connection and all *Roots* merchandising such as records, et cetera has Alex Haley's personal approval—who I think should be the true protector of the *Roots* property."[8]

Roots did have an extensive educational licensing component, but squabbles over profits emerged here as well. Wolper negotiated a deal with Miami-Dade Community College to provide educational materials (marketed by Random House and Films

Incorporated) that would allow participating colleges to offer *Roots*-based classes to students for credit. Students would purchase *From Freedom to Freedom: African Roots in American Soil* (1977), a two-volume study guide and collection of readings on black history.[9] The deal gave Films Incorporated, a Chicago-based film supply company, the exclusive rights to sell 16 mm prints of *Roots* to schools and libraries. "I am very pleased with the way our marketing organization has accepted and responded to the challenge of selling 'Roots,'" a Films Inc. executive wrote to a colleague, praising sales of the film series to the California State University consortium, Chicago City College, City College of New York, the University of Missouri, and other institutions. "Our people and the people at Miami-Dade are proceeding with almost a missionary zeal to convert inquiries into sales." A handwritten note on the bottom of the memo calculated the company's revenue from *Roots:* "11 schools × $5,400 per film = $60,000 and we haven't even started our own promotion campaign! We believe we will have at least ½ million dollars in sales prior to the telecast."[10] On the one hand, this educational marketing deal encouraged thousands of college students to watch, read, and discuss *Roots* in relation to work on black history and culture by scholars like Margaret Just Butcher, W. E. B. Du Bois, Gladys-Marie Fry, Winthrop Jordan, and Eric Williams. On the other hand, the arrangement produced another set of competing claims on the *Roots* property. Films Inc., for example, sent letters to schools across the country warning them that the only legal way to view *Roots* in the classroom was to purchase the 16 mm film from their company. "We are taking this opportunity to help protect our customers from innocent infringements of the copyright on *Roots*," the company informed educators. "Anyone recording the program on videotape infringes on the copyright

Figure 22. Alex Haley *(right)* signing a copy of *Roots* for Dr. Robert McCabe, who coordinated the nationally marketed *Roots* college course from Miami-Dade Community College. George Sims, Haley's longtime friend and research assistant, looks on. 1976. Image Courtesy of Florida State Archive.

and may be subject to prosecution under the United States Copyright Laws.... Please protect your school or organization. *Do not videotape* the ABC telecast of Roots. But by all means, do watch this great television event."[11] Wolper shared these concerns that new videocassette recorder (VCR) technology would cut into film sales of the *Roots,* but he was more concerned that the company's warning letter had not given him due credit. "I object to [your letter] strongly," Wolper wrote. "It indicates 'a celebrated movie from Films, Incorporated.' Hereinafter, all materials issued by Films, Incorporated will have product referred to as, 'David L. Wolper's Production of,' or 'A David L. Wolper Production.'"[12] These disputes over who should receive credit for *Roots* were often petty, but they were motivated by very real monetary concerns.

For his part, Haley was frustrated that Doubleday was profiting handsomely by publishing *Roots*. Though Haley had signed a contract with Doubleday for *Before This Anger* (which grew into *Roots*) in 1964 and had missed several deadlines to complete the manuscript, he felt that the publisher had been stingy with advances and travel money. Making matters worse, in 1976 Doubleday acquired Dell Publishing, to whom Doubleday had previously sold the paperback rights to *Roots*. The acquisition meant that Doubleday would get a larger percentage of the profits on the paperback sale of *Roots*, while Haley would get a smaller royalty payment on each copy.

Haley sued Doubleday in March 1977, on the advice of his entertainment lawyer Lou Blau, in an attempt to negotiate a better deal for the *Roots* paperback. "I really find myself representative of two groups of people, who have been cast in the lot of sharecroppers," Haley told the press. "One of them is black people, who have long struggled to throw off their second-class status.... And the second group is writers, who are like sharecroppers in the sense that it is we who sweat and produce the crops and then someone else owns the land, the company store, and the cotton gin, and at harvest time they give us what they think we ought to have."[13] Haley stressed that he still had good relationships with his editors Lisa Drew and Ken McCormick. "My quarrel is with the corporate Doubleday, which to me manifests that it possesses no heart nor soul," Haley emphasized. "As owners of Dell, they would gross ninety-five percent of what I sweated 12 years to produce for them. That's worse than sharecropping.... I produced the crop. Corporations do not write books. Authors do. I resent deeply being dealt with on terms made obviously when I was hungry."[14] Haley withdrew the suit in the summer of 1977 and later said he had learned that Hollywood, where people "sue each other and then have lunch," was very different from the publishing industry. "It was my naiveté," Haley said. "I felt terrible."[15]

Shortly after Haley's case against Doubleday made headlines, the *London Times* published journalist Mark Ottaway's story accusing Haley of fabricating much of his research.[16] The charges received international attention and were especially worrying for Gambian officials, who believed *Roots*'s success would lead to a tourism boom in the small African nation. "It can safely be said that with his book 'Roots,' Alex Haley has given The Gambia more publicity in the United States and around the world than the country ever had, or is likely to have had, for years to come," M.D. N'Jie wrote about the book's impact on his country. "To The Gambia, it is manna from heaven at this time when she is pushing ahead with the development of tourism."[17] After the Ottaway story broke, Haley's scheduled return trip to Gambia to promote *Roots* quickly became an effort in damage control. Haley sent Gambia tourism minister B.L.K. Sanyang an urgent telegram in advance of his April 1977 visit. "Bringing around 18 top rank journalists, television, movie, and still photographers, carefully picked during past weeks and invited to join my next visit to Gambia to accomplish our planned major media promotion of the country," Haley wrote. "But this intended goal suddenly now faces problem of world newswires carrying variously hurtful London Sunday Times long story." Haley continued describing the problems Ottaway's article presented. "Story in general cannot but hurt the Gambian gains we have seen including tourism and especially worldwide ideal public image," Haley wrote. "Please consider what might prove best steps to influence my coming press party toward effectively positive counter action of this damage to your and my ... efforts together with the offices of the Secretary General and of the President as well as so many other people devoting themselves to the advancing of the Gambia."[18] Gambian officials had facilitated Haley's research with the hope that *Roots* would pay dividends. All of this now seemed to be in jeopardy. A Gambian's tourism official told the *Guardian,* "We deeply fear that the doubt now surrounding Roots could put off many of those American pilgrims who'd come in search of their roots."[19]

Haley's trip to Gambia was the cover story in *People* and *Ebony* and received coverage in other newspapers across the country. The *New York Times* described Haley's visit as the biggest news event in the Gambia since the country had gained independence from Britain in 1965.[20] Haley told *People* that *Roots* was a mix of fact and fiction but angrily denied the *London Times* story. "When you consider how many blacks were taken out of here, it seems like the Good Lord would let one of us trace his family tree back to his ancestors," Haley said. "It just incenses me that if one *was* able to do it—after nine *years* of research—some s.o.b. would come here and question it.... I don't think this is just *my* family story; it's a saga of American blacks. If I don't put him down, everyone can say blacks have no history."[21]

While Haley described *Roots* as "faction," his insistence on the accuracy of the people, places, and dates in the Gambian part of his story painted him into a corner. Haley consistently projected an air of certainty in the face of skepticism about whether Kunta Kinte was actually his ancestor. On at least one occasion, in a letter to his editor Murray Fisher in the early 1970s, Haley considered changing a key detail in this origin story and making this fictionalization explicit to readers. "In one of the reference books I have here, I have come across a significant item," Haley wrote. "For years ... I have noted the name of a Gambian village spelled 'Jillyfree,' notably in the Mungo Park adventures in the Gambia in 1730s." Haley said he had come upon the "startling information" that "Jillyfree," a village associated with slave trading, was the same as "Juffure," which he had identified as the Edenic birthplace and home of Kunta Kinte. He worried that academics would point this out immediately after the book's publication. "I think the very best move is to create a fictional village name for Kunta to be born and reared in.... Then, in the final section, of low-key telling about the components of the book the reader has just read, say that this was done, a fictional name ... sheerly because there were the several villages where there were Kintes ... and this book is symbolic of them; as it aspires to be symbolic of all of the Gambia villages; and for that matter all of the West Africa villages, from which slaves were taken." Haley said he hoped this would "solve a potentially knotty problem in the anticipation of it."[22] Despite these concerns, Haley decided to paint an idealized picture of Juffure for business and personal reasons. In terms of marketing, Doubleday wanted to sell *Roots* as nonfiction, and ABC was eager to promote the book as factual. For his part, Haley wanted *Roots* to do uplifting and restorative work that he did not think could be accomplished by sticking strictly to the facts. This was especially true with the African section of the book. "I know Juffure was a British trading post and my portrait of the village bears no resemblance to the way it was," Haley said in the midst of the Ottaway controversy. "But ... I, we, need a place called Eden. My people need a Plymouth Rock."[23] On the one hand, Haley could have staved off some of the criticism of *Roots* if he had made his desire to write a mythic history more clear in the book. On the other hand, much of *Roots*'s cultural power accrued from

Haley's embrace of history as myth and the push by Doubleday and ABC to market this myth as a true story. The television miniseries, especially, elevated the story to a different scale and lacquered over concerns about historical inaccuracies. Most readers and viewers understood *Roots* to be a mix of fact and fiction, and it is not at all clear that the millions who read or watched *Roots* were shaken by the Ottaway controversy.

While Haley battled the Ottaway allegations in the court of public opinion, he also faced plagiarism charges from Margaret Walker and Harold Courlander. Walker claimed that Haley had copied from *Jubilee,* her 1966 historical novel set in the Civil War–era South. Walker's book, like *Roots,* was a fictionalized version of a family story that had been passed down from her grandmother. Walker researched on and off for over two decades before finally finishing *Jubilee* as her PhD dissertation at the University of Iowa. As a novelist, Walker was adept at character development and more creative in handing the fictional aspects of history. While she started with a true story, she said, "Imagination has worked with this factual material … for a very long time."[24] Judge Marvin Frankel heard the case in the US District Court in New York. Frankel ruled that the similarities between *Roots* and *Jubilee* did not constitute plagiarism because both books were based on historical facts and used common words and metaphors that were not subject to copyright protection. "No claim of copyright protection can arise from the fact that plaintiff has written about such historical and factual items, even if we were to assume that Haley was alerted to the facts in question by reading *Jubilee,*" Frankel ruled.[25]

Shortly after winning the lawsuit brought by Walker, Haley was back in a Manhattan courtroom facing similar charges from Harold Courlander. Courlander had written several well-regarded fictional and nonfictional works on African history and culture, as well as books on oral traditions among Hopi communities in the American Southwest and African retentions in Haitian culture and music. Like millions of other Americans, Courlander watched *Roots* on ABC. What he saw struck him as very similar to his 1967 novel *The African.* "Many of the incidents, phrasings and images seen on TV aroused in me a feeling of déjà vu," Courlander said.[26] Days after the *Roots* series finale, Courlander wrote to tell his publisher about these similarities. "How can I say it calmly, without feeling too much?" Courlander wrote. "There is Haley's book, *Roots,* selling so fast they can't keep track of how many. But where is *The African,* which scooped *Roots* by ten years? I have reread *The African.* There are many similarities that can't escape anyone who has read both. Whatever the literary qualities of the Haley book, I'm certain that *The African* can survive a comparison with honor."[27] Courlander was worried about the potential plagiarism of his work, but he also saw an opportunity to capitalize on the *Roots* phenomenon. "The climate engendered by *Roots* is most propitious for a new hardcover (or Crown paperback) printing," Courlander wrote. "I believe urgently that now is the time for a reissue of *The African* and enough promotion to relate it to the present moment.... If it is not done swiftly now, I won't care if it ever appears again or not. I have the feeling that I've been left standing at the airport after the plane has gone."[28] Herbert Michelman, editor-in-chief at Crown Publishing, urged Courlander to find specific examples of where *Roots* resembled *The African.* Courlander wrote back days later with a list of what he called "remarkable similarities." "It is quite obvious to me that Haley read *The African* and borrowed freely.... The examples I send ought to give some idea of Haley's plagiarism," Courlander wrote, before again imploring his publisher to get *The African* back in print. "I think that with the climate in which Roots is prospering, the African could sell quite a few copies, particularly with the right promotion.... Crown would seem to have a stake in protecting *The African* as a property."[29] Courlander later complained that *Roots*'s tremendous popularity made it difficult to get anyone to take his complaints seriously. "Roots was no longer a mere book but a kind of natural phenomenon like fire and water," he lamented.[30]

Having won his case against Walker, Haley was initially dismissive of Courlander's plagiarism charges. "It's beginning to sound as if I went around finding various books to copy," Haley said before the case went to court. "Well, it wouldn't take me 12 years to do that. I type faster than that."[31] The Courlander court case lasted six weeks, and the experience exhausted Haley. Throughout the development of *Roots,* Haley had always relied on his speaking and storytelling ability to persuade audiences. The courtroom was one of the rare places when his words failed him. "It seemed incredible to me that nobody could believe what I said," Haley said. "I worked as hard on that book as a man could. I don't want the book which is a symbol of hope and of history to be eroded, ridiculed, held in contempt or anything like that. That frightened me. It frightened me more than it angered me."[32]

The court proceedings did not go well for Haley. "The courtroom is not the world of a writer," Haley later said. "It is a world of calipers, of tweezers, of picking apart your words. I had to send literally crates of notes, all my notebooks, scraps of paper. It was my viscera. In these kinds of cases it's the defendant that has to prove everything. How can you explain every word that you write?"[33] Haley maintained that he had never heard of or read *The African,* which made it difficult for him to explain how a page from the book ended up in his notes, or how several passages in *Roots* were strikingly similar to *The African*. Haley's lawyers initially argued that the similar materials related to slavery and the Middle Passage were not protected by copyright law because they were part of the common black experience. The lawyers also argued that all of the passages made up only 1.1 percent of *Roots*.[34] Judge Robert Ward was skeptical of these arguments and became increasingly hostile toward Haley over the course of the trial. In his chambers Judge Ward told lawyers, "Haley could not have written this." Summarizing the power dynamic in the trial a lawyer said, "Judge Ward is the master and Alex is Toby."[35] While the judge was preparing his ruling, Haley's team agreed to settle with Courlander for $650,000. Haley said that *Roots: The Next Generations*, which ABC had scheduled to air in February 1979, figured into his decision to settle. "I did not want the blight of a trial going on before the miniseries Roots II was about to come out," Haley said. "So by settling, the whole affair was over by the time the film came out. Otherwise it would have been a different scene. That was my main consideration. Many people had done so much to make that series, I didn't want anything hovering over it. Looking back, I'm glad I took the action I did. I only wish I'd done it earlier."[36] In a 1991 interview, Haley struck a more defiant tone regarding the plagiarism lawsuits. "The people who sued me and claimed I took from them ... my first thought was, if your stuff was all this marvelous why didn't you do something [with it], you know.... You'll see people going on to this person, 'These words are mine.' Well damn. All [your] words didn't do much for you."[37]

Historian C. Eric Lincoln, a friend of Haley who knew the author as he struggled to finish *Roots,* suggested that Haley did not know the rules governing plagiarism. "The very fact that Alex was not an academic and had no significant academic experience would have made it unlikely that he had any real concept of the rules guarding the misappropriation of other people's literary work," Lincoln argued. "This was compounded by the fact that most of his research was done by George Sims." Lincoln offered his own opinion of how Haley came to copy from published work. "My view of what happened is this, George went into the library and found the facts that Alex needed. I know George knew nothing about attribution and he brought back a stack of data and put it in front of Alex and Alex used it, having no sense of documentation. I'm sure that that's what happened.... If Alex plagiarized anybody, and he probably did, it was innocent and unintentional."[38] Lincoln was probably right that Haley's plagiarism resulted from how he incorporated the materials Sims gathered into *Roots*. In a 1975 letter to editor Murray Fisher, for example, Haley described sending Sims to the library to gather information to build out a scene with his grandfather Tom Murray, who was a blacksmith. "I discovered with shock or nearly such that as *much* researching as I'd done, I had scarcely a page's worth about blacksmithing," Haley told Fisher. "An emergency appeal to George Sims, however, brought me soon after what I've by now transcribed and organized into a good inch-and-a-half depth on blacksmithing, atmospherically and factually."[39] Haley probably incorporated parts of Courlander's book in a similar fashion.

At the same time, Haley knew the value of his words and was far from ignorant on the nuances of copyright. While he loved talking about his rural upbringing in Henning, Tennessee, by the time *Roots* was published he was well versed in the business of publishing. Haley was represented by separate literary and film agents, he had a standing contract with a lecture firm, and he had been paid for the rights to *Roots* at different points by Doubleday, *Reader's Digest,* Columbia Pictures, and television producer David Wolper, among others. Haley's letters also make it clear that he understood that reproducing copyrighted work without permission was illegal. In one instance, Haley responded to a request to reprint the pictures from *The Autobiography of Malcolm X*. "Those pictures belonged to Malcolm, and since have become the property of Mrs. Shabazz," Haley wrote, referring to Betty Shabazz, Malcolm X's widow. "Insofar as I am concerned, you are perfectly welcome to use them, but I think that since she holds the co-copyright, you would also have to have her permission. For this, I think you would best write to her c/o our agent, Paul R. Reynolds, Inc."[40] In response to a separate inquiry about selling copies of his lecture, Haley wrote, "I really can't give the approval of the sale of transcribed copies of the speech I gave at Austin. The reason for this simply is the rights for the book—of which that speech, or its essence, will be a part—has been sold diversely. Extracts from the speech are generally disseminated, but a full copy of it would be improper, and maybe legally perilous for me. I wish that I could just say great, go ahead—as you know I would be quick to do, but I have had some experience with this before, and the lawyers get very uptight when it is brought to their ears."[41] Haley recognized that copyright laws protected his words and publications, and he guarded this property carefully. Haley did not exercise the same caution in writing *Roots*. This mistake cost him financially and emotionally.

Ultimately, the pressures of promoting and defending *Roots* overwhelmed Haley. "When 'Roots' first happened, it was like being fired out of a gun into spotlights and applause and limousines and body guards," he said.[42] Haley wrote to the head of the Leigh agency at the end of 1977 to say he needed to take a break from lecturing. "*No* one else can comprehend the aggregate of the pressures, professional and personal that 'success' has generated," Haley wrote. "*No* one can sense as deeply as I how sheer physical and psychic survival hang upon how well I alone am able to re-structure my yet-tangled skein of activities into some liveable pattern. The previous urgencies, priorities, are no longer. Money now I don't need. Public exposure, instead of more, I deliberately diminish. Above all things I need now are all possible oases of committed time ... within which to recoup being a working writer ... within which to recoup being the myself whom I will like."[43] Haley apologized to George Sims for not writing for several months, telling his friend that he felt like he had fallen into a "whirlpool." Haley's thousands of archived letters make it clear that he loved corresponding with friends, fans, and critics. This stopped after *Roots*. "It was appalling to realize that I simply humanly no longer could even start to read my mail," Haley said. Haley told Sims that he felt drained by the Courlander plagiarism case. You "put your heart, soul, blood into something, years on end; if you have the luck that it becomes very successful, it is as if you have stepped amongst predators," Haley wrote. "Probably you have read of the one suit that finally I settled, having simply grown sick, sick of having by then spent the better part of two years either preparing for court, or being in court, instead of writing. The joy, the romance, the thrill, I fear, is gone for me for writing books."[44] Haley never published another book after *Roots*. He turned his attention to consulting on television productions based on his family's history, including *Roots: The Next Generations* (1979), *Palmerstown U.S.A.* (1980–81), *Roots: The Gift* (1988), and *Alex Haley's Queen* (1993). When he died in 1992, Alex Haley had achieved his goals of making the Haley name famous and of helping make black history interesting to American audiences.

Eight months after his death, Haley's extensive manuscript collection was auctioned off in an inauspicious conference center on the campus of the University of Tennessee–Knoxville. Hundreds of boxes of Haley's letters, drafts, and notes from his years of work on *The Autobiography of Malcolm X* and *Before This Anger/Roots* were spread over tables to be perused by prospective buyers. The scene of black history and culture on the auction block horrified scholar Detine Bowers. "Anyone at the manuscripts sale would have thought he was the guest of honor at a theatrical performance as he smiled and laughed at the animations of the auctioneers in search of the highest dollar," Bowers wrote. "The wild eyes of the auctioneers glared at audience faces while their hands gestured, 'come on,' as they stared in an audience member's eyes saying, 'Don't let it go for that. Come on.'"[45] This book would not have been possible if the Schomburg Center for Research in Black Culture, the University of Tennessee–Knoxville, and Goodwin College had not acquired and archived the majority of Haley materials from his work on *Roots*. This was made clear to me when I was flying to New York to view the collection at the Schomburg. Among the archived materials from Knoxville that I reviewed on the plane was the Schomburg's receipt for the purchase of the materials I was traveling to view.[46] The receipt totals $13,557.50, and among the dozens of purchases are materials related to key parts of the story I tell in *Making "Roots"*:

Lot 213: Roots Background Reportage, $300.00

Lot 354: Roots T.V. Scripts, $300.00

Lot 478: Manuscript for D. Wolper, $175.00

Lot 486: Signed Letters by Alex Haley, $150.00

As a historian, I have never confronted the monetary value of evidence so starkly. I doubt this insight would have surprised

Alex Haley. From the first story he sold to *Reader's Digest* through the decade-plus that he worked on *Roots,* Haley understood that his words equaled money.

Roots made Alex Haley rich, but it also made him feel like property. In September 1977, a year after *Roots* broke publishing records and six months after *Roots* became the most watched television program of all time, *Parents Magazine* editor Genevieve Millet Landau traveled to Los Angeles to interview Haley. The profile was meant to be a soft focus piece where Haley would offer advice to parents and kids on starting family genealogy projects. Sitting in his office of Kinte Corporation in Century City, Haley turned introspective about the personal cost of *Roots*'s success. "Sometimes I get to feel a little like a property or a thing," Haley said. "I was having a meeting here the other day with a couple of people representing me and some of my projects. They were negotiating various plans, guarding my interests, saying, 'He'll do this or he can't do that,' and I got up and walked to the window and looked out, and then I turned around, and I realized they didn't even know I'd gone. They just went on without me."[47]

Conclusion

In the fall of 1988, Toni Morrison earned the Melcher Book Award for her haunting novel *Beloved*. In her acceptance speech Morrison told the audience that a year after she finished *Beloved* it had become clearer to her why she had to write the book. "There is no place you or I can go, to think about or not think about, to summon the presences of, or recollect the absences of slaves; nothing that reminds us of the ones who made the journey and of those who did not make it," Morrison said. "There is no suitable memorial or plaque or wreath or wall or park or skyscraper lobby. There's no 300-foot tower. There's no small bench by the road. There is not even a tree scored, an initial that I can visit or you can visit in Charleston or Savannah or New York or Providence or, better still, on the banks of the Mississippi. And because such a place doesn't exist (that I know of), the book had to."[1] While Morrison was not the first to highlight the historical erasure of slavery, her remarks became a touchstone for the urgency and difficulty of commemorating the lives and legacies of enslaved people.

Morrison is undoubtedly one of the greatest authors in American history, but what if she overlooked the most influential commemoration of slavery in her lifetime?

What if *Roots* was the first national memorial to slavery? This suggestion is probably difficult for many people to accept. As this book has shown, *Roots* was an explicitly commercial production that appealed to mass audiences. The book and television mini-series told a story of slavery through historical fiction and melodrama, popular genres that are underappreciated by critics. *Roots* took on a serious subject, but it lacked the air of seriousness and solemnity we usually associate with memorials. For her part, Morrison described *Roots* as "backward."[2] Still, it matters that *Roots* encouraged more people to engage seriously with the history of slavery than anything before or since. Alex Haley made trade-offs in order to tell his family story through these commercial venues, but more traditional kinds of memorials—sculptures, plaques, benches, and museums—also require concessions and adjustments to appease different constituencies and sensibilities. Some readers might dismiss out of hand the notion that a story published by Doubleday or broadcast by ABC could be a memorial, but in a country dominated by commercial culture it should not be surprising that historical commemoration could come through mass-market publishing and broadcast television.

I float the idea of *Roots* as the first national memorial to slavery in order to highlight two reasons why *Roots* still matters today. First, one of the most important legacies of *Roots* is that the book and television series have provided a baseline from which to create and appreciate more nuanced and challenging treatments of slavery. For artists and scholars, *Roots* created space to approach the history of slavery from different angles, often in ways that explored the challenges of representing black history.

Watts-based artist Edgar Arceneaux, for example, staged a 2002 installation called *Rootlessness* that included a copy of Haley's *Roots* that Arceneaux had dipped into a sugary solution until the book crystallized.[3] Even when artists make these connections less explicit, many gallery visitors, film and television viewers, and readers approach new representations of slavery with *Roots* in mind. *Roots* is a sort of lingua franca for representing slavery. This is one of the paramount reasons why mass commercial culture is valuable. For millions of people in the United States and internationally, *Roots* throws other representations of slavery into sharper relief.

Consider, for example, the allusions to the Middle Passage in Toni Morrison's *Beloved*. "I am Beloved and she is mine," begins a five-page chapter told from the perspective of the character/spirit who haunts the novel. The chapter evokes a slave ship and is written as a prose poem without punctuation. "All of it is now it is always now   there will never be a time when I am not crouching and watching others who are crouching too   I am always crouching   the man on my face is dead   his face is not mine   his mouth smells sweet but his eyes are locked." The passage continues with references to urine ("morning water") and vermin in the hold of the slave ship. "some who eat nasty themselves   I do not eat   the men without skin bring us their morning water to drink   we have none   at night I cannot see the dead man on my face   daylight comes through the cracks and I can see his locked eyes   I am not big   small rats do not wait for us to sleep."[4] Regarding *Beloved,* Morrison said, "I wanted the reader to be kidnapped, thrown ruthlessly into an alien environment as the first step into a shared experience with the book's population—just as the characters were snatched from one place to another, from any place to any other, without preparation or defense."[5] Nowhere is this disorientation more pronounced than in this chapter of *Beloved*.

When I teach *Beloved*, many of my students have never heard of the Middle Passage. Some assume it is referring to the middle chapters of Morrison's book or referring chronologically to a set of years between the start and end of slavery. These are smart students, they just have not been taught much about the history of slavery. This makes it really difficult for them to follow *Beloved* or to appreciate how Morrison's book is also telling a story about the limitations of telling stories about slavery. I wished for these students that their high school history textbooks had discussed slavery in greater detail or that they had read or seen *Roots*. "Kunta wondered if he had gone mad," is how Haley opens the slave ship section of his book. "Naked, chained, shackled, he awoke on his back between two other men in a pitch darkness full of steamy heat and sickening stink and a nightmarish bedlam of shrieking, weeping, praying, and vomiting. He could feel and smell his own vomit on his chest and belly. His whole body was one spasm of pain from the beatings he had received in the four days since his capture. But the place where the hot iron had been put between his shoulders hurt the worst."[6] Whether one prefers Haley's realism or the prose poetry of *Beloved*, Morrison's literary craftsmanship resonates more powerfully when compared to a familiar reference point like *Roots*.

Alex Haley went to great lengths to make his black characters respectable in terms of their sexual behavior. In the first version of the family history that Haley relayed to his agent, Haley's original African ancestor (whom he later identified as Kunta Kinte) was described as fathering several children on several different plantations. By the time Haley developed the Kunta Kinte character in *Roots*, Kunta did not have sex until his late thirties, after he had married Belle, and he fathered only one child, Kizzy. For Haley, this revision challenged portrayals that circulated widely during and after slavery of black men as sexually aggressive and of black women as sexually promiscuous. This sexual modesty also reflected Haley's personal views. "I just probably because of my background, have a private feeling that sex is something concerning two people in a room with the door closed, and so I've never cared for it much in literature," Haley said. "I know when I was writing Roots ... I wanted a book which would be written without any obscenity at all in it and which would not have a single explicit sex scene in it."[7]

Much of Kara Walker's artwork can be viewed as a rejection of this sentiment. Walker's cut-paper silhouette murals make visible that which Haley and ABC worked so hard to keep hidden in *Roots*. Walker's work is full of psychological perversions, desires, and fears, many of them sexual. In the room-sized panorama *Slavery! Slavery!* (1997), a white figure bows before a black woman perched on a fountain. Walker describes the scene this way: "A white man—something of a 'Nigger lover' bows at the feet of an all-giving black girl fountain. He farts his pleasure. Puffs of perfume and gas resemble speech bubbles. The base of the 'fountain of you' has a skull and a monkey. The fountain offers milk, blood, piss, spit or vomit. 'Coffee, tea or me?' Or from childhood water fountain games: 'Coffee, tea, milkshake, pee?'"[8] Just to the right of this image is a slave market scene where a trader engages in a sex act with the shackled black man he is buying or selling. Unlike *Roots*, Walker's work is not focused on conferring historical personhood to enslaved black ancestors. Whereas *Roots* was deeply invested in getting audiences to see and appreciate specific black characters (e.g., Kunta Kinte, Kizzy, Chicken George) as noble, hardworking, and resilient,

Walker's work questions what it means to create a "positive" representation of black people.

Walker was eight years old when ABC broadcast *Roots*. "I don't remember much of the story, but I know it was very important, we all watched it," Walker recalled. "Everyone came into school—it was fourth grade—and started making fun of it. So it became just another joke."[9] Curator Hamza Walker (no relation) has described Kara Walker as being part of a generation of black artists who are "post-*Roots*."[10] While Walker approached *Roots* across a generation divide, her work finds much of its inspiration in visual and literary works like *Uncle Tom's Cabin, Gone with the Wind,* and *Roots* that have presented the history of slavery, the Civil War, and the South to mass audiences through what she calls "melodramatic" and "outrageous gestures."[11] Walker's *Camptown Ladies* (1998) silhouette tableau, for example, alludes to the scene in *Roots* where Omoro Kinte holds baby Kunta toward the sky and declares, "Behold the only thing greater than yourself." In Walker's piece, a naked black woman with a large posterior akin to Sara Baartman (the nineteenth-century "Hottentot Venus") holds aloft a baby who urinates into the mouth of a kneeling/praying white woman. "In Walker's tableau, the 'Hottentot Venus' has become the African ancestor figure, signaling how the treatment of Baartman's body was of a piece with the denigration of the bodies of Africans enslaved in the Americas," literary scholar Arlene Keizer argues. "The rooted foot of the Hottentot Venus further emphasizes the connection to Haley's popular representation of American slavery; in contrast to the white woman's tiny foot, the black woman's foot is enormous and almost indistinguishable from the earth beneath it. While recognizing the weight ascribed to African ancestry in 'Roots,' it is difficult for viewers to escape the playfulness and feeling of parody evoked by the re-imagination of roots and rootedness in *Camptown Ladies*."[12] Walker's work asks viewers to think about what it means to create, view, and profit from representations of slavery. Understanding Haley's romantic family history and the massive promotional campaign that made this story about slavery into a national phenomenon make Walker's silhouettes stand out more sharply.

Roots's most direct inspiration is Henry Louis Gates's PBS genealogy shows *African American Lives* (2006–8) and *Finding Your Roots* (2012–16), which examine the family ancestry of celebrities. Gates described *Roots* as motivating his interest in genealogy. "You can say I had a severe case of *Roots* envy," Gates said. "I wanted to be like Alex Haley, and I wanted to be able to … do my family tree back to the slave ship and then reverse the Middle Passage, as I like to put it, and find the tribe or ethnic group that I was from in Africa."[13] Gates found Haley's story powerful despite its inaccuracies. "Most of us feel its highly unlikely that Alex actually found the village whence his ancestors sprang," Gates said. "'Roots' is a work of the imagination rather than strict historical scholarship. It was an important event because it captured everyone's imagination."[14] On the one hand, Gates's advocacy of DNA genetic testing is both an embrace of contemporary technology and, in light of the questions that plagued Haley's research, a way to add scientific evidence to the study of black genealogy: "Alex Haley in a test tube," as Gates put it.[15] On the other hand, genetic testing is similar to *Roots* in that it relies on storytelling and belief to make disparate pieces of data meaningful. "While today's popular genealogy television programs would lead us to believe that root-seekers take up wholesale the information provided to them by genetic ancestry tests and accept it unconditionally, something far more complex is at play," sociologist Alondra Nelson argues. "Genetic genealogy tests are deemed reliable to the extent that they are useful for consumers' myriad aims; for many, this involves strategically marshaling the data. Some use their genetic results as usable narratives that open up new avenues of social interaction and engagement." Nelson describes how *Roots* piqued the interest of a generation of genealogists of African descent and how "racial composite testing had proved unsatisfactory to some root-seekers who want to re-create Alex Haley's *Roots* journey in their own lives."[16]

Almost every year brings some sort of popular culture reference to Alex Haley and *Roots.* From Robert Townsend's joke about an "Epic Slaves" acting class in *Hollywood Shuffle* (1987) to the *Chappelle Show*'s parody of outtakes from the twenty-fifth anniversary DVD of *Roots* (2003), *Roots* remains a touchstone to reference what has and has not changed for black performers in Hollywood. Dozens of hip-hop artists have referenced *Roots,* including A Tribe Called Quest (the song "What?" in 1991: "What's Alex Haley if it doesn't have roots?"), Missy Elliot (the song "Work It" in 2002: "Kunta Kinte a slave again, no sir / Picture blacks saying, Oh yes'a massa / No!"), and Kendrick Lamar (the song "King Kunta" in 2015: "Now I run the game got the whole world talkin', King Kunta / Everybody wanna cut the legs off him, Kunta"). Artists keep returning to *Roots* with the expectation that their audiences will understand, or be encouraged to learn about, the reference. *Roots* remains a generative story because it has been part of the national consciousness for generations of Americans.

The second reason why *Roots* still matters is that it is a cautionary story about the inevitability of progress. With the largest black cast in the history of commercial television, *Roots* seemed to herald new possibilities for black employment in television and for the possibility that more black-themed shows would cross over to white audiences. Four months after *Roots, New York Amsterdam News* reporter Phyllis Lu Simpson interviewed representatives from ABC, CBS, and NBC regarding whether there would be more black-themed shows or black actors in the fall lineup. Each network told Simpson there were no new black programs on deck, to which she asked, "Roots inspired nothing?"[17] For television executives, *Roots* helped legitimize the miniseries format and led to several follow-up projects—*Roots: The Next Generations* (1979), *Roots: The Gift* (1988), and *Alex Haley's Queen* (1993)—but did not convince executives of the profitability of black programming more broadly. Even producer David Wolper, one the most ardent boosters of *Roots,* did not believe *Roots* changed the industry. "I don't think [*Roots*] changed race relations," Wolper told an interviewer in 1998. "I think for a moment it had an impact. Did it help African American actors? No. A lot of them couldn't get work even after *Roots* came on. Did more stories about African Americans show on television? No."[18] By these lights *Roots* should be remembered as television's unfulfilled promise to reflect the diversity of the country.

Roots is also a cautionary story about the difficulties of speaking honestly about slavery in public forums. Since *Roots* no treatment of slavery has captured the public consciousness in the same way, and it is unlikely that anything ever will. Producer David Wolper joked that with so many channels now, "You couldn't get a 71 share if you had the returning of the Lord."[19] Mass commercial culture, on rare occasions, encourages people to spend time thinking and talking about serious subjects. By making *Roots,* Alex Haley and many publishing and television professionals asked readers and viewers to see slavery as an American story.

As I finish writing this book, America is again struggling with how to memorialize slavery, how to talk about the history of racism in this country, and how to address the generational legacies of unfreedom. The lesson we can take from *Roots* and how quickly American culture moved on to the next phenomenon is that it takes consistent work to give these issues traction in public discourse. Scholars know much more about the histories of slavery and racism today than they did when *Roots* was published and broadcast. Within the academy we can work to make slavery a subject of inquiry for scholars outside of early American history and African American studies, we can produce resources to make recent scholarship available to high school teachers and students, and we can work beyond the classroom to motivate people to talk more, and more honestly, about the history of slavery. As media consumers we can push producers and publishers to make work that takes on serious subjects, such as Steve McQueen and John Ridley's adaption of Solomon Northup's narrative *12 Years a Slave* (1853; 2013), BET's miniseries based on Lawrence Hill's novel *The Book of Negroes* (2007; 2015), and WGN's *Underground* (2016). And we can adapt lessons from museums, such as the New York Historical Society's *Slavery in New York* exhibit (2005), the Whitney Plantation Museum (opened in 2014), and the National Museum of African American History and Culture (opening in the fall of 2016), to tell local, national, and transnational stories about slavery. This moment of renewed attention to America's original sin is important, but it is not guaranteed to last. The four decades since *Roots* have underscored how uncommon it is to have black actors, culture, and history featured in a mass commercial production and how difficult it is to speak honestly about slavery. If we appreciate the varied creative energies that went into making *Roots*, we can better understand what it takes to make Americans reckon with slavery and its legacies.

NOTES

The following are abbreviations used in the notes:

Goodwin   Hoffman Family Library, Goodwin College, East
            Hartford, CT
Schomburg   Schomburg Center for Research in Black Culture,
            New York Public Library, New York
UT   University of Tennessee Libraries Special Collections,
            Knoxville
USC   Doheny Memorial Library, University of Southern
            California, Los Angeles

INTRODUCTION

1. *The Tonight Show*, NBC, February 2, 1977.

2. Mary Beth Crain, "'Birth of a Nation'—The Other Side of 'Roots,'" *Los Angeles Times*, February 13, 1977.

3. John Stauffer, Zoe Trodd, and Celeste-Marie Bernier, *Picturing Frederick Douglass: An Illustrated Biography of the Nineteenth Century's Most Photographed American* (New York: Liveright, 2015); Darcy Grimaldo Grigsby, *Enduring Truths: Sojourner's Shadows and Substance* (Chicago: University of Chicago Press, 2015).

4. Shawn Michelle Smith, *American Archives: Gender, Race, and Class in Visual Culture* (Princeton, NJ: Princeton University Press, 1999); Shawn Michelle Smith, "Looking at One's Self through the Eyes of Others: W.E.B. Du Bois's Photographs for the 1900 Paris Exposition," *African American Review* 34, no. 4 (Winter 2000): 581–99.

5. Thomas Cripps, *Slow Fade to Black: The Negro in American Film, 1900–1942* (New York: Oxford University Press, 1977).

6. Melvin Patrick Ely, *The Adventures of Amos 'n' Andy: A Social History of an American Phenomenon* (New York: Free Press, 1991).

7. Joan Hauer, "'Roots' Crushes 'Gone with the Wind,'" *Baltimore Afro-American,* February 12, 1977.

8. Henry Louis Gates Jr. et al., *The Norton Anthology of African American Literature,* 3rd ed. (New York: Norton, 2014).

9. Arnold Rampersad, "Review of *Roots,*" *New Republic,* December 4, 1976, 23–24.

10. Toni Morrison, *Beloved* (New York: Alfred Knopf, 1987); Philippe Vergne, Sander Gilman, and Kara Walker, *Kara Walker: My Complement, My Enemy, My Oppressor, My Love* (Minneapolis: Walker Art Center, 2007); Saidiya Hartman, *Lose Your Mother: A Journey along the Atlantic Slave Route* (New York: Farrar, Straus and Giroux, 2007); Tiya Miles, *Ties That Bind: The Story of an Afro-Cherokee Family in Slavery and Freedom* (Berkeley: University of California Press, 2005).

11. Quoted in Murray Fisher, ed., *Alex Haley: The Playboy Interviews* (New York: Ballantine Books, 1993), vii.

1. *BEFORE THIS ANGER*

1. Alex Haley, "August 5, 1964" notecard, n.d. [ca. 1974], box 29, folder 34, Alex Haley Collection, UT.

2. Alex Haley, interview by Anne Romaine, September 29, 1991, transcript, p. 2, box 2, folder 31, Anne Romaine Collection, UT.

3. Robert Norrell, *Alex Haley and the Books That Changed a Nation* (New York: St. Martin's Press, 2015), 15.

4. Alex Haley, "Smithsonian Institution Bicentennial Speech," n.d. [ca. 1976], box 5, folder 3, Schomberg.

5. Norrell, *Alex Haley,* 16.

6. Joan Wixen, "Home Village Visit Cherished," *Lubbock Avalanche Journal,* January 23, 1977.

7. Quoted in Norrell, *Alex Haley,* 20.

8. Alex Haley to Paul Reynolds, April 23, 1967, box 3, folder 25, Anne Romaine Collection, UT.

9. "The Black Scholar Interviews: Alex Haley," *Black Scholar* 8, no. 1 (September 1976): 35.

10. Norrell, *Alex Haley,* 29.

11. Ibid., 17, 27–32.

12. Alex Haley, "The Harlem Nobody Knows," *Reader's Digest,* July 1954.

13. Martin Luther King Jr., "Letter from a Birmingham Jail," April 16, 1963, http://okra.stanford.edu/transcription/document_images/undecided/630416–019.pdf.

14. Alex Haley, interview by Anne Romaine, December 18, 1990, transcript, p. 6, box 2, folder 32, Anne Romaine Collection, UT.

15. Quoted in Norrell, *Alex Haley,* 34.

16. "Black Scholar Interviews," 36.

17. Alex Haley, interview by Anne Romaine, December 18, 1990, transcript, p. 7, box 2, folder 32, Anne Romaine Collection, UT; "Search Chapter 4," n.d. [ca. 1975], box 1, folder 5, Alex Haley Collection, Goodwin.

18. "Black Scholar Interviews," 37.

19. Alex Haley, "Search Chapter 4," n.d. [ca. 1975], box 1, folder 5, Alex Haley Collection, Goodwin.

20. "Roots: The Second Hundred Years," transcript of meeting with Alex Haley, John McGreevey, and Stan Margulies, January 9, 1978, p. 18, box 38, folder, 6, Alex Haley Collection, UT.

21. Ibid., p. 52.

22. Ralph Ellison, *Invisible Man* (1952; repr., New York: Vintage, 1995), 3.

23. "Roots: The Second Hundred Years," p. 2.

24. "Playboy Interview: Miles Davis—Candid Conversation," *Playboy,* September 1962, 60.

25. Alex Haley to Paul Reynolds, September 3, 1963, box 3, folder 24, Anne Romaine Collection, UT.

26. Alex Haley to Paul Reynolds, September 5, 1963, box 3, folder 24, Anne Romaine Collection, UT.

27. Norrell, *Alex Haley,* 63.

28. Alex Haley to Paul Reynolds, September 22, 1963, box 3, folder 24, Anne Romaine Collection, UT.

29. Alex Haley to Paul Reynolds, October 24, 1963, box 3, folder 24, Anne Romaine Collection, UT.

30. Ibid.

31. Alex Haley to Paul Reynolds, January 28, 1964, box 3, folder 24, Anne Romaine Collection, UT.

32. Alex Haley to Paul Reynolds, July 14, 1964, box 3, folder 24, Anne Romaine Collection, UT.

33. Alex Haley to Phoebe, November 7, 1964, box 3, folder 24, Anne Romaine Collection, UT.

34. Alex Haley to Ken McCormick and Paul Reynolds, November 26, 1963, box 3, folder 24, Anne Romaine Collection, UT.

35. Alex Haley to Paul Reynolds, August 16, 1964, box 3, folder 24, Anne Romaine Collection, UT.

36. Paul Reynolds to Alex Haley letter, December 12, 1963, box 3, folder 26, Anne Romaine Collection, UT.

37. Joan Cord to Paul Reynolds, August 28, 1964, box 3, folder 26, Anne Romaine Collection, UT; Paul Reynolds to Alex Haley, September 24, 1964, box 3, folder 26, Anne Romaine Collection, UT; Paul Reynolds to Lou [Blau], October 26, 1976, box 3, folder 27, Anne Romaine Collection, UT.

38. Alex Haley to Paul Reynolds, September 9, 1964, box 3, folder 24, Anne Romaine Collection, UT.

39. Alex Haley to Paul Reynolds, October 15, 1964, box 3, folder 24, Anne Romaine Collection, UT.

40. Alex Haley to Paul Reynolds, July 9, 1965, box 3, folder 24, Anne Romaine Collection, UT.

41. Alex Haley to Paul Reynolds, October 15, 1964, box 3, folder 24, Anne Romaine Collection, UT.

42. Ibid.; Alex Haley to Paul Reynolds, October 17, 1964, box 3, folder 24, Anne Romaine Collection, UT.

43. Alex Haley to Paul Reynolds, October 28, 1964, box 3, folder 26, Anne Romaine Collection, UT.

44. Alex Haley to "Susannah-O," November 3, 1964, box 3, folder 24, Anne Romaine Collection, UT.

45. Alex Haley to Paul Reynolds, January 30, 1965, box 3, folder 10, Alex Haley Collection, UT.

46. Ibid.

47. Ibid.

48. Alex Haley, *Roots: The Saga of an American Family* (New York: Doubleday, 1976), 570.

49. Ibid., 573.

50. Alex Haley to Paul Reynolds, January 30, 1965, box 3, folder 10, Alex Haley Collection, UT.

51. Ibid.

52. Paul Reynolds to Alex Haley, February 8, 1965, box 3, folder 10, Alex Haley Collection, UT.

53. Norrell, *Alex Haley,* 86–87; Manning Marable, *Malcolm X: A Life of Reinvention* (New York: Viking, 2011), 418–49.

54. Quoted in Norrell, *Alex Haley,* 88.

55. Paul Reynolds to Alex Haley, May 11, 1965, box 3, folder 26, Anne Romaine Collection, UT.

56. Alex Haley to Paul Reynolds, August 24, 1965, box 3, folder 10, Alex Haley Collection, UT.

57. Ibid.

58. Ibid.

59. Stan Margulies to Conrad Holzgang, July 14, 1975, box 105, folder 019, David Wolper Collection, USC.

60. Alex Haley, *Search for Roots* draft, n.d. [ca. 1975], p. 99, box 14, folder 13, Alex Haley Collection, Goodwin.

61. Alex Haley to Ken McCormick, November 24, 1965, box 3, folder 24, Anne Romaine Collection, UT.

62. Ibid.

63. Alex Haley, "Preface: August 19, 1966," box 6, folder 10, Alex Haley Collection, Goodwin.

64. Alex Haley, "Notes on 'America America,'" n.d. [ca. 1965], box 6, folder 10, Alex Haley Collection, Goodwin.

65. Alex Haley to Paul Reynolds, October 24, 1966, box 3, folder 25, Anne Romaine Collection, UT.

66. Ibid.

67. Ibid.

68. Dr. Kathryn Graupner to George Haley, December 16, 1966, box 8, folder 5, Alex Haley Collection, Goodwin; Karen Lawman to Alex Haley, December 21, 1966, box 8, folder 5, Alex Haley Collection, Goodwin.

69. George Haley to Alex Haley et al., February 1, 1967, box 8, folder 5, Alex Haley Collection, Goodwin.

70. Simon Haley to Alex Haley, September 8, 1965, box 8, folder 5, Alex Haley Collection, Goodwin; Alex Haley, "From Dad Night of 10–11 January 1965" notes, box 8, folder 5, Alex Haley Collection, Goodwin.

71. Simon Haley to Alex Haley, April 26, 1966, box 8, folder 5, Alex Haley Collection, Goodwin.

72. Alex Haley, "Anecdotes about Dad" notecard, n.d. [ca. 1974], box 1, folder 3, Alex Haley Collection, Goodwin.

73. Alex Haley to Paul Reynolds, March 9, 1967, box 3, folder 25, Anne Romaine Collection, UT.

74. Alex Haley to Paul Reynolds, March 5, 1967, box 3, folder 25, Anne Romaine Collection, UT.

75. Ibid.

76. Alex Haley to Paul Reynolds, March 9, 1967, box 3, folder 25, Anne Romaine Collection, UT.

77. Ibid.

78. Paul Reynolds to Alex Haley, March 10, 1967, box 3, folder 27, Anne Romaine Collection, UT.

79. Ibid.

80. Ibid.

2. THE GAMBIA

1. Lloyd Garrison, "Gambia a Nation, Tiniest in Africa," *New York Times,* February 18, 1965.

2. "Independent Gambia," February 20, 1965, *New York Times,* February 20, 1965.

3. William Hogan, "A Bookman's Notebook," *Corona Daily Independent,* January 11, 1966.

4. Alex Haley, "Primary Tribes Then in Gambia," n.d. [ca. 1973], box 2, folder 4, Alex Haley Collection, Goodwin, and "Mungo Park" notes, n.d. [ca. 1971], box 2, folder 4, Alex Haley Collection, Goodwin.

5. Alex Haley to Ken McCormick, August 8, 1966, box 3, folder 10, Alex Haley Collection, UT.

6. Alex Haley to Paul Reynolds, October 18, 1966, box 3, folder 10, Alex Haley Collection, UT.

7. Alex Haley to Paul Reynolds, October 29, 1966, box 3, folder 25, Anne Romaine Collection, UT.

8. Alex Haley, *Roots: The Saga of an American Family* (New York: Doubleday, 1976), 573–74.

9. Ebou Manga, interview by Anne Romaine, March 4, 1992, transcript, pp. 2–3, box 3, folder 15, Anne Romaine Collection, UT.

10. Alex Haley to Alexander Alpert, December 23, 1970, box 6, folder 4, Alex Haley Collection, Goodwin.

11. Alex Haley, "Search: My Mental Model" note, n.d. [ca. 1974], box 10, folder 4, Alex Haley Collection, Goodwin.

12. Ebou Manga to Alex Haley, November 1, 1966, box 3, folder 12, Alex Haley Collection, UT.

13. Alex Haley to Maurice Ragsdale, December 14, 1966, box 3, folder 10, Alex Haley Collection, UT.

14. Ibid.

15. Ibid.

16. Ibid.

17. Alex Haley to Dr. and Mrs. John Mahoney, March 16, 1967, box 3, folder 10, Alex Haley Collection, UT.

18. M. D. N' Jie to Alex Haley, March 23, 1967, box 3, folder 10, Alex Haley Collection, UT.

19. Alex Haley, "Working Calendar for Roots, Inserts for Chapter One, p. 262," n.d. [ca. 1975], box 29, folder 34, Alex Haley Collection, UT.

20. Ebou Manga, interview by Anne Romaine, March 4, 1992, transcript, pp. 4–7, box 3, folder 15, Anne Romaine Collection, UT.

21. "Top American Writer Here on Working Visit," *Gambia News Bulletin*, April 11, 1967; David P. Gamble, "Postmortem: A Study of the Gambian Section of Alex Haley's 'Roots,'" *Gambian Studies*, no. 39 (2000): 18–19.

22. Alex Haley to Paul Reynolds, April 23, 1967, box 3, folder 25, Anne Romaine Collection, UT.

23. Paul Reynolds to Alex Haley, April 25, 1967, box 3, folder 27, Anne Romaine Collection, UT.

24. Alex Haley to Paul Reynolds, May 13, 1967, box 3, folder 25, Anne Romaine Collection, UT.

25. Alex Haley, "May 12, 1967," n.d. [ca. 1974], box 10, folder 1, Alex Haley Collection, Goodwin.

26. Alex Haley, "Safari, into the Provinces, Tuesday, May 16, 1967" notes, n.d. [ca. June 1967], box 29, folder 33, Alex Haley Collection, UT.

27. Ibid.

28. See box 8, folder 5, Alex Haley Collection, Goodwin.

29. "Tape #9, Haley," transcript, n.d. [ca. May 1967], p. 4, box 29, folder 33, Alex Haley Collection, UT.

30. "Tape #9, Haley," transcript, n.d. [ca. May 1967], pp. 1–2, box 29, folder 33, Alex Haley Collection, UT.

31. Alex Haley, "Safari, into the Provinces, Tuesday, May 16, 1967," notes, n.d. [ca. June 1967], box 29, folder 33, Alex Haley Collection, UT.

32. Haley, *Roots,* 576.

33. Ibid.

34. Ibid., 577.

35. "Tape #2, Radio Gambia," transcript, n.d. [ca. May 1967], pp. 2–3, box 29, folder 33, Alex Haley Collection, UT.

36. Haley, *Roots,* 578–79.

37. Mark Ottaway, "Tangled Roots," *Times* (London), April 10, 1977, 17.

38. Bakari Sidibe to Alex Haley, May 30, 1973, box 30, folder 24, Alex Haley Collection, UT.

39. Ibid.

40. "Griot Embodies Entertainment" notecard, n.d. [ca. 1974], box 3, folder 4, Alex Haley Collection, Goodwin.

41. "Searching, Motivation," n.d. [ca. 1974], misc. box, no folder number, Alex Haley Collection, Goodwin.

3. SPEAKING *ROOTS*

1. "During Civil Rights Demonstrations" notecard, n.d. [ca. 1974], box 1, folder 3, Alex Haley Collection, Goodwin.

2. See lecture booking contracts in box 21, folder 6, Alex Haley Collection, UT.

3. Alex Haley, "Search Chapter 7," n.d. [ca. 1975], box 1, folder 8, Alex Haley Collection, Goodwin.

4. "Alex Haley Is . . . ," W. Colston Leigh Bureau brochure, n.d. [ca. 1971], box 105, folder 001, Wolper Collection, USC.

5. Paul Reynolds to Alex Haley, April 10, 1967, box 3, folder 27, Anne Romaine Collection, UT.

6. Alex Haley, "Search Chapter 7," n.d. [ca. 1975], box 1, folder 8, Alex Haley Collection, Goodwin.

7. Michael Kirkhorn, "A Saga of Slavery That Made the Actors Weep," *New York Times,* June 27, 1976.

8. Alex Haley to June Glenn, September 25, 1970, box 10, folder 1, Alex Haley Collection, Schomburg.

9. Alex Haley to Paul Reynolds, April 23, 1967, box 3, folder 25, Anne Romaine Collection, UT.

10. Alex Haley to Paul Reynolds, n.d. [ca. April 1967], box 3, folder 25, Anne Romaine Collection, UT.

11. Paul Reynolds to Alex Haley, May 16, 1967, box 3, folder 27, Anne Romaine Collection, UT; Alex Haley to Paul Reynolds, May 28, 1967, box 3, folder 25, Anne Romaine Collection, UT.

12. Alex Haley to Paul Reynolds, May 28, 1967, box 3, folder 25, Anne Romaine Collection, UT.

13. Ibid.

14. Harry Gilroy, "A Book in a New Form Earns $2-Million for Truman Capote," *New York Times,* December 31, 1965; George Plimpton, "The Story behind a Nonfiction Novel," *New York Times,* January 16, 1966.

15. Gilroy, "Book."

16. Alex Haley to Paul Reynolds, May 28, 1967, box 3, folder 25, Anne Romaine Collection, UT.

17. Paul Reynolds to Alex Haley, May 29, 1967, box 3, folder 27, Anne Romaine Collection, UT.

18. Alex Haley to Lisa Drew, July 17, 1967, box 3, folder 12, Alex Haley Collection, UT.

19. Quoted in Robert Norrell, *Alex Haley and the Books That Changed a Nation* (New York: St. Martin's Press, 2015), 122.

20. Alex Haley, "Working Report: 'Before This Anger,'" n.d. [ca. 1967], box 2, folder 30, Alex Haley Collection, Schomburg.

21. Alex Haley to Cham Joof, July 29, 1967, box 6, folder 5, Alex Haley Collection, Goodwin.

22. Alex Haley to Friends & Committee Joof, Salla & Jallow, August 11, 1967, box 3, folder 12, Alex Haley Collection, UT; Alex Haley to R.C.E. Lander, July 26, 1967, box 3, folder 12, Alex Haley Collection, UT; R.C.E. Lander to Alex Haley, August 7, 1967, box 3, folder 12, Alex Haley Collection, UT; Dorris Maguire to Alex Haley, August 9, 1967, box 3, folder 12, Alex Haley Collection, UT; Vaughn Brown to Alex Haley, August 17, 1967, box 3, folder 12, Alex Haley Collection, UT.

23. Alex Haley to Cham Joof, July 29, 1967, box 6, folder 5, Alex Haley Collection, Goodwin.

24. Gary Mills and Elizabeth Mills, "The Genealogist's Assessment of Alex Haley's Roots," *National Genealogical Society Quarterly* 72 (1984): 42.

25. Alex Haley to Friends & Committee Joof, Salla & Jallow, August 11, 1967, box 3, folder 12, Alex Haley Collection, UT.

26. Frank Chin to Alex Haley, n.d. [ca. 1969], box 3, folder 11, Alex Haley Collection, UT.

27. Alex Haley to Fulton Oursler Jr., July 29, 1969, box 3, folder 12, Alex Haley Collection, UT.

28. Ibid.

29. Henry James, *A Small Boy and Others* (New York: Charles Scribner's Sons, 1913), 160.

30. James Baldwin, *Notes of a Native Son* (Boston: Beacon Press, 1955), 19.

31. When Haley wrote these words he was collaborating with Malcolm X on the black Muslim leader's autobiography, and it is easy to see this essay as part of Haley's efforts to make it clear that the two men held different political philosophies. Haley notes in the essay that Malcolm X had called "practically every Negro leader in the nation" an Uncle Tom. Alex Haley, "In 'Uncle Tom' Are Our Guilt and Hope," *New York Times,* March 1, 1964.

32. Alex Haley, "Separate Insert: Met with Reader's Digest, p. 239–242," n.d., box 29, folder 34, Alex Haley Collection, UT.

33. Ibid.

34. Lou Blau, interview with Anne Romaine, August 9, 1989, transcript, pp. 7–8, box 2, folder 25, Anne Romaine Collection, UT; Columbia Pictures to Alex Haley, April 7, 1969, box 3, folder 12, Alex Haley Collection, UT.

35. Alex Haley to Paul Reynolds, December 29, 1970, box 3, folder 25, Anne Romaine Collection, UT.

36. Ibid.

37. Alex Haley to Paul Reynolds, February 15, 1971, box 3, folder 25, Anne Romaine Collection, UT.

38. Ibid.

39. Paul Reynolds to Alex Haley, February 5, 1971, box 3, folder 27, Anne Romaine Collection, UT.

40. Alex Haley to Elaine and Wally Wiser, March 4, 1972, box 3, folder 1, Alex Haley Collection, Goodwin.

41. Alex Haley, "My Furthest Back Person—'The African,'" *New York Times,* July 16, 1972.

42. Peggy Murrell, "Black Genealogy," *Wall Street Journal,* March 9, 1972.

43. Lafe Todd to Alex Haley, October 20, 1972, box 10, folder 3, Alex Haley Collection, Schomburg.

44. Paula Glenn to Alex Haley, July 20, 1972, box 10, folder 2, Alex Haley Collection, Schomburg.

45. Mary Wheeler to Alex Haley, July 25, 1972, box 10, folder 2, Alex Haley Collection, Schomburg.

46. Rosemary Lyons to Alex Haley, July 16, 1972, box 10, folder 2, Alex Haley Collection, Schomburg.

47. J. Fred Coots to Alex Haley, July 16, 1972, box 10, folder 2, Alex Haley Collection, Schomburg.

48. Mary Bagley to David Frost, May 4, 1972, box 10, folder 4, Alex Haley Collection, Schomburg.

49. Phyllis Woodard to Alex Haley, April 21, 1972, box 10, folder 2, Alex Haley Collection, Schomburg.

50. Lorrie Mikesell to David Frost, April 20, 1972, box 10, folder 3, Alex Haley Collection, Schomburg.

51. Walter Green to David Frost, April 24, 1972, box 10, folder 2, Alex Haley Collection, Schomburg.

52. Alex Haley to Calre Ward, June 12, 1972, box 10, folder 2, Alex Haley Collection, Schomburg.

53. Lois Alexander to Alex Haley, July 26, 1972, box 10, folder 4, Alex Haley Collection, Schomburg.

54. B. K. Joshi to Alex Haley, January 21, 1973, box 10, folder 6, Alex Haley Collection, Schomburg.

55. Genevieve Abel Stephenson to Alex Haley, August 2, 1972, box 10, folder 2, Alex Haley Collection, Schomburg.

56. Alex Haley to Charles Anderson, February 13, 1971, box 10, folder 1, Alex Haley Collection, Schomburg.

57. Alex Haley to Harry Edwards, June 12, 1970, box 10, folder 1, Alex Haley Collection, Schomburg.

58. Bernice Reagon, interview by Anne Romaine, March 3, 1992, transcript, p. 3, box 3, folder 16, Anne Romaine Collection, UT.

59. Paul Reynolds to Alex Haley, August 18, 1967, box 6, folder 5, Alex Haley Collection, Goodwin.

60. Alex Haley to Elaine and Wally Wiser, March 4, 1972, box 3, folder 1, Alex Haley Collection, Goodwin.

61. Jean Blackwell Hutson to Alex Haley, November 30, 1972, box 10, folder 3, Alex Haley Collection, Schomburg.

62. Jean Blackwell Hutson to Alex Haley, January 19, 1977, box 11A, folder 8, Alex Haley Collection, Goodwin.

63. C. Eric Lincoln, interview with Anne Romaine, June 11, 1992, transcript, p. 8, box 3, folder 14, Anne Romaine Collection, UT.

64. "Anecdotes about Dad" notecard, n.d. [ca. 1974], box 1, folder 3, Alex Haley Collection, Goodwin; "Notes on Meeting with Jan

Vansina," n.d. [ca. 1967], box 16, folder 3, Alex Haley Collection, Goodwin.

65. Alex Haley to Fulton Oursler Jr., July 29, 1969, box 3, folder 12, Alex Haley Collection, UT.

66. Alex Haley to Michael Kirley, January 26, 1971, box 10, folder 1, Alex Haley Collection, Schomburg.

67. Alex Haley to Elaine, October 20, 1972, box 10, folder 3, Alex Haley Collection, Schomburg.

68. Alex Haley to Mid York Library for *Utica Observer Dispatch*, June 10, 1969, box 3, folder 11, Alex Haley Collection, UT.

69. Frank Chin to Alex Haley, n.d. [ca. 1969], box 3, folder 11, Alex Haley Collection, UT.

70. Gil Noble to Alex Haley, n.d. [ca. October 1972], box 10, folder 5, Alex Haley Collection, Schomburg.

4. WRITING *ROOTS*

1. Alex Haley to Michael Blow, November 30, 1973, box 3, folder 25, Anne Romaine Collection, UT.

2. Alex Haley to Fulton Oursler, July 29, 1969, box 3, folder 25, Anne Romaine Collection, UT.

3. Jeffrey Elliot, "The Roots of Alex Haley's Writing Career," *Writer's Digest*, August 1980, 36.

4. Alex Haley to Fulton Oursler, July 29, 1969, box 3, folder 25, Anne Romaine Collection, UT.

5. Alex Haley, "Search Chapter 8," n.d. [ca. 1974], box 1, folder 9, Alex Haley Collection, Goodwin.

6. Alex Haley to Curtis Strong, September 25, 1972, box 16, folder 6, Alex Haley Collection, Goodwin.

7. Alex Haley, "7/2/69" *Roots* draft, misc. box, no folder number, Alex Haley Collection, Goodwin; "The Journey: August 20" *Roots* draft, misc. box, no folder number, Alex Haley Collection, Goodwin; "October 3, 1973" *Roots* draft, box 2, folder 5, Alex Haley Collection, Goodwin; "October 4, 1973" *Roots* draft, box 2, folder 5, Alex Haley Collection, Goodwin; "August 11, 1975" *Roots* draft, box 2, folder 8, Alex Haley Collection, Goodwin.

8. Alex Haley, "Writing Roots—2 Major Fetishes," n.d. [ca. 1976], box 14, folder 10, Alex Haley Collection, Goodwin.

9. Alex Haley to Fulton Oursler, July 29, 1969, box 3, folder 25, Anne Romaine Collection, UT.

10. Alex Haley, *Roots: The Saga of an American Family* (New York: Doubleday, 1976), vii.

11. Myrna Oliver, "Murray Fisher, 69," *Los Angeles Times,* June 5, 2002.

12. Alex Haley to Murray Fisher, October 9, 1075, box 10, folder 8, Alex Haley Collection, Schomburg.

13. Alex Haley to Murray Fisher, July 18, 1970, box 29, folder 25, Alex Haley Collection, UT; Alex Haley to Lafe Todd, December 12, 1972, box 10, folder 3, Alex Haley Collection, Schomburg.

14. Alex Haley to Paul Reynolds, December 29, 1970, box 3, folder 25, Anne Romaine Collection, UT.

15. See Murray Fisher comments on drafts of *Roots* in box 14, folder 1, Alex Haley Collection, Goodwin.

16. Alex Haley to Paul Reynolds, November 3, 1972, box 3, folder 25, Anne Romaine Collection, UT.

17. Alex Haley, *Roots* draft marked "1802–1," n.d. [ca. 1974], box 2, folder 14, Alex Haley Collection, Goodwin.

18. Alex Haley to Paul Reynolds, May 18, 1971, box 3, folder 25, Anne Romaine Collection, UT.

19. Alex Haley to Paul Reynolds, July 27, 1971, box 3, folder 25, Anne Romaine Collection, UT.

20. Ibid.

21. Alex Haley, "Note: Unused Selection Material," n.d. [ca. 1971], box 29, folder 35, Alex Haley Collection, UT.

22. See Alex Haley, "Unused Selection Material," box 29, folder 35, Alex Haley Collection, UT.

23. Alex Haley, "Book Outline Parts II and III Notebook," n.d. [ca. 1973], box 29, folder 23, Alex Haley Collection, UT.

24. Alex Haley to Paul Reynolds, March 15, 1975, box 3, folder 25, Anne Romaine Collection, UT.

25. Alex Haley to Paul Reynolds, March 11, 1973, box 3, folder 25, Anne Romaine Collection, UT.

26. Ibid.

27. Alex Haley to Paul Reynolds, July 11, 1973, box 3, folder 25, Anne Romaine Collection, UT; Alex Haley to Paul Reynolds, October 5, 1972, box 3, folder 25, Anne Romaine Collection, UT.

28. Alex Haley to Paul Reynolds, May 5, 1973, box 3, folder 25, Anne Romaine Collection, UT.

29. Ibid.

30. Alex Haley to Paul Reynolds, August 10, 1973, box 3, folder 25, Anne Romaine Collection, UT.

31. Paul Reynolds to Alex Haley, August 16, 1973, box 3, folder 27, Anne Romaine Collection, UT.

32. Alex Haley to Paul Reynolds, October 24, 1973, box 3, folder 25, Anne Romaine Collection, UT.

33. Ibid.

34. Alex Haley to Paul Reynolds, November 3, 1973, box 3, folder 25, Anne Romaine Collection, UT.

35. Alex Haley to Michael Blow, November 30, 1973, box 3, folder 25, Anne Romaine Collection, UT.

36. Alex Haley to Ray Possiel, June 7, 1974, "misc." box, no folder number, Alex Haley Collection, Goodwin.

37. Victoria Crews to Alex Haley, July 9, 1974, box 10, folder 6, Alex Haley Collection, Schomburg.

38. Caryl Faulk to Alex Haley, June 4, 1974, box 10, folder 6, Alex Haley Collection, Schomburg.

39. Rolfe Neill to Alex Haley, May 28, 1974, box 10, folder 6, Alex Haley Collection, Schomburg.

40. Alex Haley to Rolfe Neill, May 9, 1974, box 10, folder 6, Alex Haley Collection, Schomburg.

41. Stan Margulies, interview by Quincy Troupe, April 18, 1977, transcript, pp. 21–22, David Wolper Collection, USC.

42. David Wolper to Stan Margulies, May 23, 1974, box 13, folder 30, Stan Margulies Collection, USC.

43. Alex Haley to Paul Reynolds, March 10, 1974, box 3, folder 25, Anne Romaine Collection, UT.

44. Alex Haley to Steve Sheppard, May 3, 1974, box 3, folder 25, Anne Romaine Collection, UT.

45. Alex Haley to John Hawkins, March 24, 1974, box 3, folder 25, Anne Romaine Collection, UT.

46. Reynolds cautioned Haley, "It's awfully hard to make a motion picture deal without the book written and again, motion picture people talk, know of your Columbia deal and wonder why there isn't a book." Alex Haley to Paul Reynolds, May 3, 1974, box 3, folder 25, Anne Romaine Collection, UT; Paul Reynolds to Alex Haley, May 6, 1974, box 3, folder 27, Anne Romaine Collection, UT.

47. Harold Cohn to Wolper Productions, August 28, 1974, Alex Haley Collection, UT; Paul Reynolds to Lou Blau, August 12, 1974, box 3, folder 25, Anne Romaine Collection, UT.

48. Alex Haley to Paul Reynolds, November 7, 1974, box 3, folder 25, Anne Romaine Collection, UT.

49. Paul Reynolds to Lou Blau, October 26, 1976, box 3, folder 27, Anne Romaine Collection, UT.

50. Stan Margulies, interview by Quincy Troupe, April 18, 1977, transcript, pp. 22–23, David Wolper Collection, USC.

51. Paul Reynolds to Alex Haley, September 25, 1974, box 3, folder 27, Anne Romaine Collection, UT.

52. Stan Margulies to Alex Haley, December 26, 1974, box 3, folder 10, Alex Haley Collection, UT.

53. Alex Haley to Paul Reynolds, January 4, 1975, box 3, folder 25, Anne Romaine Collection, UT.

54. Lisa Drew to Paul Reynolds, December 11, 1974, box 3, folder 27, Anne Romaine Collection, UT.

55. Lisa Drew to Paul Reynolds, February 3, 1975, box 3, folder 27, Anne Romaine Collection, UT.

56. Lisa Drew, interview with Anne Romaine, January 27, 1989, transcript, p. 7, box 3, folder 10, Anne Romaine Collection, UT.

57. Ibid.

58. Alex Haley to Paul Reynolds, May 16, 1975, box 3, folder 25, Anne Romaine Collection, UT.

59. Lou Blau to Alex Haley, August 4, 1975, box 10, folder 7, Alex Haley Collection, Schomburg.

60. Alex Haley to Lou Blau, August 11, 1975, box 10, folder 7, Alex Haley Collection, Schomburg.

61. Alex Haley to Paul Reynolds, July 18, 1975, box 3, folder 25, Anne Romaine Collection, UT.

62. Alex Haley to Stan Margulies, June 14, 1975, box 105, folder 001, Wolper Collection, USC.

63. Alex Haley to Murray Fisher, October 9, 1975, box 10, folder 8, Alex Haley Collection, Schomburg.

64. Alex Haley to Paul Reynolds, March 10, 1974, box 3, folder 25, Anne Romaine Collection, UT.

65. Ibid.

66. Alex Haley to Murray Fisher, October 9, 1075, box 10, folder 8, Alex Haley Collection, Schomburg.

67. Ibid.

68. Ibid.

69. Haley wrote, "What I am wishing now is that you had submitted the bill around the time when I was there, when I had the money, for now I sure do not. Absolutely stopping other even lucrative forms of income in order to isolate with the book, to finish, has produced an uncommon squeeze." Alex Haley to Diane Yensen, October 7, 1975, box 10, folder 8, Alex Haley Collection, Schomburg.

70. Alex Haley to John Roman, October 15, 1975, box 10, folder 8, Alex Haley Collection, Schomburg.

71. Alex Haley to Herman Blake, October 12, 1975, box 10, folder 8, Alex Haley Collection, Schomburg.

72. Alex Haley to Howard Meyer, October 12, 1975, box 10, folder 8, Alex Haley Collection, Schomburg.

73. Dick Kleiner, "Alex Haley Still Can't Believe He's Rich and Famous," *Cincinnati Post,* January 29, 1977.

74. Alex Haley to Murray Fisher, October 18, 1975, box 10, folder 8, Alex Haley Collection, Schomburg.

75. Ibid.

76. Ibid.

77. Ibid.

78. Ibid.

79. Ibid.

80. Quoted in Robert Norrell, *Alex Haley and the Books That Changed a Nation* (New York: St. Martin's Press, 2015), 138.

81. Alex Haley to Murray Fisher, October 18, 1975, box 10, folder 8, Alex Haley Collection, Schomburg.

5. PRODUCING *ROOTS*

1. Stan Margulies to Lou Rudolph, December 5, 1975, box 104, folder 024, David Wolper Collection, USC.

2. Alex Haley to Stan Margulies, September 5, 1974, box 105, folder 001, David Wolper Collection, USC.

3. William Blinn, interview by Gary Rutkowski, October 7, 2005, Web video, www.emmytvlegends.org/interviews/people/william-blinn#.

4. Stan Margulies, interview by Quincy Troupe, April 18, 1977, transcript, pp. 34–35, David Wolper Collection, USC.

5. William Blinn, interview by Quincy Troupe, May 12, 1977, transcript, p. 11, David Wolper Collection, USC.

6. Stan Margulies, interview by Quincy Troupe, April 18, 1977, transcript, p. 35, David Wolper Collection, USC.

7. Ibid., pp. 35–36; William Blinn, interview by Quincy Troupe, May 12, 1977, transcript, p. 11, David Wolper Collection, USC.

8. Stan Margulies, interview by Quincy Troupe, April 18, 1977, transcript, p. 35, David Wolper Collection, USC.

9. Ibid., p. 37. By July 1975, Blinn and Margulies submitted the first *Roots* script to ABC, which had eliminated the use of flashbacks or a narrator. Stan Margulies to Lou Rudolph, July 8, 1975, box 104, folder 024, David Wolper Collection, USC.

10. Lynn Stalmaster, commentary, in *Roots: The Triumph of an American Family*, 30th Anniversary Edition (Burbank, CA: Warner Home Video, 2011), DVD, disc 1.

11. Stan Margulies, interview by Quincy Troupe, April 18, 1977, transcript, p. 47, David Wolper Collection, USC.

12. Ibid.

13. Ibid., p. 49.

14. Brandon Stoddard, interview by Brian Lowry, December 12, 2007, Web video, www.emmytvlegends.org/interviews/people/brandon -stoddard#.

15. Stan Margulies, interview by Quincy Troupe, April 18, 1977, transcript, p. 48, David Wolper Collection, USC.

16. David Greene, commentary, in *Roots: The Triumph*, disc 1.

17. Brandon Stoddard, interview by Brian Lowry, December 12, 2007, Web video, www.emmytvlegends.org/interviews/people/brandon-stoddard#.

18. Lynn Stalmaster, commentary, in *Roots: The Triumph*, disc 1.

19. William Blinn, interview by Gary Rutkowski, October 7, 2005, Web video, www.emmytvlegends.org/interviews/people/william-blinn#.

20. Jeannie Battersby to Alex Haley, January 30, 1977, box 11A, folder 7, Alex Haley Collection, Goodwin.

21. David Wolper, interview by Quincy Troupe, June 20, 1977, transcript, p. 63, David Wolper Collection, USC.

22. Ibid., p. 65.

23. Ibid.

24. Regarding *Roots* casting, see box 104, folders 020–023, Wolper Collection, USC.

25. "Being Too Skinny for School Team Was Lucky Break for Lou Gossett," *Philadelphia Tribune,* August 8, 1970.

26. "John Amos Leaving 'Good Times,'" *Hartford Courant,* June 27, 1976.

27. "Roots as Untold History," PBS, www.pbs.org/wnet/pioneers-of-television/video/roots-as-untold-history/.

28. "The Cast of Roots," YouTube video, posted by Wendy Williams, February 5, 2013, https://www.youtube.com/watch?v=5EqO1680evM.

29. Sharon Male, "A Return to Roots: A Conversation with John Amos," *Parade Magazine,* May 22, 2007.

30. "Roots as Untold History," PBS, www.pbs.org/wnet/pioneers-of-television/video/roots-as-untold-history/.

31. Council on Interracial Books for Children, *Stereotypes, Distortions and Omissions in U.S. History Textbooks* (New York: Racism and Sexism Resource Center for Education, 1977); Frances FitzGerald, *America Revised: History Schoolbooks in the Twentieth Century* (New York: Vintage, 1980).

32. LeVar Burton, commentary, in *Roots: The Triumph*, disc 1.

33. George Stanford Brown, commentary, in *Roots: The Triumph*, disc 3.

34. Ibid.

35. Alex Haley to Stan Margulies, August 30, 1976, box 105, folder 001, Wolper Collection, USC.

36. LeVar Burton, commentary, in *Roots: The Triumph*, disc 1.

37. David Greene, commentary, in *Roots: The Triumph*, disc 1.

38. On the Oyotunji African Village, see Kamari Maxine Clarke, *Mapping Yorùbá Networks: Power and Agency in the Making of Transnational Communities* (Raleigh, NC: Duke University Press, 2004); Carl Hunt, *Oyotunji Village: The Yoruba Movement in America* (Washington, DC: University Press of America, 1979).

39. Tom Kersey to Stan Margulies, March 16, 1976, box 104, folder 024, David Wolper Collection, USC.

40. Stan Margulies to David Wolper, March 4, 1976, box 104, folder 019, David Wolper Collection, USC.

41. Brandon Stoddard, interview by Brian Lowry, December 12, 2007, Web video, www.emmytvlegends.org/interviews/people/brandon -stoddard#.

42. Carl Sterens to David Wolper, June 15, 1976, box 282, folder 014, David Wolper Collection, USC.

43. "John Amos on Ancestor and Roots," PBS, www.pbs.org/wnet /pioneers-of-television/video/ john-amos-on-connecting-to-ancestors-in-roots/.

44. John Amos, interview by Quincy Troupe, May 9, 1977, transcript, p. 17, David Wolper Collection, USC.

45. "John Amos on Ancestor and Roots."

46. John Amos, interview by Quincy Troupe, May 9, 1977, transcript, p. 22, David Wolper Collection, USC.

47. Ibid.

48. Denise Ames, "One-on-One with Richard Roundtree," *Tolucan Times* (Glendale, CA), March 6, 2014.

49. Marvin Chomsky, interview by Quincy Troupe, May 23, 1977, transcript, p. 22, David Wolper Collection, USC.

50. William Blinn, interview by Gary Rutkowski, October 7, 2005, Web video, www.emmytvlegends.org/interviews/people/william-blinn#.

51. Woodie King to David Wolper and Stan Margulies, May 31, 1976, box 105, folder 019, David Wolper Collection, USC.

52. Gilbert Moses, interview by Quincy Troupe, April 18, 1977, transcript, pp. 3, 10, David Wolper Collection, USC.

53. Charlayne Hunter, "'We Are Starved for Images of Ourselves,'" *New York Times,* March 5, 1972.

54. Gilbert Moses, interview by Quincy Troupe, April 18, 1977, transcript, p. 29, David Wolper Collection, USC.

55. Stan Margulies, interview by Quincy Troupe, April 18, 1977, transcript, p. 67, David Wolper Collection, USC.

56. Gilbert Moses, interview by Quincy Troupe, April 18, 1977, transcript, pp. 30–31, David Wolper Collection, USC.

57. Ibid., p. 35.

58. Ibid., p. 49.

59. Stan Margulies, interview by Quincy Troupe, April 18, 1977, transcript, p. 69, David Wolper Collection, USC.

60. Joe Wilcots, interview by Quincy Troupe, April 21, 1977, transcript, pp. 1–9, David Wolper Collection, USC.

61. Dennis McLellan, "Joseph M. Wilcots Dies at 70," *Los Angeles Times,* January 5, 1970.

62. Joe Wilcots, interview by Quincy Troupe, April 21, 1977, transcript, p. 11, David Wolper Collection, USC.

63. Ibid., p. 27.

64. Gilbert Moses, interview by Quincy Troupe, April 18, 1977, transcript, p. 35, David Wolper Collection, USC.

65. Joseph Wilcots, interview by Gary Rutkowski, December 5, 2007, Web video, www.emmytvlegends.org/interviews/people/joseph-m-wilcots#.

66. Stan Margulies, interview by Quincy Troupe, April 18, 1977, transcript, p. 29, David Wolper Collection, USC.

67. William Blinn, interview by Quincy Troupe, May 12, 1977, transcript, pp. 6–7, David Wolper Collection, USC.

68. Alex Haley to Murray Fisher, October 18, 1975, box 10, folder 8, Alex Haley Collection, Schomburg.

69. David Wolper, *Producer: A Memoir* (New York: Scribner, 2003), 226.

70. Carole Stevens, "Roots," April 7, 1976, box 30, folder 7, Alex Haley Collection, UT.

71. David Wolper and Quincy Troupe, *The Inside Story of T.V.'s "Roots"* (New York: Warner Books, 1978), 134.

72. Lisa Drew to Stan Margulies, February 1, 1976, box 104, folder 025, David Wolper Collection, USC.

73. Quoted in Norrell, *Alex Haley,* 147.

74. David Wolper to Lisa Drew, May 13, 1976, box 283, folder 013, David Wolper Collection, USC.

75. David Wolper to Carole Stevens, June 17, 1976, box 283, folder 013, David Wolper Collection, USC.

76. "Promotion Managers: 'Roots' Exploitation Opportunities," n.d. [ca. 1976], box 30, folder 6, Alex Haley Collection, UT.

77. "This Is 'Roots' Week," *Afro-American,* January 29, 1977.

78. Brandon Stoddard, interview by Brian Lowry, December 12, 2007, Web video, www.emmytvlegends.org/interviews/people/brandon -stoddard#.

79. Lawrence Laurent, "An Unprecedented Eight Straight Nights," *Washington Post,* January 23, 1977.

80. "ABC Sets Precedent by Airing 'Roots,'" November 1976, box 30, folder 6, Alex Haley Collection, UT.

81. Brandon Stoddard, interview by Brian Lowry, December 12, 2007, Web video, www.emmytvlegends.org/interviews/people/brandon -stoddard.

82. Fred Silverman, interview by Dan Pasternack, March 16, 2001, Web video, www.emmytvlegends.org/interviews/people/fred-silverman.

6. READING *ROOTS*

1. Murray Fisher, "A Candid Conversation with the Author of the American Saga Roots," *Playboy,* January 1977, 78.

2. Mel Watkins, "A Talk with Alex Haley," *New York Times,* September 26, 1976.

3. Willie Lee Rose, "An American Family," *New York Review of Books,* November 11, 1976.

4. A. S. Doc Young, "Roots: Tangled and Untangled," *Los Angeles Sentinel,* April 21, 1977.

5. William Henry, "Did Haley Bring Us Together?" *Boston Globe,* February 1, 1977.

6. "Penthouse Interview: Alex Haley," *Penthouse,* December 1976, 145.

7. Mike Kelley, "'Roots' Author: Don't Forget to Look Back," *American Statesman* (Austin, TX), January 26, 1977.

8. Mary McCauley, "Alex Haley, a Southern Griot: A Literary Biography" (PhD diss., Vanderbilt University, 1983), 207.

9. Roger Wilkins, "The Black Ghosts of History," *New York Times,* February 2, 1977.

10. Maya Angelou, "Haley Shows Us the Truth of Our Conjoined Histories," *New York Times,* January 23, 1977.

11. Fisher, "Candid Conversation," 78.

12. Jeffrey Elliot, "Alex Haley Interview," *Negro History Bulletin,* January 1, 1978, 782.

13. Ibid., 783.

14. Ibid.

15. "Searching for His Roots, Alex Haley Helps Us Discover Our Own," *Los Angeles Times,* October 17, 1976.

16. Louis Rubin, "On the Need for Roots," *Sewanee Review* 85, no. 4 (Fall 1977): 702.

17. Jim Cleaver, "The Wisdom and Truth of Alex Haley's 'Roots,'" *Los Angeles Sentinel,* December 23, 1976.

18. Ibid.

19. Charles Price, "Haley Makes a Significant Contribution," *Atlanta Daily World,* October 17, 1976.

20. Chuck Stone, "Roots: An Electronic Orgy in White Guilt," *Black Scholar* 8, no. 7 (May 1977): 40.

21. US Department of Labor Office of Policy Planning and Research, "The Negro Family: The Case for National Action," March 1965, 30.

22. Herbert Gutman, *The Black Family in Slavery and Freedom, 1750–1925* (New York: Vintage, 1977), xvii, 461–67.

23. Kelley, "'Roots' Author

24. Joan McKinney, "An Author's Search for Roots," *Oakland Tribune,* October 26, 1976; Bruce Lewis, "Haley Tells Local Listeners to Find Their Roots," *Contra Costa Times,* May 24, 1977.

25. Fisher, "Candid Conversation," 92.

26. Lou Ann (Owens) Strozyk to Alex Haley, January 19, 1978, box 2, folder 28, Alex Haley Collection, Schomburg.

27. Mrs. Carl Smith to Alex Haley, February 3, 1977, Alex Haley Collection, box 11A, folder 8, Goodwin College.

28. DeWayne Wickham, "Haley to Head African-American Round Table," *Baltimore Sun,* March 1, 1976.

29. Alex Haley, *Roots: The Saga of an American Family* (New York: Doubleday, 1976), 584.

30. Fisher, "Candid Conversation," 79.

31. Arnold Rampersad, "Review of *Roots,*" *New Republic,* December 4, 1976, pp. 23–24.

32. Rose, "American Family."

33. Christopher Lehmann-Haupt, "Corroborating Evidence," *New York Times,* October 14, 1976.

34. Ibid.

35. Mark Ottaway, "Tangled Roots," *Times* (London), April 10, 1977, 17.

36. Israel Shenker, "Some Historians Dismiss Report of Factual Mistakes in 'Roots,'" *New York Times,* April 10, 1977.

37. Ibid.

38. Warren Roberts, "Statement on Alex Haley's Roots," April 12, 1977, box 4, folder 41, Anne Romaine Collection, UT.

39. C. Eric Lincoln, interview by Anne Romaine, June 11, 1992, transcript, p. 11, box 3, folder 14, Anne Romaine Collection, UT.

40. Robert Maynard, "The Making of an American," *Washington Post,* September 26, 1976.

41. Thomas Lask, "Success of Search for 'Roots' Leaves Alex Haley Surprised," *New York Times,* November 23, 1976.

42. C. Eric Lincoln, interview by Anne Romaine, June 11, 1992, transcript, p. 11, box 3, folder 14, Anne Romaine Collection, UT.

43. "Pulitzer for 'Roots,'" *Guardian* (London), April 19, 1977.

44. Ken McCormick to Alex Haley, March 29, 1977, box 10, folder 10, Alex Haley Collection, Schomburg.

45. Holly Hill, "Alex Haley and His Exceptional Book Is Given Astounding Acclaim," *Public Opinion* (Chambersburg, PA), November 3, 1976.

46. Erik Lacitis, "'Don't Do It' Haley's 'Roots' Spoke," *Seattle Times,* October 19, 1976.

47. Steve Kemme, "Haley Relates His Odyssey into the Past," *Clermont Courier* (Batavia, OH), November 18, 1976.

48. Alex Haley, "Notes," n.d. [ca. 1977], box 30, folder 24, Alex Haley Collection, UT.

49. Alex Haley, "NYT Article Notes," n.d. [ca. 1977], box 30, folder 24, Alex Haley Collection, UT.

50. McCauley, "Alex Haley," 181.

51. Joanne Williams to Alex Haley, January 23, 1977, box 11A, folder 8, Alex Haley Collection, Goodwin.

52. Alex Haley, "Search Chapter 7," n.d. [ca. 1974], box 1, folder 8, Alex Haley Collection, Goodwin College.

53. Alex Haley, "Search" note, n.d. [ca. 1974], box 6, folder 10, Alex Haley Collection, Goodwin, and "Search" note, n.d. [ca. 1975], box 3, folder 2, Alex Haley Collection, Goodwin.

54. James Baldwin to Alex Haley, May 29, [1968], box 3, folder 27, Anne Romaine Collection, UT.

55. Alex Haley, "Suicidal Slaves," n.d. [ca. 1973], box 7, folder 1, Alex Haley Collection, Goodwin.

56. Angelou, "Haley Shows Us."

57. James Baldwin, "How One Black Man Came to Be an American: A Review of 'Roots,'" *New York Times,* September 26, 1976.

7. WATCHING *ROOTS*

1. Alex Haley, foreword to *From Freedom to Freedom: African Roots in American Soil,* ed. Mildred Bain and Ervin Lewis (Milwaukee, WI: Purnell Reference Books, 1977), xvi.

2. Stan Margulies to David Wolper, March 4, 1976, box 105, folder 019, David Wolper Collection, USC.

3. Alex Haley, *Roots: The Saga of an American Family* (New York: Doubleday, 1976), 1.

4. David Greene, commentary, in *Roots: The Triumph of an American Family*, 30th Anniversary Edition, DVD (Burbank, CA: Warner Home Video, 2011), disc 1.

5. Richard Schickel, "Middlebrow Mandingo," *Time,* January 24, 1977.

6. Mary Beth Crain, "'Birth of a Nation'—The Other Side of 'Roots,'" *Los Angeles Times,* February 13, 1977.

7. Alex Haley, "Captain Davies' View," 1971, box 9, folder 13, Alex Haley Collection, Goodwin, and "Book Section Two," August 12, 1971, box 9, folder 13, Alex Haley Collection, Goodwin.

8. Ed Asner, interview with Morrie Gelman, April 7, 1999, Web video, www.emmytvlegends.org/interviews/people/edward-asner.

9. William Blinn, interview by Gary Rutkowski, October 7, 2005, Web video, www.emmytvlegends.org/interviews/people/william-blinn.

10. Jane Scott, commentary, in *Roots: The Triumph*, disc 1.

11. Nella Larsen, *Quicksand* (1929; repr., New Brunswick, NJ: Rutgers University Press, 1986), 59.

12. On casting of extras, see box 104, folder 018, Wolper Collection, USC.

13. David Greene, commentary, in *Roots: The Triumph*, disc 1.

14. Bill Blinn, commentary, in *Roots: The Triumph*, disc 1, side B.

15. Sander Vanocur, "'Roots': A New Reality," *Washington Post,* January 19, 1977.

16. Harry Waters, "The Black Experience," *Newsweek,* January 24, 1977, 59.

17. Lloyd Pilchen to Alex Haley, January 31, 1977, box 11A, folder 7, Alex Haley Collection, Goodwin.

18. David Greene, interview by Quincy Troupe, April 18, 1977, transcript, pp. 13–14, David Wolper Collection, USC.

19. Rebecca Bess Shearry, affidavit, attached to Milton Segal to David Wolper, May 11, 1984, box 282, folder 022, David Wolper Collection, USC.

20. LeVar Burton, commentary, in *Roots: The Triumph*, disc 1.

21. Ibid., disc 1, side B.

22. ABC Press Relations, "LeVar Burton," n.d. [ca. 1976], box 30, folder 6, Alex Haley Collection, UT.

23. *Roots: The Triumph*, disc 1, side B.

24. "The Cast of Roots," YouTube video, posted by Wendy Williams, February 5, 2013, https://www.youtube.com/watch?v=5EqO1680evM.

25. LeVar Burton, commentary, in *Roots: The Triumph*, disc 1, side B.

26. John Erman, commentary, in *Roots: The Triumph*, disc 1, side B.

27. Mrs. John Pelli to Alex Haley, February 3, 1977, box 11A, folder 8, Alex Haley Collection, Goodwin.

28. Murray Fisher, "A Candid Conversation with the Author of the American Saga Roots," *Playboy*, January 1977, 76.

29. John Amos, commentary, in *Roots: The Triumph*, disc 2.

30. *Roots: The Triumph*, disc 2.

31. Frederick Douglass, "What to the Slave Is the Fourth of July?" July 5, 1852.

32. Mary McCauley, "Alex Haley, A Southern Griot: A Literary Biography" (PhD diss, Vanderbilt University, 1983), 183–84.

33. "Page 253: Roots Working Calendar," n.d. [ca. 1973], box 29, folder 34, Alex Haley Collection, UT.

34. Leslie Uggams, commentary, in *Roots: The Triumph*, disc 3.

35. *Roots: The Triumph*, disc 2, side B.

36. Ibid., disc 2, side B.

37. Stan Margulies to Lou Rudolph, June 2, 1976, box 104, folder 024, Wolper Collection, USC.

38. *Roots: The Triumph*, disc 2, side B.

39. Ibid., disc 3.

40. Stan Margulies to Irwin Russell, June 8, 1976, box 104, folder 005, Wolper Collection, USC.

41. William Blinn, interview by Gary Rutkowski, October 7, 2005, Web video, www.emmytvlegends.org/interviews/people/william-blinn.

42. Benjamin Hooks, "Another Word on Roots," *New Journal and Guide*, March 19, 1977.

43. Charlayne Hunter-Gault, "'Roots' Getting a Grip on People Everywhere," *New York Times*, January 28, 1977.

44. W. Clyde Williams, "The Power of the Roots Search," *Norfolk Journal and Guide*, April 30, 1977.

45. Robert Williams, "Postscript," *Washington Post*, February 14, 1977.

46. Janice Turner, letter to the editor, *Los Angeles Sentinel,* March 10, 1977.

47. Clarissa Steedley, letter to the editor, *State* (Columbia, SC), February 9, 1977.

48. Joan Lawrence, letter to the editor, *Seattle Daily Times,* February 20, 1977.

49. Gregory Sweigert, letter to the editor, *Fort Wayne News Sentinel,* March 22, 1977.

50. "Seething Southerner," letter to the editor, *Pasadena Star-News,* February 4, 1977.

51. "Kizzy," letter to the editor, *Pasadena Star-News,* March 3, 1977.

52. Roger Wilkins, "The Black Ghosts of History," *New York Times,* February 2, 1977.

53. "Why 'Roots' Hit Home," *Time,* February 14, 1977, 71.

54. Timothy Havens, *Black Television Travels: African American Media around the Globe* (New York: New York University Press, 2013), 48–49.

55. William Chapman, "'Roots' Becomes Japan's Latest Fad: 'Roots' Is a National Hit in Japan," *Washington Post,* October 23, 1977.

56. Havens, *Black Television Travels,* 45–46.

57. Chuck Stone, "Roots: An Electronic Orgy in White Guilt," *Black Scholar* 8, no. 7 (May 1977): 39.

58. David Wolper, interview by Quincy Troupe, June 20, 1977, transcript, p. 65, David Wolper Collection, USC.

8. A TROUBLESOME PROPERTY

1. John Egerton, "Homecoming," *New Times,* July 8, 1977.

2. "The Making of a Millionaire," *Michigan Chronicle,* February 19, 1977; "Alex Haley Finds 'Roots' Means Bucks," *Staten Island,* May 19, 1977; "Bio: Alex Haley. Writer Alex Haley's Slave Ancestors Help Him Make It Rich," *People,* October 18, 1976.

3. "'Roots' Captures America's Heart," *Cleveland Call and Post,* February 5, 1977.

4. Mary Ellen Ferry, "The Commercial Success of 'Roots,'" *Oakland Tribune,* February 25, 1977.

5. Alex Haley to John Hawkins, March 24, 1974, box 3, folder 25, Anne Romaine Collection, UT.

6. David Wolper to Al Ashley, June 14, 1977, box 282, folder 027, David Wolper Collection, USC.

7. David Wolper to LeVar Burton et al., June 14, 1977, box 282, folder 027, David Wolper Collection, USC.

8. David Wolper to Georg Stanford Brown, June 17, 1977; David Wolper to Ron Yatter, September 28, 1977; Irwin Russell to David Wolper, September 2, 1977, box 282, folder 027, David Wolper Collection, USC.

9. Mildred Bain and Ervin Lewis, eds., *From Freedom to Freedom: African Roots in American Soil: Selected Readings Based on Roots* (Milwaukee, WI: Purnell Reference/Random House, 1977); Morris Johnson, William Primus, and Sharon Thomas, *From Freedom to Freedom: African Roots in American Soil: Study Guide* (Milwaukee, WI: Purnell Reference/Random House, 1977).

10. Gale Livengood to Charles Benton, December 16, 1976, box 282, folder 022, David Wolper Collection, USC.

11. Films Incorporated to "Film and Videotape Customers," n.d. [ca. January 1977], box 282, folder 022, David Wolper Collection, USC.

12. David Wolper to James Benton, February 9, 1977, box 282, folder 022, David Wolper Collection, USC.

13. Hollie West, "The Roots of Haley's Suit," *Washington Post,* March 19, 1977.

14. "Re Haley vs. Doubleday Matter," n.d. [ca. March 1977], box 10, folder 10, Alex Haley Collection, Schomburg.

15. Eleanor Blau, "For Alex Haley, Work Is a Voyage," *New York Times,* December 10, 1988; Quoted in Norrell, *Alex Haley,* 177.

16. Mark Ottaway, "Tangled Roots," *Times* (London), April 10, 1977, 17.

17. M.D. N'Jie, "Gambian on 'Roots,'" *Baltimore Afro-American,* March 26, 1977.

18. Alex Haley, telegram to B.L.K. Sanyang, April 10, 1977, box 3, folder 10, Alex Haley Collection, Schomburg.

19. Robert Smith, "Roots Country Waits for Sons of the Soil," the *Guardian,* April 16, 1977.

20. John Darton, "Haley, Assailing Critic, Says 'Roots' Is Sound," *New York Times,* April 19, 1977.

21. Linda Witt, "Stung by Accusations, Alex Haley Returns to the Village Where He Found His Roots," *People,* May 9, 1977, 31.

22. Alex Haley to Murray Fisher, August 6 [1971], box 6, folder 13, Alex Haley Collection, Goodwin.

23. A.S. Doc Young, "Roots: Tangled and Untangled," *Los Angeles Sentinel,* April 21, 1977.

24. Quoted in Robert Norrell, *Alex Haley and the Books That Changed a Nation* (New York: St. Martin's Press, 2015), 186.

25. Alexander v. Haley, 460 F. Supp. 40, 45 (1978).

26. Harold Courlander, "'Roots,' 'The African,' and the Whiskey Jug Case," *Village Voice,* April 9, 1979, 33.

27. Harold Courlander to Herbert Michelman, February 4, 1977, box 41, folder 3, Alex Haley Collection, UT.

28. Ibid.

29. Harold Courlander to Nat Wartels, February 9, 1977, box 3, folder 28, Anne Romaine Collection, UT.

30. Courlander, "'Roots,'" *Village Voice,* April 9, 1979, 33.

31. Witt, "Stung by Accusations," 32.

32. Mary McCauley, "Alex Haley, A Southern Griot: A Literary Biography" (PhD diss, Vanderbilt University, 1983), 199.

33. Ibid., 200–201.

34. "Defendants' Pretrial Memorandum: *Courlander v. Haley,*" 1978, box 41, folder 2, Alex Haley Collection, UT.

35. Quoted in Norrell, *Alex Haley,* 195.

36. McCauley, "Alex Haley," 199.

37. Alex Haley, interview by Anne Romaine, September 29, 1991, transcript, p. 10, box 2, folder 31, Anne Romaine Collection, UT.

38. C. Eric Lincoln, interview by Anne Romaine, June 11, 1992, transcript, p. 9, box 3, folder 14, Anne Romaine Collection, UT.

39. Alex Haley to Murray Fisher, October 18, 1975, box 10, folder 8, Alex Haley Collection, Schomburg.

40. Alex Haley to Sandra Stevens, March 2, 1973, box 10, folder 6, Alex Haley Collection, Schomburg.

41. Alex Haley to Amelia Fry, March 2, 1973, box 10, folder 6, Alex Haley Collection, Schomburg.

42. Charles Powers, "Haley Locked in Suit on Origin of 'Roots,'" *Los Angeles Times,* December 11, 1978.

43. Alex Haley to Bill Leigh, December 28, 1977, box 14, folder 8, Alex Haley Collection, Schomburg.

44. Alex Haley to George Sims, June 1, 1979, box 10, folder 15, Alex Haley Collection, Schomburg.

45. Detine Bowers, "On the Alex Haley Auction: Disintegrating Roots: African American Life and Culture Returns to the Auction Block," *Black Scholar* 22, no. 4 (Fall 1992): 5.

46. Diana Lachatanere to James Lloyd, January 4, 1993, box 3, folder 22, Anne Romaine Collection, UT; Kimball M. Sterling, Inc. invoice, October 1, 1992, box 3, folder 22, Anne Romaine Collection, UT.

47. Genevieve Millet Landau, "Alex Haley on Kids in Search of Their Roots," *Parents' Magazine,* September 1977, 85.

CONCLUSION

1. Toni Morrison, "A Bench by the Road," *World,* January/February 1989, 4.

2. Quoted in Dan White, "Toni Morrison and Angela Davis on Friendship and Creativity," October 29, 2014, University of California Santa Cruz Newscenter, http://news.ucsc.edu/2014/10/morrison-davis-q-a.html.

3. Jori Finkel, "A Reluctant Fraternity, Thinking Post-Black," *New York Times,* June 10, 2007.

4. Toni Morrison, *Beloved* (New York: Random House, 2004), 248.

5. Ibid., xviii.

6. Alex Haley, *Roots: The Saga of an American Family* (New York: Doubleday, 1976), 127.

7. Mary McCauley, "Alex Haley, A Southern Griot: A Literary Biography" (PhD diss., Vanderbilt University, 1983), 185.

8. Robert Hobbs, *Kara Walker: Slavery! Slavery!* (Washington, DC: International Arts and Artists, 2001), 31.

9. Jerry Saltz, "Kara Walker: Ill-Will and Desire," *Flash Art,* November/December 1996, 84.

10. Rhonda Stewart, "Still Here: Artist Kara Walker in Black and White," *Crisis,* January/February 2004, 50.

11. "Stories: Kara Walker," *Art 21,* September 9, 2003, PBS, https://www.youtube.com/watch?v=lGZ7ijeiCWo.

12. Arlene Keizer, "'Our Posteriors, Our Posterity': The Problem of Embodiment in Suzan-Lori Parks's *Venus* and Kara Walker's *Camptown Ladies,*" *Social Dynamics* 37, no. 2 (June 2011): 206.

13. "Henry Louis Gates Jr.: A Life Spent Tracing Roots," NPR, May 8, 2012, www.npr.org/2012/05/08/152273032/henry-louis-gates-jr-a-life-spent-tracing-roots.

14. Alex Beam, "The Prize Fight over Alex Haley's Tangled 'Roots,'" *Boston Globe,* October 30, 1998.

15. "Henry Louis Gates Jr."

16. Alondra Nelson, *The Social Life of DNA: Race, Reparations, and Reconciliation after the Genome* (Boston: Beacon Press, 2016), 77.

17. Phyllis Lu Simpson, "No New Black Shows on TV," *New York Amsterdam News,* May 21, 1977.

18. David Wolper, interview with Morrie Gelman, May 12, 1998, Web video, www.emmytvlegends.org/interviews/people/david-wolper.

19. David Wolper, commentary, in *Roots: The Triumph of an American Family,* 30th Anniversary Edition (Burbank, CA: Warner Home Video, 2011), DVD, disc 3, side B.

BIBLIOGRAPHIC ESSAY

In writing *Making "Roots"* I have tried to focus on the experiences and perspectives of Alex Haley and the many publishing and television professionals who transformed Haley's family story into a best-selling book and record-breaking television series. As a scholar, I have read widely on African American history, the history of slavery, and media representations of race and history. The purpose of this essay is to identify some of the sources that have influenced my analysis of *Roots*.

Given the series' commercial success and influence, the **scholarship on *Roots*** is surprising limited. The best work includes Robert Norrell, *Alex Haley and the Books That Changed a Nation* (New York: St. Martin's Press, 2015); David Chioni Moore, "Routes," *Transition*, no. 64 (1994): 4–21; Linda Williams, *Playing the Race Card: Melodramas of Black and White from Uncle Tom to O.J. Simpson* (Princeton, NJ: Princeton University Press, 2001); Donald Bogle, *Primetime Blues: African Americans on Network Television* (New York: Farrar, Straus and Giroux, 2002), 234–50; J. Fred MacDonald, *Blacks and White TV: Afro-Americans in Television since*

1948 (Chicago: Nelson-Hall, 1983); David Gerber, "Haley's Roots and Our Own: An Inquiry into the Nature of a Popular Phenomenon," *Journal of Ethnic Studies* 5 (Fall 1997): 87–111; Timothy Havens, *Black Television Travels: African American Media around the Globe* (New York: NYU Press, 2013); Malgorzata Rymsza-Pawlowska, "Broadcasting the Past: History Television, 'Nostalgia Culture,' and the Emergence of the Miniseries in the 1970s in the United States," *Journal of Popular Film and Television* 42 (2014): 81–90; Leslie Fishbein, "'Roots': Docudrama and the Interpretation of History," in *American History/American Television: Interpreting the Video Past*, ed. John O'Connor (New York: Ungar, 1983), 279–305; Alison Landsberg, *Prosthetic Memory: The Transformation of American Remembrance in the Age of Mass Culture* (New York: Columbia University Press, 2004), 81–110; Leslie Fiedler, *The Inadvertent Epic: From Uncle Tom's Cabin to Roots* (New York: Simon and Schuster, 1979); *Color Adjustment* (dir. Marlon Riggs, 1992); and Eric Pierson, "The Importance of Roots," in *Watching While Black: Centering the Television of Black Audiences,* ed. Beretta Smith-Shomade (New Brunswick, NJ: Rutgers University Press, 2012), 19–32. Two important books on Haley and *Roots* are due out soon: Erica Ball and Kellie Carter Jackson, eds., *Reconsidering Roots: The Phenomenon That Changed the Way We Understood American Slavery* (Athens: University of Georgia Press, forthcoming); and Timothy Haven, *Roots, Forty Years Later: Television, Race, and America.*

Roots is about **slavery, memory, and history.** The books that have most helped me think about the challenges involved in writing histories of slavery and recovering black identities and kinship ties that were fractured by slavery are Saidiya Hartman, *Lose Your Mother: A Journey along the Atlantic Slave Route* (New York: Farrar, Straus and Giroux, 2007); James Campbell, *Middle Passages: African American Journeys to Africa, 1787–2005* (New York: Penguin, 2006); Tiya Miles, *Ties That Bind: The Story of an Afro-Chero-kee Family in Slavery and Freedom* (Berkeley: University of California Press, 2005); Alondra Nelson, *The Social Life of DNA: Race, Reparations, and Reconciliation after the Genome* (Boston: Beacon Press, 2016); Stephanie Smallwood, *Saltwater Slavery: A Middle Passage from Africa to American Diaspora* (Cambridge, MA: Harvard University Press, 2008); Jennifer Morgan, *Laboring Women: Gender and Reproduction in New World Slavery* (Philadelphia: University of Pennsylvania Press, 2004); Heather Andrea Williams, *Help Me to Find My People: The African American Search for Family Lost in Slavery* (Chapel Hill, NC: University of North Carolina Press, 2012); Salamishah Tillet, *Sites of Slavery: Citizenship and Racial Democracy in the Post–Civil Rights Imagination* (Durham, NC: Duke University Press, 2012); Terri Snyder, *The Power to Die: Slavery and Suicide in British North America* (Chicago: University of Chicago Press, 2015); Vincent Brown, *The Reaper's Garden: Death and Power in the World of Atlantic Slavery* (Cambridge, MA: Harvard University Press, 2010); and Maria Diedrich, Henry Louis Gates Jr., and Carl Pedersen, eds., *Black Imagination and the Middle Passage* (New York: Oxford University Press, 1999). *Roots* also brought slavery into public discussions in ways that resonate with works on **slavery and public history,** such as Ana Lucia Araujo, *Politics of Memory: Making Slavery Visible in the Public Space* (New York: Routledge, 2012); James Oliver Horton and Lois Horton, eds., *Slavery and Public History: The Tough Stuff of American Memory* (Chapel Hill: University of North Carolina Press, 2008); and James DeWolf Perry and Kristin Gallas, *Interpreting Slavery at Museums and Historic Sites* (New York: Rowman and Littlefield, 2014).

Making "Roots" is indebted to works on **black popular and visual culture,** such as Gwendolyn DuBois Shaw, *Seeing the*

Unspeakable: The Art of Kara Walker (Durham, NC: Duke University Press, 2004); Huey Copeland, *Bound to Appear: Art, Slavery, and the Site of Blackness in Multicultural America* (Chicago: University of Chicago Press, 2013); Nicole Fleetwood, *Troubling Vision: Performance, Visuality, and Blackness* (Chicago: University of Chicago Press, 2010); Mark Anthony Neal, *Looking for Leroy: Illegible Black Masculinities* (New York: New York University Press, 2013); Mark Anthony Neal, *Soul Babies: Black Popular Culture and the Post-Soul Aesthetic* (New York: Routledge, 2001); Leigh Raiford, *Imprisoned in a Luminous Glare: Photography and the African American Freedom Struggle* (Chapel Hill: University of North Carolina Press, 2013); Marcus Wood, *Black Milk: Imagining Slavery in the Visual Cultures of Brazil and America* (New York: Oxford University Press, 2013); Cora Kaplan and John Oldfield, eds., *Imagining Transatlantic Slavery* (New York: Palgrave, 2010); John Stauffer, Zoe Trodd, and Celeste-Marie Bernier, *Picturing Frederick Douglass: An Illustrated Biography of the Nineteenth Century's Most Photographed American* (New York: Liveright, 2015); Darcy Grimaldo Grigsby, *Enduring Truths: Sojourner's Shadows and Substance* (Chicago: University of Chicago Press, 2015); Shawn Michelle Smith, *American Archives: Gender, Race, and Class in Visual Culture* (Princeton, NJ: Princeton University Press, 1999); and Daniel Widener, *Black Arts West: Culture and Struggle in Postwar Los Angeles* (Durham, NC: Duke University Press, 2010).

I was drawn to *Roots* by my interest in the intersections among **television, history, and race,** and my analysis of the series is influenced by Herman Gray, *Watching Race: Television and the Struggle for "Blackness"* (Minneapolis: University of Minnesota Press, 1995), Christine Acham, *Revolution Televised: Prime Time and the Struggle for Black Power* (Minneapolis: University of Minnesota Press, 2005); Aniko Bodroghkozy, *Equal Time: Television and the Civil Rights Movement* (Urbana: University of Illinois Press, 2012);

Gayle Wald, *It's Been Beautiful: Soul! and Black Power Television* (Durham, NC: Duke University Press, 2015); Devorah Heitner, *Black Power TV* (Durham, NC: Duke University Press, 2014); Darnell Hunt, ed., *Channeling Blackness: Studies of Television and Race in America* (New York: Oxford University Press, 2005); and George Lipsitz, *Time Passages: Collective Memory and American Popular Culture* (Minneapolis: University of Minnesota Press, 1990).

My thinking about *Roots* as an example of the importance, contradictions, and limitations of **mass culture** is influenced by Eric Lott, *Love and Theft: Blackface Minstrelsy and the American Working Class* (New York: Oxford University Press, 1993); David Reynolds, *Mightier Than the Sword: Uncle Tom's Cabin and the Battle for America* (New York: W.W. Norton, 2012); Joanne Sharp, *Condensing the Cold War: Reader's Digest and American Identity* (Minneapolis: University of Minnesota Press, 2000); Christina Klein, *Cold War Orientalism: Asia in the Middlebrow Imagination, 1945–1961* (Berkeley: University of California Press, 2003); Lizabeth Cohen, *A Consumers' Republic: The Politics of Mass Consumption in Postwar America* (New York: Vintage, 2003); Susan Smulyan, *Popular Ideologies: Mass Culture at Mid-century* (Philadelphia: University of Pennsylvania Press, 2010); Tom Perrin, *The Aesthetics of Middlebrow Fiction: Popular US Novels, Modernism, and Form, 1945–1975* (New York: Palgrave Macmillan, 2015); Joan Shelley Rubin, *The Making of Middlebrow Culture* (Chapel Hill: University of North Carolina Press, 1992); and Lawrence Levine, *Highbrow/Lowbrow: The Emergence of Cultural Hierarchy in America* (Cambridge, MA: Harvard University Press, 1990).

Finally, I have benefited from works on the **culture and politics of 1970s America,** such as Matthew Frye Jacobson, *Roots Too: White Ethnic Revival in Post–Civil Rights America* (Cambridge, MA: Harvard University Press, 2008); Jefferson Cowie, *Stayin'*

Alive: The 1970s and the Last Days of the Working Class (New York: New Press, 2010); Rick Perlstein, *The Invisible Bridge: The Fall of Nixon and the Rise of Reagan* (New York: Simon and Schuster, 2014); Robert Self, *All in the Family: The Realignment of American Democracy since the 1960s* (New York: Hill and Wang, 2012); and Natasha Zaretsky, *No Direction Home: The American Family and the Fear of National Decline, 1968–1980* (Chapel Hill: University of North Carolina Press, 2007).

INDEX